THIS IS OUR FAITH...

A Catholic Catechism for Adults

THIS IS OUR FAITH...

"This is our faith. This is the faith of the Church.
We are proud to profess it, in Christ Jesus our Lord."
from *The Rite of Baptism*

Michael Francis Pennock

AVE MARIA PRESS Notre Dame, IN 46556

Michael Francis Pennock has been a religious educator with adults and young adults alike for over 20 years. A graduate of Loyola University in Chicago, he holds a master's degree from St. John College in Cleveland and a Ph.D. from the University of Akron.

He teaches theology at St. Ignatius High School in Cleveland where he has been chairman of that department and has been cited by both students and alumni for his teaching. He is the author of *The Ways of Prayer* (Ave Maria Press) and is widely known and respected for his series of successful high school religious education textbooks, including the *Friendship in The Lord* series.

First printing, January, 1989
Fifth printing, June, 1993
110,000 copies in print

Nihil Obstat: The Reverend Peter M. Mihalic, S.T.D.
                  Censor Deputatus

Imprimatur   The Most Reverend Anthony M. Pilla, D.D., M.A.
                  Bishop of Cleveland

International Standard Book Number: 0-87793-390-1
                                    0-87793-389-8 (pbk.)

Library of Congress Catalog Card Number: 88-82681

Printed and bound in the United States of America.

DEDICATION

To my loving wife, Carol, and our children,
Scott, Jennifer, Amy and Christopher.

Acknowledgments _____

I wish to thank my editor, Joan Marie Laflamme. She is an author's best friend; her contributions to this book are countless. I also wish to thank Frank Cunningham of Ave Maria Press for his encouragement to write this book. His friendship, support and many kindnesses have greatly enriched my writing ministry.

Many other people deserve my gratitude: my parents, Frank and Louise Pennock, for sharing their love of the Catholic faith with me; the many dedicated, good Sisters of the Incarnate Word who demonstrated to me when I was a youngster that the Catholic church is a loving mother; my high school and college Jesuit teachers who showed through their lives that our efforts should be directed to God's greater honor and glory; my colleagues in religious education at St. Ignatius High School—their friendship has shown me the meaning of Christian community; the countless number of students over the years whose response to my teaching has made sharing the Catholic faith with them a real joy—it is truly good news to know that my students are my brothers and sisters in the Lord; the many outstanding priests who have inspired my ministry over the years, especially Father Paul Hritz and Father Mark DiNardo and Bishop Anthony Pilla whose pastoral leadership and personal example of compassion and holiness inspire every Catholic in the diocese of Cleveland; and the many friends whose support and love have sustained me in my ministry.

Above all else, though, I wish to thank the Lord Jesus for all those wonderful people, for the gift of his salvation and love, and for the privilege of working as a religious educator. May his name be praised forever.

Contents

Introduction

> Leave your country, your kindred and
> your father's house for a country which
> I shall show you; and I shall make you
> a great nation, I shall bless you
> and make your name famous; you are to be a
> blessing!
>
> —Genesis 12:1-2

A spiritual classic entitled *The Way of a Pilgrim* speaks to the hearts of contemporary searchers. Its anonymous author, who lived in 19th-century Russia, tells of his lifelong pilgrimage, a search for a way to get closer to God through prayer. The book begins humbly:

> By the grace of God I am a Christian, by my deeds a great sinner, and by my calling a homeless wanderer of humblest origin, roaming from place to place. My possessions consist of a knapsack with dry crusts of bread on my back and in my bosom the Holy Bible. This is all![1]

The Russian author reminds all seekers of God that we are pilgrims in a foreign land. Someday we will have to leave it, forsaking our possessions. For the anonymous pilgrim a knapsack and dried bread were sufficient for his physical needs; the Bible provided nourishment for his spiritual needs. By traveling simply he uncluttered his life for the journey.

In our more complex and sophisticated world we could hardly get by with the simple supplies of a 19th-century wanderer. Nonetheless, we are "strangers in a strange land" who are on a lifelong journey, the ultimate destination of which is union with the God who made and sustains us.

---

[1]*The Way of a Pilgrim*, trans. Helen Bacovin (Garden City, New York: 1978), p. 13.

INSIGHT, DETERMINATION, SUPPORT_____

The Christian life is a journey which requires insight, determination and support to keep going. There is always a danger that we will get so distracted by the sights along the way that we forget about our final destination. Thus the Christian pilgrimage requires clear vision to correctly discern the direction indicators along the way. The Bible provided vision for the Russian pilgrim; it is still a major source of insight for the Christian journey.

Determination is also needed because there are certain dangers along the way. The ancient Israelites were led by God for 40 years through a dangerous desert. God's chosen people could never have sustained their journey on their own. Many times they wished to turn back. They seemed to prefer slavery to the freedom Yahweh promised them. They persevered in their quest because Yahweh himself stayed with them in a powerful way; his presence helped them attain their goal. Christians today are assured of one thing: If we stay close to God in his Son Jesus, the power of the Holy Spirit will sustain us to the end. St. Paul writes:

> And let us never slacken in doing good; for if we do not give up, we shall have our harvest in due time (Gal 6:9).

Today's Christian pilgrims also need support. No one can survive without other people. The 19th-century wanderer begged food from others and received spiritual encouragement from many holy people. Today's spiritual pilgrims also need others to support and nourish them on their life's journey. The good news of the Christian life is that those who follow the way of Jesus become members of his body. United to the Lord they derive strength and power from him and their fellow travelers. The inspiration of his life and sacrifice on the cross, his ongoing friendship, his presence to us through other people—all of these make the journey bearable and even adventurous.

AN INVITATION_____

I offer this book to those who want to know more about how the Catholic community journeys to the Father. This book is for Catholics who wish to get a simple but thorough overview of their faith. It is also for those who approach the Catholic community for the first time, for example, catechumens who are engaged in the R.C.I.A. (Rite of Christian Initiation of Adults) process. The book can be read alone and reflected on individually or it can be adapted for group use. Especially if it is used as part of the adult initiation process, it would be good for participants to exchange their insights, witness to their faith, and share and discuss their questions.

As a religious educator for over 20 years, I have been privileged to share my own faith journey and that of the Catholic community with thousands of young people and adults in many settings. I have found that understanding typically follows the presentation of good, solid, basic knowledge. The goal of understanding the Catholic faith should be above all else the love and appreciation for the Lord who lives in and guides the faith community.

I invite you, the reader of this book, on a journey of understanding, of faith sharing, of prayer and reflection on the Catholic faith. My own prayer for all of us is that we come to love our Lord Jesus Christ even more. He has accomplished great things in us and for us. He continues to shower his love on us, and he calls us to an eternal destiny of joy. Let us never forget that teaching of and about the church has one major purpose: to draw us to Jesus. Remember his promise:

> "I shall see you again, and your hearts will be
>   full of joy,
> and that joy no one shall take from you. . . .
> "Father,
> I want those you have given me
> to be with me where I am,
> so that they may always see my glory"
>   (Jn 16:22;17:24).

ORGANIZATION OF THE BOOK

Section 1. The first eight chapters of the book take up the major articles of the Nicene Creed, a major profession of faith of all Christians. These topics include God the Father, Jesus, the Holy Spirit, the doctrine of the Blessed Trinity and the church.

Section 2. Chapters 9-11 discuss how Christians should live and interact with others on their faith journey. Topics include the Christian moral life and social justice issues.

Section 3. Chapters 12-17 treat the important topic of sacraments, the ongoing signs of the Lord's presence, friendship and love to us. Sacraments are vital ways to live the Christian life in the Catholic community.

Section 4. Chapter 18 introduces prayer, a key means to travelling a path of holiness. Chapters 19 and 20 take up the last major articles of the creed; they discuss Catholic teachings about Mary, the communion of saints and our final destiny.

Chapter 21 discusses the Catholic attitude toward other religions, and Chapter 22 summarizes what a Catholic believes while focusing in on several major issues of concern to the Catholic community in our day.

Appendices. The book includes three appendices. The first appendix alphabetically lists and discusses some Catholic beliefs and practices that did not fit neatly into one of the other major divisions of the book. The second appendix supplies some traditional and important Catholic prayers. The third provides definitions of key terms important to Catholics.

You may wish to read the book sequentially from beginning to end or read the chapters in a given section. The first three sections especially could be read independently though I recommend that you read together all the chapters in a given section before moving on to another. Feel free to skip around from topic to topic, treating the book as a resource book. Refer to the Index and Appendices for individual topics and terms.

CHAPTER FEATURES

Each chapter has a similar format. Each begins with a relevant scripture passage, a citation from the Nicene Creed or other suitable quotation. After a brief introduction the main ideas are presented as responses to questions. This format helps to organize and reference key teachings.

The concluding remarks typically summarize the key idea of the chapter and attempt to apply it to daily living.

Prayer plays a central role in the life of the Christian. The book recognizes this by providing a prayer reflection after each chapter. Exposure to different kinds and ways of prayer should help to enrich the reading and application of the book to the Christian faith journey.

Discussion/reflection questions are provided to help the reader interact with the material and to apply it to daily life. I encourage you to discuss the questions and share your faith life with others. The Lord speaks to us through our Christian brothers and sisters, so we should provide opportunities to allow him to speak to us through our friends.

Finally, each chapter includes a recommendation for further reading. These are typically references to the Bible. The Bible is God's word; it too speaks to our hearts. In addition, throughout the text itself are woven numerous scripture passages to show the intimate relationship between Catholic doctrine and the word of God.

PRAYER REFLECTION

> Do not be afraid, for I have redeemed you;
> I have called you by your name, you are mine.

Should you pass through the waters, I shall be with
    you;
or through rivers, they will not swallow you up.
Should you walk through fire, you will not suffer,
and the flame will not burn you.
For I am Yahweh, your God,
the Holy One of Israel, your Savior (Is 43:1-3).

Section 1

1

The Existence of God

Now we see only reflections in a
mirror, mere riddles, but then we shall
be seeing face to face. Now, I can
know only imperfectly; but then I shall
know just as fully as I am myself known.
—1 Corinthians 13:12

Every thinking, feeling human being at some time or other has an awesome experience, one that shakes the very ground he or she walks on. It is at such times that most of us tend to turn to God, to wonder about that hidden presence which we have somehow sensed. These experiences force us to ask questions about the meaning of life . . . and death. Why am I here? Why is there suffering? Why do my loved ones and I have to die? What is the meaning of love?

Belief vs. Unbelief

Questions like the ones above force us to face the issue of God's existence. Most people conclude that God exists. Atheists, however, deny God's existence. Their reasons vary. Some atheists say that the existence of God cannot be proven; therefore, for them, there is no God, in fact, no world other than the one they experience with the senses. Others claim that belief in God downgrades what it means to be human; for them, humanity is the only god. Still other atheists reject the notion of God because they find the suffering and evil in the world incompatible with the existence of a supreme and loving Being.

Between the believers and the atheists are the agnostics who claim that we cannot know if there is a God or not. The question of the exist-

21

ence of God makes little practical difference in their lives.

Atheists and agnostics—and also self-named believers who are in fact indifferent to spiritual realities—challenge believers to reconsider their beliefs.

This chapter will take up two issues: the questions of God's existence and whether God has communicated with humanity.

Does God Exist?

In his letter to the Romans, St. Paul teaches that we can discover God's existence by reflecting on the things God has made (Rom 1:19-21). The Catholic church taught at the First Vatican Council that "God, the origin and end of all things, can be known with certainty by the natural light of human reason from the things he created."

St. Paul and the church do not claim that each and every person can and does come to a knowledge of God's existence through reason. Rather, they assert that humans are rationally able to discover the hidden God because "ever since the creation of the world, the invisible existence of God and his everlasting power have been clearly seen by the mind's understanding of created things" (Rom 1:20). Belief in God is not unreasonable or foolish as some non-believers claim.

Some of the arguments for the existence of God include personal experience, common human experience, human history and demonstrations based on reason.

What Does Personal Experience Tell Us About God?

Our own experience can guide us to God. Our feelings of dependency, our sense of wonder and awe and joy, our feelings of being invited and called to do greater things than we are doing right now—all of these may speak of a God who has made us to discover him. When we reflect on ourselves as something very special in creation, we are given some strong insights that help us conclude there is a Creator who brought us into existence. The following are traditional arguments for the existence of God. One of them may strike a response with you.

An unquenchable thirst for happiness. We all want to be happy. We spend a lot of our time and energy trying to do things and acquire things that we think will make us happy. Yet our happiness fades and we soon find ourselves desiring something else. Are we creatures doomed to be ultimately frustrated? We want happiness, but the more we pursue it, the more it seems to slip away.

Can it be that a Creator made us with a hunger for happiness which nothing in this world can completely satisfy? Might it be that he implanted in us a kind of homing device which causes us to be restless until we find him? This restlessness for *total* happiness points to a God who made us this way.

Sense of justice. Have you ever felt that the evil people of the world will someday be called to task? It seems unfair that cheaters and liars and killers often prosper in this life while some good people suffer and are taken advantage of. We have a fundamental feeling that things will be reversed someday, that there is a Power that will right all wrongs, if not in this life, then in the next.

Love. How can we explain the greatest reality known to us, the sense of being cared for and loved? Love is a spiritual reality that is not explained by the material universe. It must come from somewhere, ultimately from Love itself, the being we call God. (The same can be said for intelligence; it must ultimately come from Intelligence itself, God.)

What Does Common Experience Tell Us About God?

From the earliest times human beings have testified to the existence of God. An overwhelming majority of cultures has believed in some being who is greater than any of its members. There have been atheistic governments which deny God, but many of the people in those countries still hold fast to a belief in God.

One can argue that such an observation does not prove that there is a God. Yet it is still very convincing that the common human experience has acknowledged a God who unites, heals and preserves the human race.

People have not agreed on the exact nature of this superior being or how many of these beings there may be. Some picture a vengeful, spiteful god. Others see a remote figure, like a clock maker who constructs his masterpiece but is then quite content to allow it to run by itself. Still others imagine a capricious god, one who toys with and torments his creatures.

Disagreement on what God is like does not disprove his existence, however. These differences merely show that, left to our own clouded intellects, we cannot perceive God clearly. We know *someone* is there, but his true identity is not clear to us. We need God's direct help if we are to know him as he really is.

What Does Human History Tell Us About God?

Human history is a powerful argument for the existence of God. There seems to be an intelligence behind our evolving history—the spread of humanity from the plains of Africa or the Mesopotamian

Valley to the very ends of the earth and now even to the moon and the outer reaches of the solar system.

What Does Reason Tell Us About God?

St. Thomas Aquinas, the great medieval theologian, summed up five so-called proofs for the existence of God. They all come down to affirming that we can discover God by looking at what he has made. For example, Aquinas points out that everything we know of in existence was caused by something or someone else. There has to be a source which was the first cause—an uncaused cause which logically always existed. This first cause the philosophers call God. The other arguments are similar.

Besides philosophical arguments, our own personal reflection on the beauty, immensity, symmetry and power of creation can give us an awareness of a God who made all things and keeps them in existence. Alfred North Whitehead once said that God is the poet of the world. God's lyricism can be discovered in truth, beauty and goodness. Our reflections and experiences of awe and wonder point to the existence of God.

Does God Communicate With Us?

Christians not only believe that God exists but that he also freely and graciously communicated himself to us. As the Second Vatican Council taught:

> In His wisdom, God chose to reveal Himself and to make known to us the hidden purpose of his will by which through Christ, the Word made flesh, man has access to the Father in the Holy Spirit and comes to share in the divine nature (*Dogmatic Constitution on Divine Revelation*, No. 2).

What Is Divine Revelation?

Christians believe in divine revelation. What do we mean by this important term? First, we must emphasize that God is primarily a mystery; his ways are above our ways, and his thoughts are above our thoughts. God is totally other; no human words, no human thoughts can totally explain who God is. In a certain sense God is hidden behind a veil. As we have seen, though, we can use our minds to figure out that there must be a God who made everything and keeps it in existence. And by studying carefully what God has made, we can say some things about him. For example, when we look at the vastness of the universe, we must conclude that the one who made it is an infinite being, that is, one who is not limited. Or when we reflect on the existence of intelligent life in the universe, we are led to conclude that the Creator himself must be an intelligent being to the nth degree, an all-knowing being who is the very source of human intelligence.

Basically, what we say about God is that he is a perfect being who is in no way limited like the creatures he has made. Our human reason alone, though, can only give us a veiled or clouded knowledge of God. People in their natural human condition can only have a very limited knowledge of what God is like.

Christians believe that God freely chose to communicate himself and his plan for our salvation to his creatures. This free gift of God's self-communication is known as supernatural or divine revelation. Literally, *revelation* means "unveiling." We believe that out of the abundance of his love, God unveiled himself in human history and speaks to us as friends, lives among us, and invites us into fellowship with him. We call this revelation supernatural because we, as God's creatures, do not have a natural right to this intimate friendship with God. His self-disclosure, his invitation to a deeper life of love is purely a gift on his part.

> At many moments in the past and by many means, God spoke to our ancestors through the prophets; but in our own time, the final days, he has spoken to us in the person of his Son, whom he appointed heir of all things and through whom he made the ages (Heb 1:1-2).

What Is Salvation History?

The story of God's self-disclosure, his saving action in history, is known as *salvation history*. The story of God's generous love began with his creation of our first parents. After their fall he promised to redeem us and gave hope of eternal life to the human race. A key event in God's plan was the calling of Abraham and the creation of the Jewish people. Through the patriarchs, and later the prophets, God taught this nation to acknowledge him as the one true God and to await the promised savior. Salvation history reached its high point in the coming of Jesus Christ, the fullness of God's revelation. Jesus is the Word of God made flesh, the Son, who lived among us, taught us in human words and deeds about his Father and completed the Father's work of salvation. To see Jesus is to see the Father.

What Role Does the Bible Play in Salvation History?

The story of salvation history lives on in the Bible and in the tradition of the Christian community. The Bible is the written record of revelation and contains the inspired testimony of people like the prophets and apostles about God's marvelous deeds in human history.

The Hebrew scriptures (Old Testament) record God's teaching to the Jewish people and his interactions in their history. They record how God called the Chosen People out of Egypt into the Promised Land, how they became a nation and a religious community, and how they grew to know and worship the one true God.

The New Testament chronicles the life and teachings of Jesus Christ and announces the good news of God's plan of salvation for all people everywhere.

What Is Our Response to God's Communication?

God's communication of himself and his plan for us require a response on our part. That response is known as *faith*. The Epistle to the Hebrews defines faith as the "confident assurance concerning what we hoped for, and conviction about things we do not see" (Heb 11:1, *NAB*). Faith, like revelation, is a free gift of God which gives conviction, commitment and trust with regard to realities that we can neither see nor clearly prove. Faith is accepting the Lord and his life both by living it and believing the truths he has revealed. We get the strength to live and believe God's truth and life from God himself.

CONCLUDING REFLECTIONS _____

We began this chapter with the question of God's existence and we end with faith. The American essayist Ralph Waldo Emerson once observed that everything he had seen taught him to trust God for all he had not seen.

It is reasonable to believe in God. Personal experiences, universal human belief, human history and rational reflection all point to a Supreme Being who has made our universe and keeps it in existence.

Christian belief does not stop with the fact of God's existence. This is only the beginning. God has revealed himself to us not only through the stamp of a creative touch on those things we can observe, but also by directly involving himself in human history. He formed a people and through them gave to the human community his Word, the Son, Jesus Christ.

Who is this God for you? How do you perceive his existence? How does he speak to you through the material world? Have you discovered him through Christian revelation?

PRAYER REFLECTION_____

"Stop and smell the roses" is common but sound advice. We can never be so preoccupied on our faith journey that we miss seeing God in his beautiful creation.

Reflection on God's creation moves the believer to adoration and praise. Both Jews and Christians turn to the psalms for inspiration in addressing the almighty God.

> Yahweh our Lord,
> how majestic is your name throughout the world!
> I look up at your heavens, shaped by your fingers,
> at the moon and the stars you set firm—
> what are human beings that you spare a thought for
>   them,
> or the child of Adam that you care for him?
> Yet you have made him little less than a god,
> you have crowned him with glory and beauty,
> made him lord of the works of your hands,
> put all things under his feet (Ps 8:1,3-6).

FOR DISCUSSION_____

1. What was the most earthshaking experience of your life? How did it speak to you of God?
2. Some people say it is impossible to "prove" one person's love for another; love must be experienced to be believed. Explain how you have experienced another's love for you. Discuss how you have experienced God's love.
3. What is the most significant question you ask about life? How might the existence of a loving God be an answer to that question?

FURTHER READING_____

Psalms 8, 19, 29, 65, 104

2

God: Our Loving Creator

> We believe in one God,
> the Father, the Almighty,
> maker of heaven and earth
> of all that is seen and unseen.
>
> —from the Nicene Creed

We live in a noisy world. We are constantly surrounded by street noises. The airwaves bombard us with music, non-stop chatter and news that shocks us, frightens us and scatters our attention in many different directions. In addition, people make constant demands on us. They request this or that and they want it . . . yesterday!

The trouble with too much unfiltered noise and the constant flow of demands is that we can become unfocused. We lose sight of what is important. Our sense of being at peace is lost. We find it extremely difficult to slow down and listen to what is really essential for our happiness and well-being.

Undoubtedly the ancient Israelites also had trouble with distractions. Like us, they had difficulty identifying the most meaningful voice speaking to them amid all the other alluring voices of their day. Surely this is why God spoke so forcefully through Moses, who was charged to preach his word. Moses' message reveals who God is and what he wants.

> Listen, Israel: Yahweh our God is the one, the only Yahweh. You must love Yahweh your God with all your heart, with all your soul, with all your strength (Dt 6:4-5).

Moses says ''Listen!'' Today we must also listen to what is essential. In the Creed we profess belief in one God, the Father, the Almighty, the Creator of all. The word God speaks to us about himself is love. In return, he asks for love because that is the way to happiness.

In this chapter we will look at what God reveals about himself and us his creatures. We will listen here primarily to the words of the Hebrew scriptures. In the next two chapters we will turn to the Christian scriptures to see what they reveal about God's Son and his message to us.

What Does God Reveal?

A prime means of listening to God is by reading and reflecting on the Hebrew and Christian scriptures. Christians believe that these writings—the Bible—are God's words in human words. Their message is a word worth listening to.

The Bible, which literally means "The Book," is a collection of books which contain different kinds of literature—poetry, history, religious myth (story), prayers, proverbs and the like. They have one thing in common though: All are *inspired* because God influenced the biblical writers in such a way that they recorded what God wanted. Inspiration refers to the guidance of the Holy Spirit in the process of writing the Holy Scriptures.

Catholics recognize 46 books as the official list (*canon*) of inspired books of the Old Testament. We can divide the Old Testament books into four major categories:

The Pentateuch treats God's covenant of love with the Jewish people and sets down their response, that is, the Law or Torah. (Five books: Genesis, Exodus, Leviticus, Numbers, Deuteronomy.)

The Historical Books recount the story of God's saving activity in the history of the Chosen People. (Sixteen books: Joshua, Judges, Ruth, 1 and 2 Samuel, 1 and 2 Kings, 1 and 2 Chronicles, Ezra, Nehemiah, Tobit, Judith, Esther, 1 and 2 Maccabees.)

The Wisdom Books contain prayers, poems and commonsense advice on how to live a faithful, good life. (Seven books: Job, Psalms, Proverbs, Ecclesiastes, Song of Songs, Wisdom, Ecclesiasticus.)

The Prophetical Books repeatedly call the Chosen People to repent and be faithful to God's covenant. (Eighteen books: Isaiah, Jeremiah, Lamentations, Baruch, Ezekiel, Daniel, Hosea, Joel, Amos, Obadiah, Jonah, Micah, Nahum, Habakkuk, Zephaniah, Haggai, Zechariah, Malachi.)

What do these books reveal about God? What do they tell us about our relationship with this Supreme Being? The following is a five-point summary of what the Hebrew scriptures reveal about God and our relationship to him.

There Is Only One God

When God chose to reveal himself to humans, he began with the Israelites (Jews), the Chosen People. Their history is one of *covenant*. In general, a covenant is a commitment between two people to do something for each other. Unlike a contract which is based on legal obligations, God's covenant with the Jews was based on his freely given love. In the covenant God promised to create a nation (his covenant with Abraham), to sustain them as a people (his covenant with Moses, the Exodus experience), to give them a land (Canaan), to help them establish self-rule and to send them a Messiah (covenant with David).

In return for God's many and great blessings, the Jews were to obey God's law which is summarized in the Ten Commandments. This law gave the Jews an identity distinct from their neighbors and gave them a special task, a mission to witness to the true God.

The most important aspect of the Israelites' response was to worship Yahweh and to testify to him as the one, true God, the source of all being and the one who keeps everything in existence. All other gods were false and thus powerless; only Yahweh was the true, living, unique God. Old Testament history is full of the sad story of how the Israelites were unfaithful to God, and how they continually fell back to the worship of false gods (for example, rain gods or the gods of worldly power and prestige). But the Old Testament also tells a happy story, the story of God's continual loving faithfulness despite the forgetfulness of the Chosen People.

What Kind of Being Is This God?

God is essentially a mystery. Human words cannot express all that God is. He reveals himself as one who is *transcendent*, that is, totally other than his creation; he is above and beyond it. He is also *immanent*, that is, present to and joined to his creation. Certain traits emphasize his majesty and beyondness, and other characteristics stress his nearness and concern for us. Some important passages from scripture help us know something about the immanence and the transcendence of God.

Transcendence

1. *God is unique.* There is no God like Yahweh.

> For thus says Yahweh, the Creator of the
> heavens—
> he is God, who shaped the earth and made it,
> who set it firm;
> he did not create it to be chaos,

he formed it to be lived in:
I am Yahweh, and there is no other (Is 45:18).

2. *God is omnipotent*. God is all-powerful; he can do all things.
   For I know that Yahweh is great,
   our Lord is above all gods.
   Yahweh does whatever he pleases
   in heaven, on earth,
   in the waters and all the depths (Ps 135:5-6).

3. God is eternal. God always was and always will be.
   Did you not know? Had you not heard?
   Yahweh is the everlasting God,
   he created the remotest parts of the earth (Is 40:28).

4. *God is immense*. God is not limited to space.
   Yet will God really live with human beings on earth?
   Why, the heavens, the highest of the heavens, cannot
   contain you. How much less this temple built by me!
   (1 Kgs 8:27).

5. *God contains all things*.
   Strongly she [wisdom] reaches from one end of the world
       to the other
   and she governs the whole world for its good (Wis 8:1).

6. *God is beyond human understanding*.
   I [Job] was the man who misrepresented your intentions
       with my ignorant words.
   You have told me about great works that I cannot
   understand,
       about marvels which are beyond me, of which I know
       nothing (Jb 42:3).

7. *God cannot be praised enough*.
   Where shall we find sufficient power to glorify him,
       since he is the Great One, above all his works?
           (Sir 43:28).

Immanence

1. *God chooses the Hebrews and makes them a people*.
   Yahweh said to Abram, "Leave your country, your kindred
   and your father's house for a country which I shall show you;
   and I shall make you a great nation, I shall bless you and
   make your name famous; you are to be a blessing!"
   (Gn 12:1-2).

2. *God establishes a covenant with the Jews, making them a holy nation*.
   "So now, if you are really prepared to obey me and keep my

covenant, you, out of all peoples, shall be my personal possession, for the whole world is mine. For me you shall be a kingdom of priests, a holy nation'' (Ex 19:5-6).

3. *God frees the Jews from Egypt.*

"And I have come down to rescue them from the clutches of the Egyptians and bring them up out of that country, to a country rich and broad, to a country flowing with milk and honey'' (Ex 3:8).

4. *God gives the Jews a land.*

"Make provisions ready, for in three days' time you will cross this Jordan and go on to take possession of the land which Yahweh your God is giving you as your own'' (Jos 1:11).

5. *God establishes the kingdom of David.*

(See 2 Sm 7:8-16.)

6. *God sends prophets to guide the Jews.*

"Turn from your wicked ways and keep my commandments and my laws in accordance with the entire Law which I laid down for your fathers and delivered to them through my servants and prophets'' (2 Kgs 17:13).

7. *God sustains the Chosen People in Babylonia and restores them to Israel.*

"Console my people, console them,''
  says your God.
"Speak to the heart of Jerusalem
  and cry to her
that her period of service is ended,
that her guilt has been atoned for'' (Is 40:1-2).

Who Is God the Creator?

The two creation stories (Genesis 1:1-2:4 and Genesis 2:5-25) reveal that God is the Creator. He made all things out of nothing. He created freely out of his great generosity. He both sustains and rules the world. We humans are created in his image.

God created man in the image of himself,
in the image of God he created him,
male and female he created them (Gn 1:27).

All that God created was good. Unlike the Babylonian creation stories which hold that there is an evil god along with a good god, and that our human existence is the result of evil, the Hebrew scriptures' picture of God is one of goodness, power, freedom and generosity.

We humans, the crown of God's creation, are endowed with both

a physical body and a spiritual nature. Our spiritual nature enables us
to think, to choose between right and wrong, and to love. We are also
immortal in the sense that, although we each have a personal beginning, we will never cease to exist. And we are social beings who live in
community. Our task is to renew the face of the earth.

> God blessed them, saying to them, "Be fruitful, multiply, fill the
> earth and subdue it. Be masters of the fish of the sea, the birds of
> heaven and all living creatures that move on earth" (Gn 1:28).

Why Is There Evil?

The Old Testament tells us why there is evil in the world. In the
Adam and Eve story, for example, we see that originally human beings
were in harmony with God. But because God created free beings and
not mere puppets, humans had the chance to either accept or reject
God's love. Original sin is the unhappy story of Adam and Eve's rejection of God's love, which resulted in humanity's loss of Yahweh's
friendship.

The sin of our first parents brought about a disunity between God
and us. Genesis also tells us that this fractured relationship resulted in
a corresponding disharmony between nature and us and our alienation
from one another.

The church teaches that original sin has been transmitted to all
generations since Adam and Eve. When the church teaches that we inherit original sin, it is not saying that original sin is an actual sin we
personally commit. Rather, we are born into a condition where we are
inclined to give in to the powers of evil which surround us. We cannot
be freed from that condition by our own strength. Only Jesus, God's
Son, can liberate us from the power of sin.

> But the Lord Himself came to free and strengthen man, renewing
> him inwardly and casting out that prince of this world (cf. Jn 12:31)
> who held him in the bondage of sin (*Pastoral Constitution on the
> Church in the Modern World*, No. 13).

What Is God's Will for Human Beings?

The major theme of salvation history is God's loving faithfulness
to his unfaithful creatures. The prophet Hosea compares Yahweh to a
faithful husband who refuses to abandon his harlot wife, Israel. The
Song of Songs praises Yahweh as a passionate lover whose love and fidelity to his wife (Israel) know no bounds.

God's love is manifested through deeds as well as words. His
deeds reflect a God who saves, one who rescues the Jews from the

bondage of slavery in Egypt, one who sustains them in the desert, one who gives them a land and a king, one who keeps them alive in captivity, one who returns them to their land.

The high point of God's loving concern is his promise to send a Messiah, a savior, a comforter who will restore humanity's proper relationship with God.

> But you (Bethlehem) Ephrathah,
> the least of the clans of Judah,
> from you will come for me
> a future ruler of Israel;
> whose origins go back to the distant past,
> to the days of old (Mi 5:1).

In fulfillment of his promise God sent his only Son, Jesus Christ. The account of his coming is the culmination of the New Testament story.

If God Knows All, How Can We Have Free Will?

The Bible reveals many truths about God, but we are still left with difficult questions such as this one. God's knowledge does not force us to do anything. He gave us freedom, and he respects that freedom even if it leads us away from his love. There is no cause-effect relationship between his knowledge and our actions. The following analogy may help clarify this point: You are on the fifth floor of a building looking down at the street below. You see a man crossing the street. You also see a car speeding down the same street. You know that the car will strike the pedestrian. The man does, in fact, get struck by the car. Your foreknowledge did not cause the accident or force the man to cross the street. So it is with God's knowledge.

If God Is Good, Why Is There Evil in the World?

This is another of the questions that have puzzled believers and non-believers through the centuries. The existence of evil is a great mystery. In fact, some people claim that religion is an attempt to reconcile good and evil in the universe. The answer to this question again revolves around a loving God who creates intelligent beings with free will. God does not create evil; evil is the absence of good. Rather, God permits evil. Evil enters the picture when free, intelligent creatures turn from God's love. The origin of some evil is easy to see. For example, it is relatively easy to understand how abortion, prejudice and war come from people's deliberate choice to turn from a loving God. We also believe that some evil in the universe results from fallen angels (devils) at odds with their Creator. Other kinds of evil such as tornadoes and hurricanes that destroy innocent human life are simply beyond understanding.

CONCLUDING REFLECTIONS _____

This chapter has looked at some basic Catholic teachings about God, especially as he has revealed himself in the Hebrew scriptures. We have seen that God is one, true, living, unique, omnipotent, eternal, immense and contains all things. God is above human understanding, a pure spirit, a thinking, absolutely loving being who is intimately concerned with his creation.

God has created all things out of nothing and keeps them in existence. He has made us in his image and likeness with a supernatural destiny. He desires our happiness and is faithful to us even when we reject him. He always stands ready to redeem us through his Son, Jesus Christ.

But how do these truths affect our lives? Do they make any difference?

Sometimes we are so bombarded with distractions that we don't hear God's word speaking to us. He is the farthest thing from our minds. But we should pause periodically and hear what God is saying. His message can make a difference in our daily lives. The following observations may help to make these teachings about God more real.

- God loves each of us greatly. He shows this through all he has created, especially through his creation of us. God's goodness and love have many concrete implications for us. He loves us unconditionally. He brought us into existence and gave each one of us certain talents. He sees what he has made—you and me—and declares that what he has made is good.

   Others may measure us against their expectations and find us wanting. But God loves us for who we are. If we let this knowledge sink into our inner awareness, we will begin to take great joy in all creation—and especially in our own existence.
- Life has meaning, even in the moments we find most confusing. Reality is good, and God cares about us. He wants us to be happy.
- The Hebrew scriptures reveal that God is involved in our lives. He is everywhere; he is closer to us than we are to ourselves. In addition, the Lord God promised his people that he would never abandon them, and he did not. He also promises never to abandon us, regardless of how we sin or turn from his love. His generous love is always available to us.

Behind our current concerns, our worries, our situation in life is the more fundamental truth of this great love of God for us. The Lord asks us: "How do you feel about this? What should you do right now to make my Father's love for you the most important reality in your life?"

PRAYER REFLECTION _____

Psalm 23 is the most beloved of all psalms. It epitomizes the closeness of God's love so richly revealed in the Hebrew scriptures. This recent translation speaks to our age in a fresh way.

> Yahweh is my shepherd, I lack nothing.
> In grassy meadows he lets me lie.
> By tranquil streams he leads me
>   to restore my spirit.
> He guides me in paths of saving justice
>   as befits his name.
> Even were I to walk in a ravine as dark as death
> I should fear no danger, for you are at my side.
> Your staff and your crook are there to soothe me.
> You prepare a table for me
>   under the eyes of my enemies;
> you anoint my head with oil;
>   my cup brims over.
> Kindness and faithful love pursue me
>   every day of my life.
> I make my home in the house of Yahweh
>   for all time to come.

FOR DISCUSSION _____

1. The Christian God is a God of covenant. He will always be faithful to his people. What does this say to you about God? What does it require of you?
2. If scripture is God's inspired word, then it should play a central role in Christian life. Borrow a copy of the parish missalette and read next Sunday's readings. What do these readings reveal about God? What do they reveal about you?
3. When have you sensed the majesty (transcendence) of God? Describe a personal experience when God seemed especially close to you (immanence).
4. Does the Christian view the world as basically good or basically evil? Explain.

FURTHER READING

Genesis 1:1—2:4; 2:5-25 (creation accounts)
Genesis 12 and 15 (God's covenant with Abraham)

3

Jesus: Lord and Messiah

We believe in one Lord, Jesus Christ
   the only Son of God,
   eternally begotten of the Father
   God from God, Light from Light,
   true God from true God,
   begotten, not made, one in Being
      with the Father.
   Through him all things were made.
   For us men and for our salvation
      he came down from heaven:
   by the power of the Holy Spirit he
      was born of the Virgin Mary,
      and became man.

—from the Nicene Creed

For this is how God loved the world: he gave his only Son, so that everyone who believes in him may not perish but may have eternal life.

—John 3:16

Who are the inspiring people in your life? Whom do you look up to and admire?

Today's world thrusts upon us varied models of the so-called great. Grocery-store tabloids want us to admire the Hollywood-types, the money-hungry sports figures, those who are clever in the marketplace and various other "beautiful people." They urge us to emulate the lifestyles of the materially successful.

But who is truly great? The dictionary tells us that a great person is superior in quality, noble, excellent. Shakespeare mused that some people are born this way; others achieve greatness; and still others have it thrust upon them.

For countless people Jesus Christ is the model of greatness. Christians believe that Jesus was born great because he was God's only Son. But Jesus was born in the most humble of circumstances. And he was killed, condemned as a criminal. Jesus' life teaches us that the meaning of greatness does not lie in personal wealth, privileged status or popular acceptance. Jesus reveals that the way to greatness is to live a life serving others and loving them without condition. His life, death and resurrection have brought about the greatest achievement of all: our eternal salvation.

Jesus is at the very heart of the Christian faith journey. He is the Father's total revelation. Jesus teaches:

> "I am the Way; I am Truth and Life.
> No one can come to the Father except through
>   me.
> If you know me, you will know my Father too"
>   (Jn 14:6-7).

This chapter will examine what the gospels tell us about Jesus and discuss some beliefs that Christians have about their Lord. As you read, keep in both mind and heart what Jesus means to you.

"Who Do You Say I Am?"

The French author Voltaire once wrote: "Judge a man by his questions rather than by his answers." By this standard we ought to think very highly of Jesus. He liked to ask questions, especially of his apostles. One of the most important scenes in the gospels depicts Jesus and his disciples out in the countryside travelling to the town of Caesarea Philippi. It was a crucial time in Jesus' career. He wanted the apostles to reflect on exactly who was calling them away from their families and occupations in order to learn the good news of God's love. So he asked a question.

Jesus asked the apostles who people thought he was. Because of his wise words and wonderful deeds, many of his contemporaries thought Jesus was a great prophet, or John the Baptist come back to life, or even the prophet Elijah. But what Jesus really wanted to know was what the apostles thought:

> "But you," he asked them, "who do you say I am?" Peter spoke up and said to him, "You are the Christ" (Mk 8:29).

Peter answered in faith and provided the correct answer which would change his life forever.

Jesus' question echoes down through the ages. He asks us today, "Who do you say I am?" For Christians, this question demands an answer.

Did Jesus Really Exist?

Few people today seriously doubt the historical existence of Jesus. Ancient Roman writers like Tacitus and Pliny the Younger and the Jewish historian Josephus take his existence for granted. Contemporary archeological studies confirm certain places and events recorded in the New Testament.

Most people reason that the Christian religion must be founded on a real person. After all, what did anyone have to gain from making up a story about Jesus? There was absolutely nothing to gain politically or economically. As a matter of fact, with the exception of John, all the apostles were put to death for their preaching about Jesus.

Finally, a careful analysis of the gospels and what they record as the words of Jesus reveal that he must have existed. The teachings of Jesus bear the stamp of an individual who taught with unique insight and authority. The parables, for example, are powerful, life-giving and original. They argue quite convincingly for the existence of a memorable teacher behind them.

What Is the Primary Source of Knowledge of Jesus?

The primary source of knowledge about the historical Jesus is the New Testament. Every page of its 27 books proclaims the Incarnation, the teaching that God became man in Jesus Christ. Like the Hebrew scriptures (Old Testament), the New Testament is a collection of books which announces the fulfillment of God's promises in his Son, Jesus Christ. The books of the New Testament can be categorized as follows:

The Gospels are faith summaries proclaiming salvation through Jesus Christ. They contain both facts about the historical Jesus and the faith of early Christians on the meaning of Jesus' life, death and resurrection. (Four books: Matthew, Mark, Luke, John.)

The Acts of the Apostles deals with the early history of the church under the guidance of the Holy Spirit, from Pentecost Sunday to the arrest of Paul in Rome around A.D. 63.

The Epistles of Paul, the earliest New Testament writings, take up particular problems faced by the early churches and continually proclaim the centrality of faith in Jesus. (Thirteen books: Romans, 1 and 2 Corinthians, Galatians, Ephesians, Philippians, Colossians, 1 and 2 Thessalonians, 1 and 2 Timothy, Titus, Philemon.)

The Epistle to the Hebrews is often attributed to Paul but was not written by him. It deals with the priesthood of Jesus.

The Seven Catholic Epistles were written to encourage the universal (catholic) church to keep the true faith and to remind Christians to live Christ-filled lives. (Seven books: James, 1 and 2 Peter, 1, 2 and 3 John, Jude.)

Revelation (The Apocalypse) is a highly symbolic work written to aid Christians under persecution to remain steadfastly loyal to Jesus.

The gospels are our main source of information about the historical Jesus. They are best described as faith summaries which announce the good news of salvation. They are primarily interested in telling the good news of Jesus. The authors, the four evangelists (literally, "proclaimers of the good news"), let their faith in Jesus as Lord shine forth. They are not interested in all the historical details of Jesus' life on earth, but rather in the good deeds he performed, the words of salvation he taught, and the meaning of his passion, death, resurrection and glorification.

When Were the Gospels Written?

Catholics believe that the gospels were written at the end of a three-stage process.

Stage 1: The Historical Jesus. This period lasted from the birth of Jesus around 4-6 B.C. to his death around 30 A.D. It includes what Jesus did and taught. Preeminent in Jesus' life is his death and resurrection.

Stage 2: Oral Preaching About Jesus. This period lasted from the founding of the church on Pentecost Sunday until the gospels were written. During this time the apostles reflected on the meaning of Jesus and God's work through him. They used hymns, catechetical lessons, prayers, stories, testimonies and other literary forms to present the words and deeds of Jesus.

Stage 3: Written Gospels. The different gospels were written over a period of about 35 years. Mark wrote around A.D. 65, Luke and Matthew between A.D. 75 and 85, and John in the last decade of the first century. Each evangelist adapted his materials keeping in mind the circumstances of the particular audience for whom he was writing. Thus, we have four versions of the gospel (the Good News of Jesus Christ) because each of the evangelists was writing for a different community of Christians in different circumstances.

What Do We Know About Jesus' Early Life?

The evangelists tell us little about Jesus' early life. Matthew and Luke write that he was born of the virgin Mary in Bethlehem. Joseph, his foster father, taught him carpentry. Jesus grew up quietly in the obscure village of Nazareth. Luke records that Jesus accompanied Mary and Joseph to Jerusalem for the great religious feasts of the Jews. Luke also writes that the 12-year-old Jesus astounded the Temple teachers with his intelligence. We hear nothing of Jesus' early life after this event other than that he "increased in wisdom, in stature, and in favor with God and with people" (Lk 2:52).

When Did Jesus' Public Ministry Begin?

Jesus next appears on the scene in the "fifteenth year of Tiberius Caesar's reign" (from A.D. 27-28) when he was in his 30s. At this time he launched his public ministry after being baptized by John the Baptist. The story and meaning of Jesus' public ministry of preaching and healing—a ministry that led to his death—occupies center stage in the gospel accounts of Jesus' life.

What Qualities of Jesus Do the Gospels Reveal?

Jesus' actions and teachings during his short public life disclose an incredibly generous man doing God's work. St. Peter summarized his master's work best when he said:

"Because God was with him, Jesus went about doing good and curing all who had fallen into the power of the devil" (Acts 10:38).

Jesus was a healer. The gospels tell us that Jesus was a healer. He received everyone who came to him with love and compassion. He cured not only friends—like Peter's mother-in-law—but also lepers, the blind, the deaf, epileptics, the crippled, the possessed, and many others with various afflictions. He also brought the dead back to life. Jesus' healings were considered miraculous by the people, and they were. Jesus demonstrated God's love in concrete actions in behalf of his people and also showed that God's love has the power to overcome evil.

Jesus was compassionate. Jesus' marvelous deeds show us a compassionate Savior. He associated with the real losers of his day, outcasts who for one reason or another were despised by the establishment. The poor, the sinners, the abandoned, widows and children—all flocked to receive his love and understanding. Crowds smothered him with attention; when he discovered that 5,000 of those who had come to hear him had no food, he fed them. But more important, he gave them what they really needed: the healing touch of God's forgiveness and the good news that they were loved.

Jesus was down-to-earth. He walked dusty roads with his apostles. He attended weddings and ate meals and drank wine. He showed his anger, for example, when the moneychangers violated the sanctity of the Temple. He expressed his impatience at the apostles' slowness to understand him.

Jesus was courageous. He stood up to the false teachers of his day; he called them blind guides and hypocrites. He rescued the woman who was about to be stoned to death because she was caught in adultery. He boldly preached the Father's will, knowing it would lead to his death. But he did not back down, even though he feared death just as any normal person would:

> "Abba, Father!" he said, "For you everything is possible. Take this cup away from me. But let it be as you, not I, would have it" (Mk 14:36).

Jesus was humble. He was poor and owned no possessions. He came from a place that was ridiculed even by his disciples. He washed the feet of his disciples, a task that even a slave was not required to do.

Jesus was self-giving. His love, his concern for all people, his miracles, his message of God's forgiveness, his preaching about God's kingdom—all of this got him in trouble with the leaders of his nation. They plotted his death. Jesus knew of the plot but freely allowed himself to be arrested. This arrest led to a trial before the Jewish leaders and before Pontius Pilate, the Roman governor in charge of the Jewish nation. And this trial led to his incredible suffering and an excruciatingly painful death on a cross. He freely gave his life for all people everywhere.

> "No one can have greater love than to lay down his life for his friends" (Jn 15:13).

There was nothing more that he could give.

Did Jesus Have Brothers and Sisters?

Some people who read the gospels notice that Matthew mentions "brothers" of Jesus and that Mark even names them (Mk 6:3). Thus they conclude that Jesus had siblings, and that Mary had other children.

Catholics have traditionally believed that Jesus did not have physical brothers and sisters and that Mary was always a virgin. These beliefs are based on both the Bible and tradition. For example, the gospels state that Mary was a virgin and that Jesus was conceived miraculously by the power of the Holy Spirit (Mt 1:20 and Lk 1:34). The gospels give no indication that Mary had children after the birth of Jesus. Furthermore, church tradition has always taught the perpetual virginity of Mary.

The texts which refer to Jesus' brothers (and sisters) use a word which can also mean cousin or even some distant relations of the same generation. Even today people who live in Near Eastern countries and in other tightly knit communities refer to their cousins as brothers and sisters. Thus both the biblical evidence and the constant teaching of the Catholic church argue strongly for the virginity of Mary and the special intervention of God in the conception of Jesus.

It is important to note what Jesus himself said about his true kinsmen:

> "Anyone who does the will of my Father in heaven is my brother and sister and mother" (Mt 12:50).

What Do the Titles of Jesus Reveal About Him?

When the early Christians reflected on Jesus' life and the meaning of his death and resurrection, the Holy Spirit led them to deeper insights into who Jesus is. The titles they used when they spoke of Jesus teach us valuable truths about his identity.

Christ. "Christ" is one of the most important titles given to Jesus. It is the Greek word for the Hebrew title *Messiah.* The Messiah was the "anointed one of Yahweh" through whom all God's promises made to the Chosen People were fulfilled. Jesus was anointed with the Spirit of God to accomplish our salvation through a life of suffering service.

Suffering Servant. Jesus was not the kind of Messiah his contemporaries expected; that is, an earthly leader who would throw off the yoke of their foreign oppressors. Jesus, rather, was the Suffering Servant of Isaiah who took on the burdens of his people and redeemed them.

Son of God. Through his work and words, Jesus revealed himself to be the unique Son of God. "The Father and I are one" (Jn 10:30).

Lord. "Lord" is a title which the Hebrew scriptures used of God alone. When Christians use this title of Jesus, they proclaim their belief that in Jesus, the Christ, God himself is present and at work.

Word of God. John's gospel underscores the divinity of Jesus:

> In the beginning was the Word:
> the Word was with God
> and the Word was God (Jn 1:1).

Human words reveal our thoughts. They express in a symbolic way what is hidden. In a similar way, the Word of God (Jesus) perfectly reveals God the Father. To see the human Jesus is to see God for Jesus is God-made-man.

Son of Man. Jesus used this title of himself more than any other.

Borrowed from Daniel 7:13, it means two things. First, it refers to Jesus as a human being, one like us who will suffer for and serve all people. Second, it describes his role as the judge and the savior through whom God will fully establish his kingdom at the end of time.

How Was the Faith of the Apostles Preserved?

The first few centuries of the church's history were marked by a growth in numbers and in an understanding of Jesus and the meaning of the paschal mystery. The Fathers of the Church, leading church thinkers and writers, preserved the apostolic faith in Jesus as they attempted to explain his message to people of their day.

What Is a Heresy?

During the first five centuries or so of Christianity, a number of false teachings about who Jesus was arose in the church. These false beliefs, called heresies, did not reflect the Jesus that the apostles experienced or believed in.

The heresies about Jesus clustered into two main categories. One category denied that Jesus was really a human being. Its followers believed that he only took the *appearance* of a man and only *appeared* to suffer and die for us. The other type of heresies, preached by a priest named Arius, denied the divinity of Jesus. For Arius and his followers, Jesus was the greatest of God's creatures, but he was not God himself.

How Was Heresy Dealt With?

These heresies confused and misled people. The official church had to counteract these false notions. Thus, under the guidance of the Holy Spirit, the bishops called a series of ecumenical (worldwide) councils to carefully define the nature of Jesus Christ. The teachings of these councils state the classic dogmas of Catholics and other Christians about Jesus Christ. A dogma is a central doctrine (teaching) of the church which is issued with the highest authority and solemnity by the church leaders.

What Did These Early Councils Teach?

The teaching of these major ecumenical councils about Jesus is summarized here:

- Jesus Christ is true God. He was born of the Father and is of one substance with the Father. There was never a time when he was not God.

- There is only one person in Christ, the divine person, the Word of God, the second Person of the Blessed Trinity.
- There are two distinct natures in the one person of Christ. Jesus has a divine nature and a human nature. He is perfect in divinity and perfect in humanity. He is true God and true man.
- There are two wills in Christ, a divine will and a human will. The human will is perfectly subject to the divine will and without sin.
- The union of the human and divine natures in the one person of Jesus is so perfect that we say, in Jesus, God truly shared our life with us, truly suffered, truly underwent death and truly rose victorious over death.
- Jesus, God-made-man, is our Savior. By uniting ourselves to his death and resurrection through faith, we will share in the eternal life he has won for us.

CONCLUDING REFLECTIONS

''But you, who do you say I am?'' Jesus put this question to Peter, and he asks it again of every person who has or ever will hear his name. Jesus confronts us with an unavoidable question: Do we believe in him?

The New Testament strengthens our faith in Jesus. It tells us that Jesus was a real, historical person. The gospels, faith summaries testifying to the good news of Jesus, proclaim that Jesus is the Savior of the world. They paint a picture of a remarkable person: a generous healer; a compassionate, forgiving and down-to-earth friend of everyone he met; a courageous individual who lived the love he preached; a humble servant who sacrificed his very life for all people; the ''man for others'' who witnessed to God's active love for his children.

The New Testament also reveals what early Christians believed about Jesus. Jesus is the Christ, the Messiah promised to the Chosen People. He is the Suffering Servant, the Son of God, the Lord (God), the Word of God, the Son of Man.

In the early centuries of Christianity, doctrine about Jesus developed in response to certain heresies concerning Jesus. Ecumenical (worldwide) councils met to teach in a definitive way that Jesus is truly God and man; that Jesus is one divine person who has both a divine nature and a human nature; that Jesus has two wills; and that Jesus is our Savior.

Many people throughout history have said yes to Jesus; others have rejected him and his message; still others have not heard his good news. What about you? What do you think of Jesus Christ?

Is Jesus Christ the Lord of your life? Many of us today think of Lord as a title of power, of one who "lords it over others." But once again, Jesus reveals a unique kind of lordship. "I am among you as one who serves" (Lk 22:27). At the Last Supper Jesus says, "You call me Master and Lord, and rightly; so I am" (Jn 13:13), but he shows what true greatness is by washing the feet of his disciples. And he commands us to do likewise.

PRAYER REFLECTION

Praying to Jesus in the Gospels. Put yourself in the presence of the Lord. Hear him reassure you of his great love for you.

Then read a short selection from Jesus' life from one of the gospels. Pause after every few verses. Reflect on the meaning of the passage. Picture all the details of the scene. What might the Lord be saying to you and your life through these verses?

Speak to the Lord in an intimate way. He is your best friend. You might use words such as these:

> Lord Jesus Christ, I believe in you, hope in you, love you with all my strength. Help me be a pleasing child of your loving *Abba*. Show me how to love.

FOR DISCUSSION

1. What do you admire most about Jesus? How would you like to be like him?
2. The doctrine of the incarnation holds that Jesus is God-made-man. If God became one of us, then what does this mean about us as humans?
3. Which title of Jesus answers best for you the question, "Who do you say I am?" Explain your choice.
4. What is your favorite gospel story about Jesus? What does it reveal about him? What might this choice be saying about your own image of Jesus?

FURTHER READING

Read Mark's gospel. (It is the shortest of the gospels and can be read in one sitting. It gives a basic picture of Jesus.)

4

Jesus: Savior and Redeemer

For our sake he was crucified
under Pontius Pilate:
> He suffered, died, and was
> > buried.
> On the third day he rose
> > again in fulfillment
> > of the Scriptures;
> he ascended into heaven
> > and is seated at
> > the right hand
> > of the Father.
> He will come again in
> > glory to judge the
> > living and the
> > dead,
> and his kingdom will
> > have no end.

—from the Nicene Creed

In fact, however, Christ has been raised from the dead, as the first-fruits of all who have fallen asleep. As it was by one man that death came, so through one man has come the resurrection of the dead.

—1 Corinthians 15:20-21

Jesus changes people. Simon bar Jonah encounters Jesus and his life changes forever. He becomes Peter, which means "rock," and will eventually die for his Lord.

Jesus finds a Samaritan woman at a well. He reads her soul and sees her faults, but he accepts her and loves her, even though her people are enemies of the Jews. The Lord asks her to believe in him. She does and spreads the good news of the advent of the Savior to the village and countryside.

Jesus meets a man born blind, a beggar. Jesus makes a mudpack, applies it to the wretched man's eyes and instructs him to wash in a pool. The man does and for the first time in his life he can see. The Pharisees are upset because Jesus cured on the Sabbath. Is he or is he not God's man? The beggar knows. "Lord, I believe" (Jn 9:38).

The historical Jesus met and touched people. His touch always demanded some kind of response. The Lord continues to touch us today—through his church, in his holy word, in the sacraments, through other people. He continues to teach us. What he wants is change, conversion.

This chapter will look to the teaching of Jesus and what he wants from those who believe in him. It will also touch on one of the greatest truths his life reveals: to follow Jesus means to partake in the paschal mystery (see page 55). If we unite ourselves to our Lord, we will share in his everlasting life.

As your read this chapter, ask yourself what the Lord wants of you.

In What Way Can We Call Jesus a Teacher?

The Jesus of history was both a healer and a teacher. He gathered around him 12 apostles and carefully instructed them so that they could carry on his work and preach his message. In addition, he travelled throughout the Holy Land preaching to the people in the fields, on the hillsides, by the seashores, in the marketplaces and in the synagogues.

What Characterized Jesus' Teaching Style?

Jesus' teaching style was imaginative and provoked much interest. His whole life, every action and word he spoke, was his teaching. People took notice when he healed lepers or associated with sinners or dined with tax collectors. They listened when he boldly scolded the hypocrites. But they were especially delighted with his parables. Jesus' parables were short stories with a religious message. They were drawn from ordinary life: fishing, farming, weddings, banquets, housekeeping, children at play. They were memorable and caused people to ponder his message.

Does Jesus' Teaching Have Meaning for Today?

Christians believe that what Jesus taught—both by his life and by his words—conveys the most important message God ever delivered to us. One of Jesus' titles, Word of God, stresses that Jesus communicates the good news of salvation, the message that saves us and wins for us eternal life. The Word of God is the message of God.

The gospels proclaim the meaning of the life, suffering, death, resurrection and glorification of Jesus. But they also record the words of the Word of God. These words are life giving. They show us the way to true happiness; they unlock the meaning of life. When we read the gospels with faith or hear them proclaimed at Mass, we are listening to the Lord himself who said he was the way, the truth and the life.

What Was Jesus' Teaching?

What follows is a short summary of some of the major points of Jesus' teaching, his good news. Read and prayerfully reflect on the scripture passage given for each point.

God's Kingdom Is Already Here. The term *kingdom of God* refers to God's active concern for us. It means that God's will is being done on earth as it is in heaven. It means that God's justice, peace and love are helping to unite his children here on earth. Jesus himself ushers in the kingdom. His healing of people's physical, emotional and spiritual hurts is a sign of the kingdom. Although the kingdom starts small and will meet resistance, it will inevitably grow and powerfully transform all humanity. *(Read Mark 4:1-20; 26-29; 30-32.)*

God is a loving Father. Jesus teaches that God is a loving Father. His love is tender and beyond anything we can comprehend. His love is so great that he sent his only Son to live among us and gain eternal life for us. We can approach God with total confidence that he will provide for us and meet our most pressing needs. *(Read Luke 11:1-13.)*

God is merciful. Jesus proclaims that God forgives all sin. He is like a merciful father who accepts his wayward son back into his household even though the son has squandered his inheritance in a sinful, wasteful life. Because God is so forgiving, we should be joyful, happy people and imitate the Father by forgiving those who have hurt us. *(Read Luke 15:1-32.)*

God's love is for everyone. God's kingdom is open to all. Everyone is invited to the banquet. It is a free gift; we cannot earn it. We show our appreciation when we love others. Jesus taught that the love of God and neighbor are one:

> "*You must love the Lord with all your heart, with all your soul,* and with all your mind. This is the greatest and first commandment. The second resembles it: *You must love your neighbor as yourself*" (Mt 22:37-39).

And who is our neighbor? Everyone, even our enemy.

(*Read Luke 10:29-37 and Matthew 22:1-14.*)

Repentance and imitation of Jesus. If we want to enter the kingdom, we must turn from our sins and put on the mind of Jesus Christ. We should be humble and admit that we need God's help to live good lives. We must believe that Jesus is God's Son, the way to happiness, and we must become his disciples. We must be light to the world, allowing the Lord to shine through us by living lives of service. What we do to others, especially the "least of these," we do to the Lord.

(*Read Luke 18:9-14 and Matthew 25:31-46.*)

The Lord is with us. Jesus promises that he will be with us until the end of time. His kingdom will triumph and be fully established when he comes again in glory. We should risk everything for the kingdom. We should be constantly watchful, living joyfully in God's love for the day of his arrival. In the meantime he has sent us the Holy Spirit who united us in love to the Father and the Son and to all our brothers and sisters. The Spirit—the living God who dwells within us—guides us, strengthens us and sanctifies us as we try to follow in the Lord's footsteps.

(*Read Matthew 13:47-50; 24:45-51; 25:1-10.*)

To accept Jesus is to accept the cross. To follow Jesus into the kingdom means to do the will of God. His will involves doing the right thing and serving others. To do these two things will inevitably lead to suffering, to renouncing sin and the allurements of the world's false enticements to happiness. Doing God's will involves self-denial and sacrifice. But Jesus promises that he will make the burden "light and easy" and that we will share in the peace and joy of the resurrection. A life of service means dying to selfishness, but leads to an eternal life of happiness.

(*Read Luke 12:13-21; 13:22-30; 16:19-31.*)

What Did Jesus Say About. . .?

Possessions

"Watch, and be on guard against avarice of any kind, for life does not consist in possessions, even when someone has more than he needs" (Lk 12:15).

Sincerity

"Be careful not to parade your uprightness in public to attract attention; otherwise you will lose all reward from your Father in heaven" (Mt 6:1).

How to Live

"So always treat others as you would like them to treat you" (Mt 7:12).

Prayer

"Ask, and it will be given to you; search, and you will find; knock, and the door will be opened to you" (Mt 7:7).

Forgiveness

Then Peter went up to him and said, "Lord, how often must I forgive my brother if he wrongs me? As often as seven times?" Jesus answered, "Not seven, I tell you, but seventy-seven times" (Mt 18:21-22).

Faith

"If you had faith like a mustard seed you could say to this mulberry tree, 'Be uprooted and planted in the sea,' and it would obey you" (Lk 17:6).

Discipleship

"If anyone wants to be a follower of mine, let him renounce himself and take up his cross every day and follow me" (Lk 9:23).

True Happiness

"More blessed still are those who hear the word of God and keep it!" (Lk 11:28).

Humility

"Many who are first will be last, and the last, first" (Mk 10:31).

Judgment

"Do not judge, and you will not be judged" (Mt 7:1).

Enemies

"Love your enemies and pray for those who persecute you" (Mt 5:44).

Worry

"Set your hearts on his [the Father's] kingdom first, and on God's saving justice, and all these other things will be given you as well. So do not worry about tomorrow: tomorrow will take care of itself. Each day has enough trouble of its own" (Mt 6:33-34).

Love

"My command to you is to love one another" (Jn 15:17).

Why Do We Call Jesus Christ Our Savior?

Christians hold that Jesus Christ is the key to the mystery of the universe. He is the fullness of God's revelation: "To have seen me is to have seen the Father" (Jn 14:9). Or, as St. Paul writes:

> He is the image of the unseen God,
> the first-born of all creation,
> for in him were created all things
> in heaven and on earth (Col 1:15-16).

This biblical faith statement reminds us that everything that Jesus said and did revealed God. Jesus himself taught that the Father was in him and he in the Father. The words he spoke were from the Father, living in him, doing his work. Above all else Jesus asks for faith.

> "You must believe me when I say
> that I am in the Father and the
>   Father is in me;
> or at least believe it on the
> evidence of these works"
> (Jn 14:11).

What is it that Jesus spoke of? What did he do that demands our attention? Simply put, he came to bring salvation.

What Is Salvation?

Salvation refers to the good and happiness that God intends for us. It refers to the healing of our hurts. It means God's peace. It is the mending of broken relationships which keep us from being whole and at one with God and with our neighbor. It is the showering of God's blessings and attention, his grace, his adoption into his family, his sharing of his life with us. It means the forgiveness of our sins.

Jesus is the Savior. It is his love, his service, his sacrifice, his presence, his death and resurrection that have won eternal life for us. No one else and nothing else can accomplish what Jesus has accomplished: the forgiveness of sin and the gift of eternal life. Jesus is the good news the apostles preached after his resurrection. "For of all the names in the world given to men, this is the only one by which we can be saved" (Acts 4:12).

What Is the Meaning of the Passion and Death of Jesus?

The teaching and life of Jesus is summed up in his passion and death on a cross. Jesus totally identified with the sufferings of all humans. He freely allowed himself to suffer and be put to death. Jesus lived the law of love he calls us to live. His fidelity to his Father's will led him to a life of total service, of giving everything he had for us—his very life.

The death of Jesus would be a tragic ending to the gospels except for the unparalleled fact of his resurrection. Through the death and resurrection of Jesus Christ, death itself died. By accepting our human condition, Jesus allowed the forces of sin to lead him to a brutal death on a cross. Death, in fact, is the worst consequence of sin. Jesus did not want to die. "'Father,' he said, 'if you are willing, take this cup away from me. Nevertheless, let your will be done, not mine'" (Lk 22:42).

Jesus accepted his Father's will. The consequence of his incredible love for us was that he surrendered his life for our sakes. But the Father accepted his life as a gift on behalf of all of us and restored him to a superabundant, glorious, resurrected life.

What Is the Meaning of the Resurrection?

Jesus is risen! This is the good news in miniature. The Lord appeared to his close followers and with his Father sent them the Holy Spirit to go out and continue his good work and to preach the forgiveness of sin and the good news that sin and death have been conquered. Paul calls Jesus the new Adam. Through the sin of Adam, death entered the world; through the passion, death, resurrection and glorification of Jesus, eternal life has been given to us.

What Is the Paschal Mystery?

The Easter mystery (paschal mystery) is the heart of the good news. It sums up God's total love for us. The paschal mystery refers to Jesus' passion, death, resurrection and glorification. Through these key events of our salvation, Jesus redeemed us from slavery to sin and the devil. Christians everywhere believe that Jesus is the source of life and the outpouring of the Holy Spirit on all humanity. The Holy Spirit enables us to call God our Father. Jesus, our brother and Savior, unites perfectly the human and divine. He shares his life with us and through the Holy Spirit instructs us that love of God and neighbor is the vocation of all who belong to God's family.

The paschal mystery is the story of God's love. It is the fulfillment of the promises made in the Hebrew scriptures. It reveals perfectly who and what God is: Love. It is the sign of the new covenant, sealed in our Lord's blood. This story of God's love gives all of us hope. Our life has meaning because Jesus has won eternal life for us. We should rejoice and live the good news as Jesus did—loving, forgiving, healing and reconciling. This is the meaning of Jesus Christ and the vocation of his followers.

CONCLUDING REFLECTIONS _____

Jesus is a teacher *par excellence*. He verbally delivered a life-saving message; more important, he lived what he preached. We have been privileged to hear Jesus' message and to reflect on what he did for us. What difference does Jesus make in your life? For those who believe, Jesus' message is a life-changing one. It is truly "good news."

Jesus revealed that God is a loving *Abba*, "daddy," one whose love knows no limits, one whom we can approach in utter confidence. God's love for us has no strings attached to it; he loves us for who we are. This is great news—we are worth so much that God's only Son gave up his life for us.

Jesus has saved us. He announces God's forgiveness and heals us of all the hurts which evil and sin can cause. He has conquered sin and death. If we join ourselves to him in faith, accept his forgiveness, and turn from sin, we need fear nothing. Jesus' life witnesses to the greatest news possible: Good triumphs over evil; life wins out over death!

Jesus teaches us how to live. As God's Son who entered fully into our human life, he shows us the path to follow: a life of loving service to others. All of us want to know how to lead meaningful, productive lives. We need but look to our Lord's example. He wants to join us on our journey as we throw ourselves into the task of living. Everything that concerns us is of value to him. It all boils down to one thing: Love God above all things and our neighbor as ourselves. God is love and will help us to love.

Jesus is our friend. We can meet the risen Lord in prayer, in the depths of our heart. We can encounter him in scripture and in the sacraments. We can receive him in the Eucharist. We can find him in one another, in the Christian community of which he is the head. We can meet him in a special way in all the needy, hurting people who come into our lives.

Jesus invites us to change so that we may find true life. Conversion is a lifelong challenge. One question remains: Are we willing to cooperate with the Holy Spirit who is at work in us?

PRAYER REFLECTION

A major challenge on our journey through life is to be constantly aware of Jesus' presence. A true test of our sincerity in turning to our Lord is our ability to see him in others and our willingness to respond to him through them. In life we meet many people who are Jesus in disguise. Mother Teresa of Calcutta is one who constantly sees Jesus in those she serves, the poorest of the poor.

Meditate on the following quotation. Then, in the presence of the Lord, examine yourself on the questions which follow.

"In truth I tell you, in so far as you did this to one of the least of these brothers of mine, you did it to me" (Mt 25:40).

1. Who are the "least of these," the brothers and sisters you encounter on a daily basis? Picture them in your mind. See the image of our Lord shining through their faces.

2. What are their most pressing needs? Ask the Lord to give you

insight on how these brothers and sisters need you, your touch, your smile, your acceptance, your support.

3. Will you respond to these needs? Ask the Lord to empower you with the strength of the Holy Spirit to manifest his love to the least of these.

Conclude your prayer session by making a resolution to do something with the insights the Lord sent you.

FOR DISCUSSION

1. Jesus is the Savior of the world. What does it mean for you to say "Jesus saves me"?
2. Jesus calls us to conversion. What needs changing in your life right now so that you can better respond to the Lord Jesus?
3. Jesus came to "comfort the afflicted and afflict the comfortable." How does Jesus comfort you? How does he challenge you?
4. The Lord says we can call God *Abba*, "daddy." What does this mean to you? In what way is God's love also like the love of a mother?
5. How can you live the paschal mystery in your daily life?

FURTHER READING

Read the following parables of Jesus:
The Laborers in the Vineyard (Matthew 20:1-16)
The Rich Man and Lazarus (Luke 16:19-31)
The Good Samaritan (Luke 10:29-37)
The Good Shepherd (John 10:1-21)
The Prodigal Son (Luke 15:11-32)

5

The Holy Spirit: The Power of Love

> . . .by the power of the Holy Spirit
> he was born of the Virgin
>   Mary and became man.
> We believe in the Holy
>   Spirit, the Lord,
>   the giver of life,
>   who proceeds from
>   the Father and the
>   Son.
> With the Father and the
>   Son he is
>   worshipped and
>   glorified.
> He has spoken through
>   the Prophets.
>   —from the Nicene Creed

Life is full of mystery. The natural world is full of silent, invisible power. The imperceptible power of erosion which is at work for eons carved out the magnificent Grand Canyon. The potency hidden in the acorn causes the inevitable growth of the oak tree. The unseen explosions of nuclear energy in our sun millions of miles away give life to our planet. Hidden, silent, powerful realities lurking in the background account for the wonderful and awesome things we see about us. God is also actively working in the world, but in a way that is veiled from direct human observation. Christians believe in the active presence of the Holy Spirit whose life-giving friendship works for us until the end of time. The Father and the Son have sent the Spirit—the power of God's love—to draw us to God. The Spirit transforms our lives from within.

His gifts enable us to accomplish God's saving work for others and the world in which we live. The Spirit is the mystery of God's love alive in the world. This chapter will consider the Spirit's role in our lives as we journey to the Father.

What Does *Spirit* Mean?

A common philosophical definition describes *spirit* as "the life force of living beings." We occasionally use this same concept when we talk about groups, especially athletic teams. Without spirit, there is no enthusiasm, no life. *Spirit* can also mean the real sense or significance of something. The expression "the spirit of the law" reflects this meaning; so does the expression "the spirit of '76."

What Does *Spirit* Mean in a Religious Sense?

We often refer to God as Spirit. The New Testament has many references to the Spirit in connection with Jesus and his followers. Jesus is conceived by the Holy Spirit; God's Spirit descended on him at his baptism; and the Spirit leads him into the desert. Jesus himself promised to send his followers the Spirit of truth who will glorify him. Christians believe that the Holy Spirit is the third person of the Blessed Trinity. He is the Spirit of the Father with whom Jesus is totally filled. He is the Father and Son's Love who is given as a gift to all of Jesus' followers.

What Does Scripture Say About the Holy Spirit?

St. Luke wrote not only the gospel named for him but also the Acts of the Apostles. Acts records the exciting early days of the church, a story which began in an upper room in Jerusalem and spread to the very ends of the Roman Empire. We turn first to the upper room. The apostles were gathered there with some of the women, including Mary, to pray. Perhaps they were still frightened and confused about the events leading to our Lord's death and resurrection.

> Suddenly there came from heaven a sound as of a violent wind which filled the entire house in which they were sitting; and there appeared to them tongues as of fire; these separated and came to rest on the head of each of them. They were all filled with the Holy Spirit and began to speak different languages as the Spirit gave them power to express themselves (Acts 2:2-4).

The apostles went out and spoke to the crowds in tongues, and people from all the different places in the Roman Empire understood them. At first the crowds were skeptical; in fact, they thought the apostles were drunk! But Peter assured them that they were quite sober—after all, it was only 9 a.m.! Peter explained that what was happening was clearly promised by the prophet Joel:

> "In the last days—the Lord declares—*I shall pour out my Spirit on all humanity. Your sons and daughters shall prophesy, your young people shall see visions, your old people shall dream dreams. . . . And all who call on the name of the Lord will be saved"*
> (Acts 2:17,21).

The fire of Pentecost recalls the fire on Mt. Sinai, a symbol of the presence of God. There God made a covenant with Moses. With the fire of Pentecost, the Father and Jesus brought to completion the greatest of all covenants. The Spirit of the risen Jesus and his Father, the Spirit of Love, invaded the disciples of the Lord. Jesus was with his disciples in a totally new way. The age of the church had dawned. The Holy Spirit had called together the community of Jesus' followers and united them into a family of love.

What Does the New Testament Say About the Spirit?

There are many references to the Holy Spirit in the Acts of the Apostles and in the letters of St. Paul. But the gospels also contain important references to the Holy Spirit. John the Baptist is filled with the Spirit in his mother's womb. We are also told that his parents, Elizabeth and Zachary, are filled with the Spirit. The Holy Spirit overshadows the Virgin Mary at the time of the Lord's conception. The Spirit is also present at the Lord's baptism.

John's gospel gives the Holy Spirit center stage. At the Last Supper the Lord tells the apostles that he must leave them for a while, that where he is going they cannot yet go. But he promises:

> "I shall ask the Father,
> and he will give you another Paraclete
> to be with you for ever" (Jn 14:16).

A paraclete is an advocate, someone who will give aid, help, comfort. Jesus himself fits these terms well, but he promised to send *another* paraclete—

> "the Spirit of truth
> whom the world can never accept
> since it neither sees nor knows him;
> but you know him,
> because he is with you, he is in you" (Jn 14:17).

Jesus told his friends that he must go the way of suffering, death and resurrection:

> "Still, I am telling you the truth:
> it is for your own good that I am
>   going,
> because unless I go,
> the Paraclete will not come to you;
> but if I go,
> I will send him to you. . . .
> When the Spirit of truth comes
> he will lead you to the complete
>   truth" (Jn 16:7,13).

Jesus tells us that he goes for our own good. He goes that the Spirit may come. After the Lord's resurrection and ascension into heaven, he is no longer visible to us as he was to the disciples. But he is very much with his followers. The Holy Spirit is the very presence of the risen, glorified Lord, the Spirit of Love who exists with the Father and Son from all eternity.

John explains in a different way than Luke how the Holy Spirit came to the disciples. On Easter Sunday the risen Lord appeared to the apostles who were afraid and confused in the upper room. Twice he offered them his greetings of peace, and then he sent them on a great mission: "As the Father sent me, so I am sending you" (Jn 20:21). After saying this he breathed on them and said:

> "Receive the Holy Spirit.
> If you forgive anyone's sins,
> they are forgiven;
> if you retain anyone's sins,
> they are retained" (Jn 20:22-23).

Just as God breathed life into our first parents at the beginning of creation, so Jesus creates his disciples anew. He gives them a new life, a life of the Spirit, a life as children of God. The Holy Spirit helps Christians on the great mission of continuing Jesus' work of forgiveness and reconciliation.

The gift of the Holy Spirit enabled the apostles, and enables us, to know and to love Jesus in a new way. The Holy Spirit takes away fear and fills us with the strength of the risen Lord so we can accomplish his work on earth. The Lord gives us the life of his Father, the Spirit "enabling us to cry out, 'Abba, Father!' The Spirit himself joins with our spirit to bear witness that we are children of God" (Rom 8:15-16).

How Does the Spirit Appear in the Hebrew Scriptures?

The writers of the Hebrew scriptures also refer to the *spirit* of God, but for them it has the meaning "wind" and "breath"—the breath that gives life. They also describe the spirit of Yahweh in personal terms—guiding, instructing, causing people to rest. But they did not give the Spirit a separate identity; Jesus revealed that the Holy Spirit is a distinct person of the Trinity.

The Hebrew scriptures treat God's spirit as God's action. For example, God's spirit (wind) creates the earth by sweeping over the watery void (Gn 1:1-2); God creates humans by breathing his spirit into their nostrils (Gn 2:7). When the prophet Isaiah speaks of the Spirit, he means God's presence and guidance. Isaiah writes:

> "The spirit of the Lord Yahweh is on me
> for Yahweh has anointed me.
> He has sent me to bring the news
>   to the afflicted,
> to soothe the broken-hearted"
> (Is 61:1).

Thus, the spirit (breath) of God creates and gives life. It also enables the prophets to speak on God's behalf. Furthermore, the Hebrew scriptures tell us that God's spirit will help God's people keep his law (Ez 36:26-28) and that it will be poured out on all people when the Messiah comes. This extraordinary presence of God will enable people to do marvelous works (see Joel 3:1-3).

With the eyes of Christian faith, we can now read the Hebrew scriptures' references to God's spirit and see deeper significance in God's action than did the people of those times. Jesus tells us that the Holy Spirit is a distinct person; the creative breath of life; the presence of the Father and the Son which guides us and gives us courage to speak on God's behalf; the source of the many gifts showered on us.

What Are Some Images of the Holy Spirit?

In Christian art the Holy Spirit is most often depicted as a dove. This image—a symbol of peace, innocence and God's mysterious presence—has roots in salvation history. For example, a dove returns to Noah's ship with an olive branch to signal the end of the great flood. The dove figures most prominently, however, as an image of the Holy Spirit at Jesus' baptism.

The Bible uses other images, among them wind, fire, tongues of fire and water, when it speaks of the Spirit's powerful, mysterious, invisible but nevertheless very real presence.

Wind. A driving wind signalled the advent of the Holy Spirit at Pentecost. But Genesis also speaks of God's Spirit (*ruah* means "wind," "breath" or "spirit") hovering over the watery chaos at the time of the creation of the world. Wind is a powerful image—something invisible but with quite evident effects. God breathes life into Adam; the breath (wind) of God parted the Red Sea and freed the fleeing Israelites from the clutches of Pharaoh; the divine wind sent quail to wandering Israelites in the desert. The image of spirit as wind underscores the life and freedom given God's people through the Holy Spirit.

Fire. Fire is an elemental symbol. It evokes images of light, warmth, transformation, power, mystery. It is an apt image for the Holy Spirit.

In the Hebrew scriptures God is referred to as a consuming fire, even appearing to Moses in a burning bush. Pillars of fire guided the Israelites through the desert at night. Fire also symbolized Yahweh's judgment on his people: It makes pure those who are holy, yet it destroys the wicked city of Sodom.

In the New Testament Jesus refers to himself as the light of the world and calls on his disciples to be light as well. The gift of the Holy Spirit empowers the followers of Jesus to be light to the world. The Spirit is the inner light who gives us the capacity to know Jesus and to burn courageously with his love as we serve others.

Tongues of Fire. The tongue is an organ of speech. Filled with the Holy Spirit, Jesus spoke for God; his words were the Father's words. When Jesus spoke, the storm calmed, demons fled, the sick became well, the dead came back to life, the lowly received hope.

When tongues of fire descended on the apostles, they were given the power to preach the truth about Jesus. And they were understood, even by people who did not speak their language. There is an important lesson in this. In earlier times, when the people tried to reach heaven on their own by building the tower of Babel, they were punished and thrown into confusion. Their pride led to alienation, to disunity; their punishment was to speak in different languages so that they could not understand one another.

The Pentecost experience reverses the Babel experience. The Holy Spirit unifies, breaks down the barriers between individuals and between people and God. The Spirit helps us to communicate—to "come-into-unity." The presence of the Spirit brings joy and helps people turn from sin and accept Jesus.

The image of tongues also brings to mind the Spirit's special presence in prophets. The prophet is one who speaks for God, who testifies to the truth. Burning with the fire of God's love, prophets are men and women of courage who speak for God regardless of the price. Both their words and actions remind others of God's presence and activity in ordinary life.

Water. Genesis reminds us of two important functions of water: destruction and life. When people sinned, God punished them with the waters of the flood. He rescued them when they were wading across the water to escape the Egyptians. Yet, God created out of the watery chaos. And he sent springs to the Chosen People in the desert. The Psalmist compares the thirst for God and the need for water:

> As a deer yearns
> for running streams,
> so I yearn
> for you, my God (Ps 42:1).

Jesus describes himself to the Samaritan woman as the one who quenches our parched souls:

> "But no one who drinks the water
>   that I shall give him
> will ever be thirsty again:
> the water that I shall give him
> will become in him a spring of
>   water, welling up for eternal
>   life" (Jn 4:14).

When the Lord speaks to Nicodemus, he makes clear the association between water and the Holy Spirit:

> "No one can enter the kingdom of God
> without being born through water
>   and the Spirit" (Jn 3:5).

This is an obvious reference to the sacrament of baptism. In baptism, water symbolizes death to an old life of sin and a rebirth to an eternal life. For the Christian, baptism represents initiation into the Body of Christ and bestows on the disciple the gift of the Holy Spirit.

What Are the Gifts of the Spirit?

The goal of Christian life is to let Jesus the Lord live in us and work through us. The Holy Spirit enables this to happen.

The gift of the Holy Spirit makes us children of God and brothers and sisters to one another. The Spirit stamps us with a new identity and makes it possible for us to relate to others with love and compassion as followers of Jesus.

St. Paul teaches that the Holy Spirit enables us to believe in Jesus Christ. Faith in the Lord, like the Spirit himself, is a free gift from God. It helps to free us from the enticements of a sinful society so that we can model our lives on the Lord, producing good works for our brothers and sisters.

The Holy Spirit showers us with many gifts to accomplish God's work in the world. The Spirit teaches us to pray. He grants us the means to live a Christian life, the seven gifts of the Holy Spirit: *wis-*

dom, understanding, counsel, fortitude, knowledge, piety and *fear of the Lord*. In addition, he gives each of us special gifts to build up the Lord's body. Some of us are called to be prophets; others to proclaim the good news; some to heal; still others to minister and teach.

What Are the Fruits of the Spirit?

The greatest gift of all is the gift of love. St. Paul said, "Make love your aim" (1 Cor 14:1). The Holy Spirit is the Spirit of Love.

> No one has ever seen God,
> but as long as we love each other
> God remains in us
> and his love comes to its perfection in
>   us.
> This is the proof that we remain in him
>   and he in us,
> that he has given us a share in his
>   Spirit.
> God is love,
> and whoever remains in love
>   remains in God
> and God in him (1 Jn 4:12-13,16).

The Holy Spirit makes us Christlike. The Holy Spirit *sanctifies* us, that is, makes us holy. And love is, in short, what it means to be holy.

Love is always patient and kind; love is never jealous; love is not boastful or conceited, it is never rude and never seeks its own advantage, it does not take offence or store up grievances. Love does not rejoice at wrongdoing, but finds its joy in the truth. It is always ready to make allowances, to trust, to hope and to endure whatever comes (1 Cor 13:4-7).

Thus it is the Holy Spirit who empowers us to live as companions of Jesus Christ. The Spirit is the source of the good that we see in those who are alive with Christ. The fruits of the Holy Spirit—*love, joy, peace, patient endurance, kindness, generosity, faith, mildness* and *chastity*—are the signs and sources of our happiness.

What Is the Charismatic Renewal?

The Charismatic Renewal in the church gets its name from the Greek word *charism* which means "a free gift" or "favor." It is a movement that has grown in the Catholic church in recent decades as an outgrowth of a renewed interest in the work of the Holy Spirit in the church. Many people are convinced that the Holy Spirit is working in a specially dramatic way in our day, and that he is showering his gifts and powers much as he did in the early church.

Those involved in the Charismatic Renewal generally belong to prayer groups which charismatics believe help them live a holier "life in the Spirit." Participation in charismatic prayer has helped many people deepen their commitment to Jesus Christ.

Certain gifts of the Holy Spirit have been bestowed on some of those who participate in charismatic prayer. For example, some charismatics testify to the gift of healing, especially the healing of emotional hurts. This often takes place when other members of a prayer group lay hands on the person and pray for his or her wholeness. Healings of physical ailments have also taken place. Charismatics believe in the power of prayer and take to heart Jesus' invitation to pray over the sick.

A phenomenon among charismatics is glossolalia, or speaking in tongues. This is a special manifestation of the Holy Spirit in which an individual or group speaks in an unknown language. Along with the gift of tongues is the gift of interpreting the tongues so that the community prayer takes on more meaning for the individuals participating in it.

A sign that the gifts given to charismatics are authentic is that they build up the Body of Christ. The sign of God working in any spiritual movement is that the fruits of the movement tend to aid the spirit of cooperation, love and mutual support of fellow Christians.

See 1 Corinthians 12-14 for St. Paul's discussion of charismatics.

CONCLUDING REFLECTIONS _____

In the Bible, the Lord reveals the Holy Spirit to us in a number of images. The Spirit, the power of love, is life-giving breath, a wind that creates and guides. The Spirit is the fire that enables us to love, burning in our hearts to create community with others and the Lord; the life-giving water that brings growth; and tongues of fire that embolden us to proclaim the prophetic word with courage.

Common human experiences with these elemental images can reinforce our understanding and appreciation of the role of the Holy Spirit in our lives. For example, just as a cool breeze refreshes us on a sweltering day, so does the Spirit comfort us when we are troubled. Just as the sailor needs the breeze to fill the sails, so do we need the gentle guidance of the Spirit on our journey to the Father.

The warmth of a fireplace in the dead of winter conjures up nostalgic images of home and hearth and love. It is the Holy Spirit who thaws our cold hearts, teaching us how to love. The secret attraction of a roaring bonfire at a family picnic celebrates family unity. The Holy

Spirit burns in the hearts of Christians as he draws them into community around the Lord's table.

A word of comfort to a troubled colleague or a hurting family member demonstrates the healing power of human speech rightly used. The Holy Spirit, who appeared as tongues of fire, inspires us even today to seek out and speak on behalf of the ''least of these'' in our midst, for example, speaking in defense of the unborn.

All of us have relished a sip of cold, refreshing water for our dry throats. The Holy Spirit is living water. The Spirit quenches our thirst for meaning in life by attracting us to Jesus Christ. A gentle rainfall on a dusty day brings growth to crops; the Holy Spirit gives growth to our faith, especially when we feel spiritually dry.

These powerful images of the Holy Spirit remind us that God's presence sustaining our very lives is a dynamic power of love.

PRAYER REFLECTION

Pray the following with deep faith and conviction:

> Come, Holy Spirit, fill the hearts
>   of your faithful
> and kindle in them the fire
>   of your love.
> Send forth your Spirit, O Lord,
>   and renew the face of the
>   earth.
> O God,
> on the first Pentecost
> you instructed the hearts of those
>   who believed in you
> by the light of the Holy Spirit;
> under the inspiration of the same
>   Spirit,
> give us a taste for what is right
>   and true
> and a continuing sense of his joy-
>   bringing presence and power,
> through Jesus Christ our Lord.
>   Amen.

FOR DISCUSSION

1. What is the most meaningful image of God for you? Explain.
2. The Holy Spirit enables us to be members of God's family. This means that others are our brothers and sisters. What is the practical

meaning of this truth in your daily relations with other people?

3. The Holy Spirit is a spirit of truth, a truth that leads to freedom. How can you personally witness to the truth? Give personal examples of how the truth set you free.

4. The Holy Spirit enables God's children to love. Loving others often increases our faith. Give examples of times in your life when your love of others increased your faith in a loving God.

FURTHER READING

Hebrew Scriptures:
  Genesis 1:1-2; 2:7
  Isaiah 11:1-3; 61:1-2
  Ezekiel 36:26-28; 37:1-14
  Joel 3:1-3
New Testament:
  1 Corinthians 12:4—13:13

6

The Blessed Trinity: Unity in Community

Glory be to the Father,
and to the Son,
and to the Holy Spirit,
as it was in the beginning,
is now,
and will be forever.   Amen.

Some people are so proud of their intelligence that a pundit once observed that they are like condemned criminals who are proud of the vastness of their prison cells.

The famous poet Milton taught that the end of all learning is to know God, and out of that knowledge to love and imitate him.

True knowledge of God does not begin with intellectual prowess but with humility. It is the one sure path to God. When asked what is the first thing in religion, St. Augustine replied, "The first, second, and third thing therein—no, all—is humility."

Christians learn this lesson well when they contemplate the fathomless mystery of the Blessed Trinity. We believe that God has revealed himself to us as a trinity of persons—the Father, the Son and the Holy Spirit. This is the central doctrine of Catholic faith. All other teachings of the church are derived from it. God's true nature is a deep mystery, beyond mere human knowledge. Yet, the Lord Jesus has privileged us with the profound truth that "The Father is God, the Son is God, and the Holy Spirit is God, and yet there are not three gods but one God" (Athanasian Creed).

In this chapter we will summarize some of the major teachings of the last few chapters. We will look to Jesus to see that he reveals the *one* true God as a Blessed Trinity. Finally, we will briefly state what the church teaches about this mystery: unity in community.

Who Is God?

When Moses asked God for his name, God responded, "Yahweh." Yahweh, a name so sacred that pious Jews avoided even saying it, means "I am who am." This means, simply, Yahweh is being itself. Yahweh is truth.

Everything Jesus did and everything he taught reveals to us the truth, that which is real. Jesus tells us the true nature of God. Let us highlight here some of his teachings concerning the Trinity, one God in a community of three persons.

What Does Jesus Teach Us of God the Father?

The God of the Hebrews revealed in the early scriptures is none other than the Father of the Lord Jesus Christ. Jesus is his unique Son, a Son who shares in the nature of the Father.

In his prayer Jesus addresses God as *Abba*, a simple term of endearment. In speaking about the Father, Jesus reveals his special and unique relationship to him by saying "my heavenly Father" (Mt 15:13) and "your Father in heaven" (Mt 5:45).

Jesus tells the apostles that they—and we—can address God as *Abba*, too. We have been adopted into the family. What is our Father like? Jesus taught us that the Father loves us in a way that is beyond our comprehension. He is like the father in the parable of the Prodigal Son who welcomes back his wayward son with open arms—no questions asked. He is like a woman who rejoices when she finds a lost coin, and like a good shepherd who goes out of his way to seek a lost sheep. The Father loves immeasurably and unconditionally. We can't earn this love; it is a gift showered on good and evil people alike.

Jesus' whole life centered around doing his Father's will. He wants us to obey the Father's will, too. He wants us to pursue his kingdom, giving up everything else if necessary, like the man who sold everything he had to buy the pearl of great price. He wants us to imitate his Father—our Father—by forgiving those who hurt us, by refraining from judging others, by seeking perfection in everything. He tells us not to fret because our loving Father will take care of all our needs; after all, he provides for the birds of the field, and we are more important than they.

Jesus tells us to pray to the Father, that he will answer us. He urges us not to give up. God knows our needs and will give us what is good for us.

St. Paul reminds us that the Father creates all things and wills the salvation of everyone through his Son. He sent his only Son to redeem us and call us to faith and glory. God is the Father of all people, but he is the special Father of Jesus Christ. The Father, who raised Jesus up, will also raise us up on the last day.

> Thank God, then, for giving us the victory [over death] through Jesus Christ our Lord (1 Cor 15:57).

Jesus used the idea of Father often in his teaching about God. The medieval mystic Juliana of Norwich and others point out that the idea of God as Mother also adds to our understanding of God's love for us. Willing to sacrifice her own life, a mother gives her child life by entering the valley of the shadow of death. A good mother tenderly protects, unblinkingly forgives and unconditionally accepts her child. Every child who experiences true motherly love knows that it is the most natural, available, compassionate, and serving kind of love known to us. God's love is exactly like that. A Jewish proverb says it best: "God could not be everywhere, and therefore he made mothers."

For most of us thinking about God as Mother or Father is helpful, but we must remember that God is neither male nor female. The best of human parents have their limitations. God embodies all the positive traits we traditionally associate with both fathers and mothers—creativity, sustenance, nuture, guidance, availability, tenderness, compassion, love. But God possesses these traits without limit. God's love is unimaginably greater than the love of any human father or mother.

What Do We Know of God the Son?

Christians believe that Jesus is "the human face of God." When Philip asked Jesus to show him and the other apostles the Father, Jesus replied:

> "Anyone who has seen me has seen the
> Father,
> so how can you say, 'Show us the
> Father'?
> Do you not believe
> that I am in the Father and the
> Father is in me?" (Jn 14:9-10).

It was only after the resurrection of Jesus and the outpouring of the Holy Spirit on Pentecost that the apostles and other disciples began to really understand who Jesus was. Yet Jesus had done many startling things while he was with them: He cured lepers, made deaf people hear, gave sight to the blind, enabled the lame to walk, drove out demons. He demonstrated his power over nature when he calmed the storm and multiplied the loaves and fishes. He claimed unity with the Father and backed up his claim by forgiving sin, something only God could do. He raised the dead to life. He claimed to be the resurrection and the life, the living water that leads to eternal life, the light of the world.

As we have seen, Jesus called God Father and related to him in a unique way. He taught that only the Son knows the Father, that all the Father has is his, that the Father has given him all power, that his words are the words of the Father who sent him. If we know Jesus, we know the Father. And if we love Jesus, both Jesus and the Father will take up their dwelling within us.

The early Christians, who had seen Jesus risen from the dead and who were filled with the power of the Holy Spirit, proclaimed with no hesitation: Jesus is Lord! Jesus is the Son of God! Jesus is God!

Everything about Jesus reveals the Father. His presence, his words, his healing touches, his forgiving glances and especially his death and resurrection show us what is really real. They reveal God because Jesus is the Word of God. Christians believe:

> For this is how God loved the world:
> he gave his only Son,
> so that everyone who believes in
>   him may not perish
> but may have eternal life (Jn 3:16).

As Matthew said, Jesus is Emmanuel, "God-is-with-us." Jesus is God-made-man who comes to deliver us from sin and death and to bestow on us a share in the eternal life he shares with the Father from all time. And he gives the greatest of all promises: "And look, I am with you always; yes, to the end of time" (Mt 28:20).

What Do We Know of the Holy Spirit?

In the last chapter we saw the many references to the Holy Spirit in the teaching of Jesus and the early Christians. For example, the Spirit empowered the early Christians on Pentecost Sunday and was with the Lord throughout his ministry. Moreover, Jesus promised to send the Paraclete to his followers. He promised that the Spirit of truth and love would take up his dwelling in God's people.

One very important gospel passage testifies to the Spirit's presence at the Lord's baptism:

> Now it happened that when all the people had been baptized and
> while Jesus after his own baptism was at prayer, heaven opened and

the Holy Spirit descended on him in a physical form, like a dove. And a voice came from heaven, *"You are my Son; today have I fathered you"* (Lk 3:21-22).

These verses are important for two reasons: First, they explicitly mention all three persons of the Trinity, that is, the Father, the Son and the Spirit. Catholics use this, and other passages, to help root their belief in the key doctrine of the Trinity, one God and three divine persons. Second, this passage shows how Jesus was filled with the Spirit as he launched out on his public ministry. The Spirit was with Jesus in the desert and during his entire teaching and healing ministry. For example, Jesus cast out demons by the power of the Holy Spirit.

The Holy Spirit attracts us to the Son so that we are able to recognize him as the Messiah, our Savior. He enables us to proclaim that God is our Father. He is the source of all good gifts given us by our gracious, loving God.

What Is the Blessed Trinity?

> In the name of the Father
> and of the Son
> and of the Holy Spirit. Amen.

With this short prayer Christians profess their belief in the greatest of all mysteries—the mystery of the Blessed Trinity. The doctrine of the Trinity is central to Christian faith.

This doctrine is rooted in the first Christians' experience of Jesus. His life, death and resurrection revealed to them one God who exists in a relationship of three persons: Father, Son and Holy Spirit. St. Paul expressed this early belief eloquently when he ended a letter to the Corinthians with the following blessing:

> The grace of the Lord Jesus Christ, the love of God and the fellowship of the Holy Spirit be with you all (2 Cor 13:13).

How Does the Trinity Relate to Us?

We can never fully comprehend the doctrine of the Trinity. God is beyond full human knowledge. God is more intimate to us than we are to ourselves. He chose to approach us through Jesus and take up his dwelling in us through the Holy Spirit. This is the mystery of love itself: We have been given a glimpse of God's own life.

The mystery of God is revealed in Jesus. When we develop a relationship with Jesus, we become aware that the one God who is at work in Jesus is also present in his followers. The Holy Spirit brings life to each individual Christian and to the Body of Christ, the church.

One way to approach the mystery of the Trinity is to reflect on the one God experienced as three distinct persons, each relating to us in a special way. God the Father creates all things and continues to give life and being to everything in creation. God the Son lived among us, taught us of the Father's love, and won for us eternal salvation. God the Holy Spirit is the Love of God who dwells in us and in the church. The Spirit is the source of unity, courage, truth and love for all humanity.

What Are the Relationships Within the Trinity?

Another way to approach the mystery of the Trinity is to reflect on God as three persons, Father, Son and Holy Spirit, relating among themselves. But we must not think of *person* in the same sense as we are persons. There are not three separate consciousnesses in God. There is only one simple being. There are not three separate intelligences or wills in the one God. When one person of the Trinity acts, the other two persons also act. Each person is *distinct* but does not act separately from the others. God is one, a community in unity.

God acts as one, though we *appropriate* certain actions to each of the persons; for example, *creation* to the Father, *redemption* to the Son, and *sanctification* to the Holy Spirit. These are called the *missions* of each of the three divine persons. But even here all three persons act as one and are fully present in all the missions. God loves us with one and the same love and knows us with one and the same knowledge.

What, then, is the difference in the three persons? The differences are in *relationships*. Traditional Catholic teaching explains the relationships among the three persons of the Trinity this way:

The Father. The First Person of the Trinity is absolutely without origin. From all eternity he "begets" the Son, the Second Person of the Trinity. The Son proceeds from the Father. There was never a time when the Son did not proceed from the Father.

The Son. The Father's begetting the Son is described as God knowing himself perfectly. The Father expresses himself perfectly to himself, and this is the Son, the Word of God. Thus the Son is the Father's perfect, divine expression of himself. They are one, yet distinct.

The Holy Spirit. The relationship of the Father and Son is a perfect relationship. The Father and Son love each other with an eternal, perfect, divine love. The love *proceeds* from the Father and the Son and is called the Third Person of the Trinity, the Holy Spirit. The Holy Spirit proceeds from both the Father and the Son as the perfect expression of their divine love for each other. Thus the Holy Spirit is the

Spirit of Love between the Father and the Son; the Spirit binds them into a community of unity.

In a classic expression of faith, the Athanasian Creed expresses the relationships of the three persons of the Trinity this way:

> **The Father is not made by anyone, nor created, nor begotten. The Son is from the Father alone, not made, not created, but begotten. The Holy Spirit is from the Father and the Son, not made, not created, not begotten, but proceeding. . . .The entire three Persons are co-eternal with one another and co-equal, so that. . . .both Trinity in Unity and Unity in Trinity are to be adored.**

CONCLUDING REFLECTIONS

Our minds can never grasp the mystery of God. We can never explain three divine persons in the one divine nature. We simply believe it as a truth that Jesus revealed to us.

We believe that our one God is a Father who loves us and will never forget us. We believe that God is our Savior Jesus Christ who loved us so much that he gave up his life so that we can have eternal life. We believe that God is a Spirit of love who dwells within us.

This privileged knowledge of our God can fill us with a sense of peace and confidence about our future. Friends may abandon us; family members may disappoint us; setbacks will inevitably come our way. But God will never let us down. He lives in us. We need but spend some time in prayer to be aware of his presence and allow his love to penetrate us.

Our God is a God who knows and loves. God is a community of persons. To be godlike means to know him, to love him and to serve him by joining others in community. Our eternal destiny is to pray *to* the Father, *through* the Son, *in* the Holy Spirit of love. The Holy Spirit unites us to the Father and to Jesus and to every other person. The Holy Spirit helps us look at others and ourselves with love and appreciation. Our knowledge of God is a great gift we have been given, and it can help us live our lives in a hopeful way.

Jesus came to reveal the nature of reality. He came to tell us about God and about ourselves, God's children. In revealing the nature of God as unity-in-community, community-in-unity, Jesus told us a profound truth about human life as well. As we journey on our pilgrimage to the Father, with Jesus our brother, in the Holy Spirit, we should remember that a goal of Christian life is to join with our fellow pilgrims in approaching our Father. A Christian simply cannot approach God alone.

PRAYER REFLECTION _____

This chapter began with a Christian doxology, a prayer of praise to the Blessed Trinity. It now concludes with the "Greater Doxology," a hymn in praise of Jesus Christ who is in union with the Father and Holy Spirit. This hymn is recited or sung at most Sunday liturgies.

> Glory to God in the highest,
>   and peace to his people on earth.
> Lord God, heavenly King,
> Almighty God and Father,
>   we worship you, we give you thanks,
>   we praise you for your glory.
> Lord Jesus Christ, only Son of the Father,
> Lord God, Lamb of God,
> you take away the sin of the world:
>   have mercy on us;
> you are seated at the right hand of the Father:
>   receive our prayer.
> For you alone are the Holy One,
> you alone are the Lord,
> you alone are the Most High,
>   Jesus Christ,
> with the Holy Spirit,
> in the glory of God the Father.   Amen.

FOR DISCUSSION _____

1. One of the most popular and important of all Christian prayers is the simple yet profound Sign of the Cross. What do you do *in the name of* the Father, the Son and the Holy Spirit?
2. What does the doctrine of the Blessed Trinity reveal to you about God? about reality? about your own life?
3. In your own prayer life, how do you relate to each person of the Trinity?

FURTHER READING _____

Ecclesiasticus 11:12-28 (trust in God alone)
Galatians 4—5 (sons of God and Christian liberty)

7

The Christian Community

> "All authority in heaven and on earth has been given to me. Go, therefore, make disciples of all nations; baptise them in the name of the Father and of the Son and of the Holy Spirit, and teach them to observe all the commands I gave you."
>
> —Matthew 28:18-20

The famous line penned by the English poet John Donne—"No man is an island"—is truer now than ever. The concept of community is very real in our global village. The survival of "spaceship earth" depends on peoples and nations striving to live as a human community.

Community comes into being when people share common interests and work for common goals. The more people share and work together the deeper, the richer is the community.

Using this description of community, it is easy to see that the church is also a community which shares common interests and works for common goals. The church is the family of believers in Jesus Christ, a community formed in his name.

Look at a typical parish liturgy. You will find all kinds of people— young and old; male and female; some who are financially well off, others less so; some who are of Irish extraction, others of Polish; some who are vitally interested in the proceedings, others who appear bored. Surely Christians are unique individuals with lots of differences. But they do have something vital in common: By virtue of their baptism into the Christian family, they come together as a community to acknowledge and celebrate the Lordship of Jesus Christ.

This chapter will examine the church, this community formed and sustained by the Spirit of Jesus Christ. The Lord's concern for each of us is both individual and communal. He brings us together and unites us into his people, his family, in order to continue his work on earth. We are united in that work with our Christian brothers and sisters who have gone before us in death and with those who will come after us.

As we look at our Christian family, we should note that people bring various preconceptions to a discussion of church. If you were to ask different Catholics to say the first thing that comes to mind when they hear the word *church*, you would get a variety of answers. Some would answer that the church is a building. Others might respond "people," "the Body of Christ," "laity," "priests and nuns," or "the pope." The church is all of these things, but some concepts are more important than others.

What Is the Church?

The word *church* translates the scriptural word *ekklesia,* which means "those called apart." Christians are called apart to openly proclaim belief in our Lord Jesus Christ. The church is the community of those who are called to acknowledge that Jesus is the Lord; it is a community of believers who live a sacramental life and who commit themselves to fellowship and service for the sake of God's kingdom. Above all else, the church is the mystery of God's loving grace.

Because the church is unlike any other human community, no one definition or description can exhaust all its rich meaning. Thus the bishops at the Second Vatican Council described the church by using biblical images: mystery, the People of God, the Body of Christ, the sacrament of Jesus Christ.

Although the images listed above are the key images we will discuss, the Bible alludes to many other images of the church, for example, pilgrim, God's building and farm, Christ's bride and the flock of Christ. Each of these adds to our understanding and appreciation of the mystery of the church. For example, the pilgrim image stresses that the church is a community on its way to a final destination. The building and farm images connote that the Lord has constructed his community and that he still cultivates it like a farmer tending his crops. The bride imagery demonstrates the great love Jesus has for his church and that intimate union with him is a major benefit of being a member of the Christian community. The flock image reminds the community that it has a sacrificing shepherd whose voice must be listened to if it is to escape being lost and even destroyed.

What Does the Church as Mystery Mean?

St. Augustine defined a *mystery* as a visible sign of some invisible grace. Pope Paul VI had something similar in mind when he described the church as "a reality imbued with the hidden presence of God."

Therefore, to call the church a mystery is to say that the invisible, almighty God is working through this faith community, this institution which exists to continue the saving work of Jesus Christ.

The mystery of the church is intimately related to the mystery of God working through Jesus Christ. In chapters 1-3 of his letter to the Ephesians, St. Paul describes how God the Father is unfolding his plan of salvation and reconciliation of all people through his Son, Jesus Christ. Paul calls God's plan the mystery hidden for ages, a mystery that is now being unfolded in the church, the mystery of Christ.

What Does the Church as the People of God Mean?

The image of the church as the People of God has its roots in the Old Testament covenant between God and Israel. In this covenant God wished to sanctify and save not only individuals, but individuals formed into a loving community. The Hebrew scriptures tell a story of God teaching, preserving and cherishing his people. This was in preparation for the new people of God formed through the blood of Jesus Christ. The new covenant calls all people to unity in the Holy Spirit.

The Greek word for people is *laos*, from which we get the word *laity*. This image emphasizes the dignity of each individual Christian who has been called into a fellowship of life, love and truth. The Lord Jesus invites the members of this fellowship to continue his work of redemption in the world, to be light of the world and salt of the earth. To be truly alive and active members of the church means we must help bring others to the Lord Jesus both by example and direct effort.

The People of God are those of us who are baptized and acknowledge that Jesus Christ is Lord and Savior. Our mission is to live our lives in such a way that the Lord's light shines forth in the world through us. When we love, God's love can be seen. When we act like Christ, we are like salt. Just as the presence of salt in food enhances its flavor, so the presence of God's people should bring to the world the exciting news that Jesus is the Savior and that God's kingdom has been established in our midst.

Is the Church the Same as God's Kingdom?

God's kingdom, his saving activity in human history which draws all people to him, is different from the church. The church includes only baptized members. Thus the kingdom of God is broader than the church. The kingdom of God extends to all people who are saved, from the time of Adam to the end of the world. But there is an intimate connection between the church and the kingdom of God.

The church is the initial budding forth of the kingdom of God; its members work on behalf of the kingdom in an explicit, conscious way. The church grows slowly, straining toward the fulfillment of the kingdom. As God's people, we hope for a day of glory when we will be united to our king. Because the church ministers to the world on behalf of the Lord, the church helps advance the fulfillment of the kingdom in all persons of good will. The full flowering of the kingdom will take place at the end of human history. It is the privileged task of Christians to help promote God's saving activity for all people everywhere and in all times.

What Does the Church as the Body of Christ Mean?

This important image of the church can be traced to both Jesus and St. Paul. Jesus often identified himself with his followers. He proclaimed:

> "In truth I tell you, in so far as you did this to one of the least of these brothers of mine, you did it to me" (Mt 25:40).

And he said to his disciples:

> "Anyone who listens to you listens to me; anyone who rejects you rejects me" (Lk 10:16).

At the Last Supper Jesus spoke of the unity between himself and those who accept him in faith and love:

> "I am the vine,
> you are the branches.
> Whoever remains in me, with me in him,
> bears fruit in plenty;
> for cut off from me you can do nothing" (Jn 15:5).

Just as the vine and branches are one living reality, so it is with Christ and his church, Jesus and his loving disciples.

St. Paul considered the Body of Christ imagery central in his preaching. He was powerfully influenced by the risen Lord's question put to him when he was on his way to persecute the Christians in Damascus:

> "Saul, Saul, why are you persecuting me? . . . I am Jesus, whom you are persecuting" (Acts 9:4-5).

By persecuting Christians, Saul (Paul) had been persecuting the Lord himself. This revelation prompted Paul to write to the Corinthians:

> Now Christ's body is yourselves, each of you with a part to play in the whole (1 Cor 12:27).

The risen, glorified Lord is present in the world today through Christians. We are his hands, his loving touch, his understanding glance, his sympathetic word of comfort to the lonely and suffering, his instrument used to preach the good news of salvation and forgiveness.

Christ is the head of the body, we are its members. We become incorporated into the body through baptism. The Holy Spirit unites the members into one body:

> We were baptised into one body in a single Spirit, Jews as well as Greeks, slaves as well as free men, and we were all given the same Spirit to drink (1 Cor 12:13).

The Holy Spirit, then, is the soul of the church, a Spirit of unity who overcomes all natural divisions of race, color, nationality and sex.

The church as the Body of Christ also underscores the dignity of each individual member. Just as each member of a person's body has a specific and important function to play, so, too, in the church each member has a specific and important role to play. Some are apostles, some prophets, others teachers, and still others miracle workers, healers, assistants or administrators. We all have specific gifts, but the greatest gift of all is the capacity to love with the love of our God.

Is the Church Perfect?

When Christians love, they are building up the Body of Christ. Each person is gifted by the Lord to do his work in a way no one else can. However, sometimes Christians fail to love. Because the church includes a human, as well as a divine dimension, the church can sin. And the church has sinned through its history by not being Christ. The story of the Christian people reveals that we are both holy and sinful. This is the paradox of Christian life: Jesus Christ comes to us through people like ourselves, people who are weak and sinful and not loving. We are a pilgrim people, a people on our way to total union with God. We are not yet perfect. God is not finished with us yet.

What Is a Sacrament?

A sacrament is a special kind of sign or symbol. A symbol, by definition, is something concrete that points to another reality. A stop sign, for example, uses shape, color and a word (all symbols) to point to the *idea* of stopping. A wedding ring points to the reality of perpetual love. A country's flag brings to mind the values of that particular nation. But all of these symbols do not bring about what they point to. A stop sign does not *cause* a driver to stop; a wedding ring does not guarantee marital happiness; a nation's flag does not automatically bring about patriotism or devotion to the values of the country.

A sacrament is also a symbol, an *efficacious symbol*. An efficacious symbol brings about what it points to; an efficacious symbol embodies the very reality that it represents. Hence, a sacrament is a very special symbol. It is a concrete reality that, in some way, is what it represents. Thus it is accurate to say that Jesus is the sacrament of God's love. Jesus not only points to God; he is God. He not only symbolizes God's love; he is God's love. He is what he represents. He is the first and most important sacrament of all. "Anyone who has seen me has seen the Father" (Jn 14:9).

How Is the Church a Sacrament?

The church is like a faceted stone. We get a different view each time we consider it from a new perspective. The Second Vatican Council shed more light on the nature of the church with its insight about the church as sacrament:

> By her intimate relationship with Christ, the Church is a kind of sacrament or sign of intimate union with God, and of the unity of all mankind. She is also an instrument for the achievement of such unity (*Dogmatic Constitution on the Church*, Article 1).

Simply put, the church is a concrete sign of Christ's presence to all people. It is an outward, visible sign of God's loving gift of himself in human history. Like every other sign and symbol, the church must point to something. This is especially true of an efficacious symbol that embodies what it represents. Thus, the church must lead us to what it signifies, that is, to Christ who is united to people through the church. The church helps put us in touch with the Lord that it represents.

How Does the Church Lead Us to Christ?

The church is a sacrament of Christ—his visible presence in the world—when it presents the message of God's love in Jesus Christ, builds up the Christian community, and serves all people, especially those in need.

Message. Down through the centuries the church has announced the good news that the God of love invites all people to the fullness of life. Some people have never heard this good news; others have only heard it in a partial or confused way. A major mission of the church is to proclaim the good news of God's love in Jesus Christ. Jesus himself commanded his disciples to do this when he told them:

> "As the Father sent me, so am I sending you" (Jn 20:21).

The heart of the good news is found in the *kerygma*, the central message of the gospel proclaimed by the apostles. We find a masterful summary of the kerygma in Peter's first sermon on Pentecost Sunday (Acts 2:14-41). Peter reviewed the high points of Jesus' life, death and his resurrection. He proclaimed that Jesus is Lord, the key to the mystery of life. He invited people to turn from their sinful lives, to accept Jesus Christ in faith, and to be baptized with water in the Holy Spirit. The church must continue to preach this message to all people everywhere. By doing so the church helps lead people to the Lord Jesus.

Community. The church builds up the community of believers when it lives the gospel it proclaims. If Christians do not live the gospel message, the church cannot be a believable symbol of Christ. To be an effective and credible sign of the gospel, others must be able to see in the church a community united by faith, hope and love.

> "It is by this love you have for
>   one another,
> that everyone will recognize you,
> as my disciples" (Jn 13:35).

If non-believers see loving, caring people, they naturally take notice and ask themselves what this group stands for. The technical term for this reality of Christian community is *koinonia*, or fellowship.

Service. The third task of the church is *diakonia*, which means service. The image of a servant best describes this task. Jesus showed us the way when he, the king of kings, took off his cloak and washed the feet of the apostles at the Last Supper. Footwashing was a menial task that even servants were not required to perform. But Jesus washed the feet of his disciples to show that to be great in the kingdom of God, a person must become a servant to others.

A Christian should be one who serves. A follower of Jesus must be a minister to the needs of others. The church must witness to God's love by translating its words of love into concrete acts of service for all, especially the poor, the lonely, the imprisoned, the sick and the suffering. Actions speak louder than words. The church which announces that our loving God cares for people in their misery must be willing to take that message and make it real by the deeds it performs for others.

CONCLUDING REFLECTIONS

Song lyrics are sometimes so inane that we chuckle at them. At other times, though, they seem to reveal profound truths. For example, the song "People" was right on target when it said that "people who need people are the luckiest people in the world." The church recognizes this reality. Christians need the love of Jesus, the support and strength of the Holy Spirit and the encouragement of fellow-believers on their pilgrimage to the Father.

Christians need the church which is primarily a mystery of God's profound love for us in Jesus Christ. We can never totally fathom this love; we can accept it and try to live it. The Christian community is a special people—God's people—set aside to witness in word and deed to God's activity in the world.

The church is also the Body of Christ. Jesus established the church and is its head. Each baptized Christian is a member of Christ's body, gifted in a special way to carry on the work of the Lord.

In addition, the church is a sacrament of Christ—his visible presence in the world. All Christians are called to be signs of God's love by heralding the good news of God's love in Jesus Christ, by building up Christian community, and by serving all people, especially "the least of these."

Christians need the support of their fellow-believers to continue to be faithful symbols of Jesus Christ. The world also needs the Christian community because the church is entrusted to proclaim and live the good news of eternal salvation for all people.

PRAYER REFLECTION

The Body of Christ is St. Paul's favorite image of the church. In the following passage Paul writes of the different gifts the Holy Spirit gives to Christians.

Read the passage slowly and meditatively. In the presence of the Lord, reflect on the two questions that follow.

> There are many different gifts, but it is always the same Spirit; there are many different ways of serving, but it is always the same Lord. There are many different forms of activity, but in everybody it is the same God who is at work in them all. The particular manifestation of the Spirit granted to each one is to be used for the general good. To one is given from the Spirit the gift of utterance expressing wisdom; to another the gift of utterance expressing knowledge, in accordance with the same Spirit; to another, faith, from the same Spirit; and to another, the gifts of healing, through this one Spirit; to another, the working of miracles; to another, prophecy; to another, the power of distinguishing spirits; to one, the gift of different tongues and to another, the interpretation of tongues. But at work in all these is one and the same Spirit, distributing them at will to each individual (1 Cor 12:4-11).

1. Ask the Lord to help you identify your greatest gift. How are you using it to help others?

2. Think of a fellow Christian with whom you might currently be having a problem. With the eyes of faith, what good can you see in this person?

FOR DISCUSSION

1. It is virtually impossible to be a Christian and not be a member of the Christian church. Do you agree? Explain.
2. If you were to create a new image for the church, what would it be? How does it reveal something about Christ who lives in this community?
3. What factors do you see present in today's church which might be keeping it from being a more effective sacrament of Christ? What must Christians do to help remedy this situation?
4. What do each of the images of the church say about the church as a *community*?

FURTHER READING

Exodus 2:23-25; 3—12; 15—20; 24 (creation of God's people, Israel)

Ephesians 1—3

8

The Church: Its Mission and Nature

We believe in the one, holy, catholic and apostolic church.
                                        —from the Nicene Creed

One possible danger in talking about the church in general is that we can become so abstract that the observations never hit home. The church is a Christian community, but we must never forget that it is *our* Christian community. For most of us, our local parish is where the church begins. Unless it becomes for us a center of guidance and light, of inspiration and strength, the reality of church as a vital, active community can never touch us.

We sense community most when we contribute to building it up. The richness of the Christian community is not what we take from others, but what we give of ourselves. This is why the Lord wants each individual member of his body to herald the gospel, build Christian community and serve others. Message, community and service summarize our Christ-given mission.

But another way of looking at our mission as members of the Christian community is through the roles of prophet, priest and king. Each individual Christian has a prophetic, priestly and kingly function. However, the church is also an institution organized in a particular way to do God's work. A major value of an institution is that specific roles can be assigned to the members of the organization so that certain tasks get done. In this chapter, we will look at the church as an institution that has the duty to continue the prophetic, priestly and kingly roles assumed by Jesus himself.

How Does the Church Function as Prophet?

A prophet speaks the word of God. Every member of the church shares in the prophetic mission of Jesus. For example, parents have the privilege of sharing their faith with their children. Because all of us are baptized into God's family, Jesus asks us to witness to his truth. We do this in words and in actions.

> "In the same way your light must shine in people's sight, so that, seeing your good works, they may give praise to your Father in heaven" (Mt 5:16).

Over the centuries the church has been blessed with Christian heroes who have boldly witnessed to the gospel. They have shared their Christian faith with non-Catholics and non-Christians and have called the church to be true to its mission. St. Francis of Assisi reminded the people of his day that the kingdom of God is open to those who are poor in spirit. St. Catherine of Siena reminded church leaders that petty quarrels hurt the unity of the Body of Christ. In our own day Mother Teresa opens our eyes to Jesus' presence in the poor and suffering.

What Is the Institutional Church's Role as Prophet?

The institutional church is also empowered by this gift of prophecy. Jesus entrusted to his church the task of authentically and truthfully proclaiming the word as it appears in scripture and tradition. The teaching of the Catholic church, its ongoing life and its worship as they have been handed on from the time of the apostles to our own day—all of these constitute the *tradition* of the church. Everything that contributes to holiness and helps increase the faith of God's people is part of the church's tradition.

The church has been led through the centuries by the Holy Spirit. The Spirit helps the church authentically recognize and hand on what is essential to the Christian life. Jesus himself promised to be with his church in a special way when he established the church, choosing Peter to be chief shepherd. The Catholic church is a structured society, organized along hierarchical lines. *Hierarchy* refers to the ordered grade of leadership of ordained persons in the Catholic church. Catholics believe that Jesus chooses to teach, to rule and to sanctify his church through this sacred leadership of pope, bishops and pastors. These men lead through service. They continue the ministry of Peter and the apostles who were singled out by the Lord during his historical lifetime to continue his work on earth. An organized leadership, especially appointed by the Lord, helps preserve authentic tradition and helps in the spreading of the true gospel.

Catholics believe that the successor of Peter, the pope, has a special role in the church. In the center and at the head of the bishops—the successors of the apostles—the pope has primacy over the whole church. We base this belief on Christ's own teaching:

> "Simon, son of Jonah, you are a blessed man! Because it was no human agency that revealed this to you but my Father in heaven. So I now say to you: You are Peter and on this rock I will build my community. And the gates of the underworld can never overpower it. I will give you the keys of the kingdom of Heaven; whatever you bind on earth will be bound in heaven; whatever you loose on earth will be loosed in heaven" (Mt 16:17-19).

The pope and the bishops form a single entity called the college of bishops. The bishops in communion with one another and with the pope have the task of teaching truthfully the word of God. They do this when they come together in an ecumenical (worldwide) council. The pope's special role is to be a sign of unity when the bishops speak as one. As the bishop of Rome, the successor of Peter, the pope has a special responsibility to be a living sign of unity in Christ for the universal church. He is the head. He speaks with the bishops as the voice of Jesus Christ alive in the church.

How Does the Church Teach?

Normally the pope and bishops teach through the ordinary magisterium of the Catholic church. *Magisterium* refers to the office of teaching in the church which the Lord gave to the apostles and their successors. This teaching can be found in encyclicals, pastoral letters, sermons and the like. This teaching is aimed at the correct proclamation of the gospel, the building up of Christian love and service, and the proper administration of the sacraments and other spiritual and temporal benefits administered by the church. All Catholics recognize the right of the pope, bishops, pastors and priests to teach on behalf of the Lord Jesus. Our general attitude to the teachings of our leaders is one of prayerful listening and obedience.

What Is Infallibility?

Based on our Lord's promise that the church could not go astray because of his continuous presence, Catholics believe that on essential matters of faith and morals, the church is *infallible*. Infallibility refers to the belief that a certain doctrine (teaching) is free from error.

The bishops as a group, in union with the pope, teach infallibly when teaching or protecting Christ's revelation concerning belief or morality. The same Holy Spirit which directs the holy Father and the whole body of the faithful also directs the college of bishops.

Although the individual bishops do not enjoy the prerogative of infallibility, they can nevertheless proclaim Christ's doctrine infallibly. This is so, even when they are dispersed around the world, provided that while maintaining the bond of unity among themselves and with Peter's successor, and while teaching authentically on a matter of faith and morals, they concur in a single viewpoint as the one which must be held conclusively (*Lumen Gentium*, 25).

This kind of teaching is best exemplified when the bishops are gathered together and teach with the pope in an ecumenical council.

What Is Papal Infallibility?

The pope speaks infallibly when he teaches *ex cathedra*, that is, under the following conditions:

- when he teaches as the visible head of the whole church
- to all Catholics
- on a matter of faith or morals
- intending to use his full authority in an unchangeable decision.

This kind of teaching is rare. Only once in the last 100 years has the Holy Father proclaimed an infallible teaching. The doctrine of the assumption of Mary into heaven was proclaimed in 1950 by Pope Pius XII.

Papal infallibility refers solely to the pope's power or gift as successor of Peter to teach correctly Christ's revelation, especially when that revelation is being attacked or denied, thus leading to confusion among God's people. The pope's personal opinions and beliefs, like any person's, can be wrong, for example, in politics, science or sports. In addition, because the pope is human, he can sin and make mistakes, even in the way he governs the church. Like all gifts of the Holy Spirit, the gift of infallibility is meant to build up the Body of Christ. It helps give us access to the truth of Christ.

What Is the Church's Role as Priest?

The church has other roles, but its primary purpose is to lead directly to the sanctification of others. Jesus came to make us holy, that is, to make us one with his Father in friendship, to give us a life of love and holiness. He wished to form a priestly people so that all people could come into contact with the saving deeds of his passion, death, resurrection and glorification—deeds which redeem and make holy the entire universe. A priest is one who is a mediator between God and people. The Christian vocation is to help bring others to Christ.

Many activities in the church lead to holiness. For example, the teaching and ruling office of the church has as its purpose the leading of people to the source of truth and holiness: Jesus Christ. But teaching and ruling do not exhaust all the sanctifying powers given by the Lord. Jesus instructed his disciples to baptize, to break bread in his name, to pray, to help others, to forgive sins.

All Christians share in the common priesthood of Jesus:

> But you are a *chosen race, a kingdom of priests, a holy nation, a people to be a personal possession* to sing the praises of God who called you out of darkness into his wonderful light (1 Pt 2:9).

Some are called to act as official teachers in the church, others to preside at the eucharistic sacrifice and to forgive sin in our Lord's name. Priests are called apart to serve and to work in a special way for the holiness of all their Christian brothers and sisters. This special priesthood within the Christian community is not meant for the sake of the individual's personal glory but for the good of all.

Though only some are called to be ordained, everyone in the church—clergy and laity alike—has the baptismal call to holiness. The measure of our personal greatness in God's eyes is not the special gifts we have been given, but rather the intensity of love we have for God and others.

What Do We Mean by the Church as King?

When we think of a king, we think of a ruler, an authority figure. Jesus reminds us that all authority resides in him, "All authority in heaven and on earth has been given to me" (Mt 28:18). However, the Lord has chosen to share his authority with shepherds in the church. He shares his teaching authority in a special way with the pope, bishops and pastors. He also shares his ruling authority. All institutions need a governing structure for tasks to be done. The office of ruling in the church has but one purpose: the growth of faith and holiness. Church law, sometimes called *canon law*, includes those precepts and rules which regulate the life of the community of the church. Canon law, along with the legitimate commands of the pope and bishops, exists for the sake of God's people and deserves our respectful obedience.

The church's ruling must be done with humility, love and compassion. The church's standards must be those of Christ, never the standards of worldly rulers:

> Jesus called them to him and said, "You know that among the gentiles the rulers lord it over them, and great men make their authority felt. Among you this is not to happen. No; anyone who wants to become great among you must be your servant, and anyone who wants to be first among you must be your slave, just as the Son of man came

not to be served but to serve, and to give his life as a ransom for
many'' (Mt 20:25-28).

The model of church as king must be that of a serving king. As a constant reminder of this truth the pope has taken the motto: The servant
of the servants of God.

What Is the Nature of the Church?

Traditionally the church has been known by four signs or marks
which help identify its true nature: one, holy, catholic (universal) and
apostolic. These marks of the church help to strengthen the faith of
Catholics and can attract the attention of non-believers.

But the signs are paradoxical in nature. They refer to the divine
element—Christ and the Holy Spirit—working in the church. And yet
the church is made up of human members who sometimes betray the
very marks which should point to the Lord. For example, the church is
holy, and yet it is made up of sinners. The church is one, and yet there
is a wounded unity among various Christian denominations. The
church is open to all people, and yet individual Christians show prejudice to non-believers. These marks need some explanation.

How Is the Church One?

There are three different kinds of unity in the Roman Catholic
Church.

Unity of Creed (faith). A creed is a body of beliefs, for example,
the Nicene Creed which Catholics profess each Sunday at Mass. The
creed is officially taught by the magisterium of the church, and all
Catholics are united in their belief.

Unity of Moral Teaching (code). The code of the church refers to
the moral teachings of the church and their application to concrete
contemporary issues. Catholics are united in the church's ongoing
quest to discover God's will in the solution of moral problems. They
look to the moral directives of the church when forming their consciences on moral issues.

Unity of Worship (cult). Cult here means a particular way of worship. The sacred liturgy—the Mass, the other sacraments and the Divine Office—is celebrated around the world and has been a source of
unity for Catholic worship down through the centuries. Other ways of
prayer such as the Rosary, novenas and devotions have also brought
Catholics together in their journey to the Father.

Unity does not necessarily mean *uniformity*. Even though Catholics from around the world believe the same truths, seek guidance from
the same moral directives, and worship the same way, there is room for

local custom. For example, the Mass is celebrated today in the vernacular, the language of the people, yet this does not destroy unity. It is the same Mass. Celebrating the eucharistic liturgy in the vernacular recognizes healthy differences among people and respects their right to understand the Mass in their own language.

When conflict arises because of differences among people, Catholics look to the pope. He is the symbol and the servant of unity.

How Is the Church Holy?

Jesus Christ, the founder of the church, is the model of all holiness in the church. He and the Father send the Holy Spirit to dwell in the church, filling it up and uniting it. God is the ultimate source of holiness in the church. In a sense, only God is holy, but because the Holy Spirit lives in the church we can call the church holy. The church is a special presence of the risen Jesus Christ.

We sometimes speak of a person being holy because he or she lives wholly for God. But people cannot make themselves holy. Only God can sanctify a person, and a major way he chooses to do this is through the church. Thus, we may also say the church is holy because in it can be found the means to holiness, the means to the wholeness of personal development.

God wants us to develop as fully as possible as individuals and as a community. The church possesses in a unique way the means necessary to achieve full personhood: the word of God which is found in the Bible, in apostolic tradition, in the writings of great saints and theologians and in the teaching office of the church; the liturgical life of the church which includes the sacraments and most especially the Holy Eucharist; and in the various kinds of prayer practiced by Catholics through the centuries. Even when individual Christians and the institutional church have appeared less than holy, the Lord has always sent men and women who have led heroic lives of witness to Jesus and the gospel.

The true test of a Christian's holiness is a life of service to others. Jesus teaches that "it is not anyone who says to me, 'Lord, Lord,' who will enter the kingdom of Heaven, but the person who does the will of my Father in heaven" (Mt 7:21). The Father's way to holiness is translated into deeds of active service: "So always treat others as you would like them to treat you" (Mt 7:12).

How Is the Church Catholic?

The word *catholic* means "general" or "universal." St. Ignatius of Antioch, a martyr who wrote in the first part of the second century, was the first to apply this adjective to the church.

The church is universal in three ways. First, by following the Lord's command to teach all nations, the church has reached out to all men and women at all times in all places. Poor and rich, learned and unlearned, all people everywhere are invited to be members of our Lord's body.

Second, the church is catholic in the sense that it continues to teach all that Christ taught. The same essential faith and worship are held by a wide variety of people, separated geographically across our wide globe, culturally across the races, and historically across almost 2,000 years.

Finally, catholic refers to fullness. We believe that a Catholic has access to the fullness of a faith relationship to Jesus Christ. This is particularly true because of the availability of the seven sacraments, especially the Eucharist.

How Is the Church Apostolic?

The present leadership of the Catholic church can trace itself back to the first leaders of the church, the apostles. Christ founded his church on the apostles who in turn appointed successors. The hierarchy of the church is in direct succession to the apostles.

The church is also apostolic in the sense that it professes the same doctrine and Christian way of life taught by the apostles. It has preserved the good news of Jesus and his salvation and has not changed anything essential in his preaching or that of his closest disciples. The church, in other words, is founded on and continues the faith of the apostles.

Can Non-Christians Be Saved?

Traditionally Catholics have taught that the church is necessary for salvation. This belief is based on the teaching of both scripture and tradition. We believe that Jesus is present in his body, the church, and that he is the one mediator and the unique way to salvation.

> For of all the names in the world given to men, this is the only one by which we can be saved (Acts 4:12).

Since the time of the Lord's ascension into heaven and his glorification with the Father, he is met on earth in an *explicit* way only through his body, the church. As people seek salvation, they will be drawn to Christ and membership in his body. The church is a *sign*, a *sacrament* of God's love. Its task is to witness to the mystery of God's love and salvation in human history through Jesus Christ. Its mandate is to show others the way to Jesus.

Furthermore, Jesus himself taught the need for faith and baptism

(Jn 3:5). Consequently, the church teaches that if anyone knows "that the Catholic Church was made necessary by God through Jesus Christ, [and] would refuse to enter her or to remain in her could not be saved" (*Lumen Gentium*, 14).

What about all those many people who have never heard of Jesus Christ? What about those who have been given a distorted picture of him by followers who didn't always live what they preached? Can they be saved? The church answers yes.

> Those can also attain to everlasting salvation who through no fault of their own do not know the gospel of Christ or His Church, yet sincerely seek God and, moved by grace, strive by their deeds to do His will as it is known to them through the dictates of conscience. Nor does divine Providence deny the help necessary for salvation to those who, without blame on their part, have not yet arrived at an explicit knowledge of God, but who strive to live a good life, thanks to His grace. Whatever goodness or truth is found among them is looked upon by the Church as a preparation for the gospel. She regards such qualities as given by Him who enlightens all men so that they may finally have life (*Lumen Gentium*, 16).

Thus God's kingdom includes those who are mysteriously drawn to it through the workings of the Holy Spirit in their lives. Their task is to seek the kingdom of God as they know it. Their vocation is to live as lovingly as they possibly can.

> God is love
> and whoever remains in love remains in God
> and God in him (1 Jn 4:16).

However, if a person truly knows and accepts the gospel which has been given to him or her as a gift, then he or she should recognize the necessity of the church for salvation. For those who have been privileged to receive the gift of faith, it would be seriously wrong to turn away from the Body of Christ, the church.

> "Anyone who listens to you listens to me; anyone who rejects you rejects me, and those who reject me reject the one who sent me" (Lk 10:16).

CONCLUDING REFLECTIONS

The church is a Christian community organized in a certain way in order to carry on the Lord's work. The institutional church as well as individual members share prophetic, priestly and kingly roles. The church as prophet must represent the Lord's truth. The church as priest must serve as a mediator between God and people. The church as king must exercise the Lord's authority, an authority of loving service to all.

The church can be recognized by four marks: one, holy, catholic and apostolic. The hierarchy—the official leaders of the church—is entrusted with the responsibility of seeing that the church is true to its nature and mission.

Some religious groups are extremely active evangelists. They want to tell everyone about their religion. Even if their tactics are not always appreciated, their commitment to their beliefs is unquestionable.

Why do so many Catholics seem to lack the kind of enthusiasm for spreading their faith that some other Christian denominations seem to have? Do we take our religion for granted?

It is a privilege to know the good news of God's love for us and to be a member of his body which has the task of teaching and demonstrating that love to others. This privilege also brings a challenge for us to be a prophetic, priestly and kingly people. United with other Catholics, nourished by the Eucharist, and strengthened by the gifts of the Holy Spirit, we have the task of spreading the Lord's word by the way we live. We are called to be Jesus' helping hands, his forgiving voice, his understanding eyes, his loving gesture. Through us the gospel message can come alive in the world.

PRAYER REFLECTIONS

The biblical word of God contains many wise words for harmonious Christian living. Reflect on the following passage:

> Finally: you should all agree among yourselves and be sympathetic; love the brothers, have compassion and be self-effacing. Never repay one wrong with another, or one abusive word with another; instead, repay with a blessing. For

> *Who among you delights in life,*
> *longs for time to enjoy prosperity?*
> *Guard your tongue from evil,*
> *your lips from any breath of deceit.*
> *Turn away from evil and do good,*
> *   seek peace and pursue it.*
> *For the eyes of the Lord are on*
> *   the upright,*
> *his ear turned to their cry.*
> *But the Lord's face is set against*
> *   those who do evil* (1 Pt 3:8-12).

FOR DISCUSSION

1. What are some benefits of clear lines of authority and definite leadership in the church? Do you see any drawbacks to this kind of structure in the church? Apply your observations to your local parish.
2. The church as prophet should speak the truth; the church as priest should draw people to God; the church as king should use its authority to serve the needs of people. In today's world, on which issues should the church be taking a prophetic stand? Which spiritual needs should the church be addressing? Who needs to be served in a special way?
3. How can you be a sign of holiness to others; that is, how can you best exercise your own priestly ministry?

FURTHER READING

Jeremiah 1—2 (the call of a prophet and his initial preaching)
Hebrews 3—5 (Christ as the model of priestly ministry)

Section 2

9

Catholic Morality: Living the Christian Life

> After all, brothers, you were called to be free; do not use your freedom as an opening for self-indulgence, but be servants to one another in love, since the whole of the Law is summarized in the one commandment: You must love your neighbor as yourself. If you go snapping at one another and tearing one another to pieces, take care: you will be eaten up by one another.
>
> —Galatians 5:13-15

There is a story told about a searcher who was seeking out spiritual wisdom. He heard about a renowned spiritual Master; he approached one of the Master's disciples:

"What miracles has your Master worked?" he said . . .
"Well, there are miracles and miracles. In your land it is regarded as a miracle if God does someone's will. In our country it is regarded as a miracle if someone does the will of God."[1]

Christians should live in the land of miracles of the second type: doing the will of God. Doing God's will is the source of personal holiness and happiness.

Our key Catholic beliefs center on faith in Jesus Christ as Lord and Savior. But Christianity is more than a set of beliefs; it is a way of living. Christian faith must result in a life of loving service or it is an empty faith. This chapter will examine some biblical themes of Christian morality. The study of Christian morality helps us discover how we should

---

[1] Anthony de Mello, *One Minute Wisdom* (Garden City, New York: Doubleday & Company, Inc., 1986), p. 4.

live our lives as a result of our faith in God's word which has been revealed to us. The epistle of James challenges us to purify our faith:

> How does it help, my brothers, when someone who has never done a single good act claims to have faith? Will that faith bring salvation? If one of the brothers or one of the sisters is in need of clothes and has not enough food to live on, and one of you says to them, "I wish you well; keep yourself warm and eat plenty," without giving them these bare necessities of life, then what good is that? In the same way faith: if good deeds do not go with it, it is quite dead (Jas 2:14-17).

What Is Christian Morality?

Christian morality can be summarized in the word *responsibility*. There are two components to this term: *response* and *ability* to respond. To what do we respond? Christian life is a response to God's freely given love and his gift of salvation offered to us through Jesus Christ. Our salvation is a gift; we cannot earn it. But we can accept it and live our lives in accordance with the Father's will.

God, however, respects our freedom. He does not thrust salvation on us as though we were mere puppets. He extends his love, but leaves us free to respond or not. Christian morality comes to the forefront when people say yes to God, when they freely respond to his love. The essence of Christian morality is, simply, love. Reflect on the words of Jesus:

> "*You must love the Lord your God with all your heart, with all your soul,* and with all your mind. This is the greatest and first commandment. The second resembles it: *You must love your neighbor as yourself*" (Mt 22:37-39).

The second aspect of Christian morality is the ability to respond to God, the ability to love, the ability to say yes to God. This is also a gift, also freely bestowed on us. It is part of what it means to be a human being.

What Does It Mean to Be Human?

One of the first and most important principles of Christian morality is summarized in this statement: To be moral is to be human. Our intellects and divine revelation help us define and describe what being human is. A clear, refreshingly optimistic view of the human person can be found in Vatican II's *Pastoral Constitution on the Church in the Modern World*. Here is a very brief summary of some of the key sections of Chapter One of that document.

Human persons have basic dignity which flows from their being created in God's image (with a soul); this implies that we can think and love and are in relationship to others in community (No. 12). We are created with bodies which are fundamentally good (No. 14); yet, we are capable of doing evil (No. 13). Our conscience aids us in a life directed to God and other people (No. 16). It is in our freedom of choice that we assert our basic dignity because it directs us to do good (No. 17).

But true Christian morality does not rest primarily on our own talents, strengths, insights or deeds. Rather, true Christian morality is rooted in the Holy Spirit who has been given to us at baptism. When we reflect on the Christian life as a response to God's invitation to life and to love, we are stressing the *covenant* relationship between God and his children. He has made a permanent commitment to us; living a moral life is our part of the covenant, our response to his gift of friendship.

What Is a Covenant?

A covenant is the strongest possible pledge between two parties, often of unequal rank, wherein certain commitments are made. In the ancient world, covenants were established between the ruler and those ruled. The Hebrew scriptures reveal Yahweh as a God who entered into a number of covenants with humans in general and the Jews in particular. The most important covenant of all is the covenant of love Yahweh has made with all people through his Son Jesus.

All covenants consist of agreements that bind people together in the deepest kind of relationship. They require the fulfillment of promises and the living out of responsibilities. The covenants Yahweh established with his people are rooted in his unconditional love. Salvation history shows that God always established a covenant by revealing himself and committing himself without reserve to his people.

Covenants are contrasted with contracts. Contracts are legal agreements that require an even exchange, a *quid pro quo*. A covenant is an open-ended contract, a mutual, never-ending commitment of persons to each other in love.

What Were God's Covenants With the Chosen People?

Yahweh's covenant with Noah promised to continue life on earth. Abraham's covenant resulted in the promise of numerous posterity and the land of Canaan. In the Sinai covenant, Israel was blessed as God's special people. The covenant with David intensified and formalized the Sinai covenant. The relationship between Yahweh and his people had moved beyond mere preservation of a species or the giving of a land or the calling of a special people. The relationship had become a blood relationship—a relationship that was to be written on the human heart.

A covenant involves commitments, and Yahweh is always faithful to his word. In return, God wanted his people to be faithful to the covenant. He asked men and women to live as though they were specially blessed and called to witness to him, the one true God. For the Chosen People this meant that living the Law was a way to *respond* to God, a way to say yes to the special gifts God bestowed on them as a people. The Law, summarized in the Ten Commandments, was not seen as a list of burdensome obligations to be tolerated, but as a way to live out the special identity bestowed on the Jewish people. Being special means acting special. Through loving, responsive actions, people can be a prayerful sign that there is a loving, caring God who deeply desires all of humanity to be united with him.

What Is the New Testament Covenant?

The New Testament covenant is a new pledge in Christ's blood. Jesus' death and resurrection seal our relationship with the Father. It is the most important covenant of all, for the Holy Spirit given to us at baptism enables us to call God our Father. As St. Paul writes:

As you are sons, God has sent into our hearts the Spirit of his Son crying "*Abba*, Father"; and so you are no longer a slave, but a son; and if a son, then an heir by God's own act (Gal 4:6-7).

Christians respond to their vocation as children of God in two ways: first, by living the Ten Commandments, for as Jesus said, "Whoever fulfills and teaches these commands shall be great in the kingdom of God" (Mt 5:19, *NAB*); second, by trying to live the Sermon on the Mount as summarized in the Beatitudes.

What Are the Ten Commandments?

The Ten Commandments are found in Exodus 20:2-17 and Deuteronomy 5:6-21. The summary below is from the *New American Bible* translation.

I	I, the Lord, am your God. You shall not have other gods besides me.	VI	You shall not commit adultery.
		VII	You shall not steal.
II	You shall not take the name of the Lord, your God, in vain.	VIII	You shall not bear false witness against your neighbor.
III	Remember to keep holy the sabbath day.	IX	You shall not covet your neighbor's wife.
IV	Honor your father and your mother.	X	You shall not covet anything that belongs to your neighbor.
V	You shall not kill.		

"Love God Above All Things": The First Three Commandments

I, the Lord, am your God. You shall not have other gods besides me. The first commandment sets the priority for the Christian life. Simply put, friendship with God which leads to eternal union with him must be the ultimate goal of our life. There is always the temptation to make something else the be-all and end-all of our existence. Sex, money, power, possessions and prestige are all good in their place, but when we end up worshipping them, we have failed to recognize the one who created them; thus, we are unfaithful. The Christian puts his or her faith in God and in God alone, not in substitute gods like the ones above or in astrological charts, good luck charms, witchcraft and the like. We honor the first commandment when we gratefully acknowledge, worship and thank the source of everything in existence—God, our loving Creator.

You shall not take the name of the Lord, your God, in vain. The second commandment stresses our need to respect the Lord's name and to practice our religion humbly. The Christian realizes that what we say reflects who we are. Some things are sacred, including God's name, and our language and attitude to our religion should be respectful; for example, it would be wrong to call on God to do harm to another person. Finally, the second commandment instructs us to pray with humility and trust. Jesus taught us to approach God confidently as children who believe that their loving Father will take care of them.

Remember to keep holy the sabbath day. Fidelity to God requires that we adore him, and adore him with others. Our salvation is not something we work at in isolation from others. We make time for the Lord and our Christian brothers and sisters.

Catholics take seriously Jesus' mandate to break bread in his name; that is, to worship the Father united to Jesus by the power of the Holy Spirit. We gather weekly for community worship and set aside a day when we slow down from our other duties to create some time for rest and reflection. This special time should help us consider the true meaning and current direction of our lives. Catholics typically worship on Sunday to commemorate the day of the Lord's resurrection. Current church law, however, does permit Catholics to celebrate the Sunday liturgy from late Saturday afternoon on.

"Love Your Neighbor as Yourself": The Last Seven Commandments

Honor your father and your mother. The covenant between Christians and God is reflected in the family. Just as God loves his children, so human parents should love and care for their children, educating them and giving them enough freedom to grow into independence. And children should offer respect, obedience, courtesy and gratitude to their parents. Likewise, brothers and sisters owe each other patience, friendship and respect so that the family can be a harmonious community of love. This commandment also has social implications. All proper authority is deserving of our obedience and respect since all authority ultimately comes from God. And because authority comes from God, those in a position over others are obligated to exercise their authority with kindness and humility.

You shall not kill. God has given us the gift of life, and the fifth commandment stresses its sanctity. It condemns anything which assaults human life. The values of the fifth commandment include taking care of ourselves, physically and mentally. Christians are also concerned about protecting the lives of others. Jesus showed that God's love extends in a special way to the weak and helpless. Thus, Christians should stand for justice and life through involvement in the great social issues of the day: war and peace, poverty and prejudice, abortion and euthanasia, and the like.

You shall not commit adultery. In the Song of Songs God's covenant love with his people is compared to the passionate love a husband has for his bride. The church itself is called the bride of Christ; Jesus is the bridegroom. In addition, Christian marriage is a powerful sign of covenant love. Thus, infidelity is unbecoming to covenant love; in a marriage, for example, adultery is a serious failure to be faithful to a love commitment.

The sixth commandment challenges us to respect the procreative powers with which God has blessed us. Sexual love is a share in God's own creative act. Acts which exploit others or which are indulged in selfishly distort God's intent. The sixth commandment praises the virtue of chastity, that is, respectful self-control that preserves one's capacity to see and to fulfill one's sexuality in a perspective of love.

You shall not steal. Theft of any kind destroys trust. To steal is to break down the smooth human relationships needed for harmonious and peaceful living.

Failing to use our God-given talents might also be considered a form of theft. By not using our gifts we keep others from sharing in something given for the good of all. The seventh commandment also reminds us to share the surplus goods we have been given with those who are in need. Not sharing with those who lack the very necessities of life is a serious failure to love.

You shall not bear false witness against your neighbor. To be honest is to witness to the truth. Revenge, gossip, scandal and lies all destroy the love which binds together the human community.

You shall not covet your neighbor's wife. You shall not covet anything that belongs to your neighbor. Covetousness is often motivated by jealousy, materialism or self-indulgence. Uncontrolled desires in the areas of sex or material possessions can breed hatred and rivalry. These two commandments stress the importance of pure intentions and decent motives when relating to others. The external action which violates love usually flows from an internal desire which was left unchecked.

What Are the Beatitudes?

The Beatitudes summarize the morality followers of Jesus should strive to live in response to both God and neighbor. They introduce and capsulize the essence of New Testament morality found in the Sermon on the Mount (Mt 5-7).

Unlike some teachers of his day, Jesus did not try to give a detailed list of rules and regulations. Rather, he taught guidelines which get at the basic *attitudes* his followers should have in relationship to other people and to God.

> How blessed are the poor in spirit:
> the kingdom of Heaven is theirs.
> Blessed are *the gentle:*
> *they shall have the earth as inheritance.*
> Blessed are those who mourn:
> they shall be comforted.
> Blessed are those who hunger and thirst for
>   uprightness:
> they shall have their fill.
> Blessed are the merciful:
> they shall have mercy shown them.
> Blessed are the pure in heart:
> they shall see God.
> Blessed are the peacemakers:
> they shall be recognized as children of God.
> Blessed are those who are persecuted in the
>   cause of uprightness:
> the kingdom of Heaven is theirs.

Explaining the Beatitudes

How blessed are the poor in spirit: the kingdom of Heaven is theirs. A key sign that God's kingdom had broken into human history was that it was announced to the poor. Jesus himself had special affection for the downtrodden and unfortunate.

In this beatitude Jesus is not praising poverty as such. Rather, he is saying that those who are deprived of material goods, power, prestige and other signs of worldly success are left in a position of openness before God. They know they must trust God completely for everything. Jesus asks that we have that same poverty of spirit, that we place our trust and confidence in God alone. In the last analysis, everything of this world is found wanting; our salvation is in trusting and obeying the Father.

Blessed are the gentle: they shall have the earth as inheritance. The gentle person is humble. He or she does not act out of jealousy or seek revenge when hurt and despised. Jesus challenges his followers to solve problems without hatred, rancor, ill-will or violence.

Blessed are those who mourn: they shall be comforted. The third beatitude gives us hope that in the midst of our difficulties we will eventually find consolation. We do not have to become bitter. Despite what modern advertisements and the media seem to be telling us, patient suffering and endurance of trials do have their reward.

Blessed are those who hunger and thirst for uprightness: they shall have their fill. One of the tasks of Jesus' followers is to get involved in the affairs of the world, to work for God's kingdom by seeking respect, dignity and equality for all. "To hunger and thirst for uprightness" means to seek justice—to give people their due and to make sure that everyone has access to those things necessary for a truly human life.

Blessed are the merciful: they shall have mercy shown them. In the Our Father we ask God to forgive us as we forgive others. The Father's love is given to us without our ever deserving it. He forgives our sins and accepts us into his family as adopted children. In return, he asks us to extend mercy, love and forgiveness to one another. When we forgive those who have hurt us, even our enemies, we show all people that God is loving and merciful and that he cares for us all.

Blessed are the pure in heart: they shall see God. The pure in heart have a single-hearted commitment to God. Nothing should distract us from God. Money, job, family, friends, reputation are all good, but they should play a secondary role in our lives. Seeking and accomplishing God's will are the primary duties of a disciple of Jesus Christ.

Blessed are the peacemakers: they shall be recognized as children of God. Like the fourth beatitude, this one emphasizes the active role Christians should take in the world. Lives lived in love and peace are the twin signs of being God's adopted children. Christians have the duty to unite those who are in strife, disharmony and opposition by helping them realize our common brotherhood and sisterhood with Jesus Christ.

Blessed are those who are persecuted in the cause of uprightness: the kingdom of Heaven is theirs. There is no greater sign of our union with our Lord than being willing to suffer for him. Jesus' words and deeds brought him misunderstanding and abuse. To be Christian means to be willing to stand up for our convictions, even if this means rejection, abuse or martyrdom. The reward promised to those who live the Christian life is nothing less than God's kingdom and the eternal happiness it brings.

CONCLUDING REFLECTIONS

In summary, true faith demands a responsible and active response to the Lord's invitation to live as children of his loving Father. Christian morality requires us to model our lives on our brother and Savior, Jesus Christ. Jesus teaches us that faith is empty without love and a commitment to do his Father's will. God's covenant relationship with his people requires this response: Love God above all things and neighbor as self.

A positive way to live the Christian life is by putting the Ten Commandments and the Beatitudes into action. These do not represent a closed system of law; rather, they are sure guides in helping us to imitate the risen Lord and respond in a responsible way to the inner promptings of the Holy Spirit. Mastering abstract propositions is not the way to become good people. The commandments and the beatitudes embody the values of Jesus and point us to the kind of life his disciples are called to live.

PRAYER REFLECTION

Though I command languages both human and angelic—if I speak without love, I am no more than a gong booming or a cymbal clashing (1 Cor 13:1).

After reflecting on this famous quotation from St. Paul, prayerfully examine your conscience. How are you currently responding to God's command to love?

To help in this examination, study the spiritual and corporal works of mercy, traditional ways Christians have used to express Christian love. If the Spirit prompts you to work more actively at living one of these works, make a positive resolution to do something specific this coming week. Check yourself next week to see if you followed through on your resolution.

Spiritual Works of Mercy	*Corporal Works of Mercy*
1. Counsel the doubtful.	1. Feed the hungry.
2. Instruct the ignorant.	2. Give drink to the thirsty.

3. Admonish sinners.
4. Comfort the afflicted.
5. Forgive offenses.
6. Bear wrongs patiently.
7. Pray for the living and the dead.

3. Clothe the naked.
4. Visit the imprisoned.
5. Shelter the homeless.
6. Visit the sick.
7. Bury the dead.

FOR DISCUSSION

1. Early Christians were known by their deeds of love. Following the way of Jesus set the Christian apart from non-believers. How has your Christian faith in action distinguished you as a follower of Jesus Christ?
2. How do the Beatitudes add to the Law as summarized in the Ten Commandments?
3. What are the major idols a Christian must guard against in today's world?
4. What obligations do adult Christians owe their parents?

FURTHER READING

2 Samuel 7 (Yahweh's covenant with David)
Matthew 5—7 (the Sermon on the Mount)

10

The Church and Social Justice: Some Principles

"Anyone who wants to become great among you must be your servant, and anyone who wants to be first among you must be your slave, just as the Son of man came not to be served but to serve, and to give his life as a ransom for many."

—Matthew 20:26-28

Jesus is attractive to us for many reasons. For example, he invites us to approach him, to learn from him of the Father's love, to accept and be nourished by his healing, forgiving touch. He beckons us to observe his life of love and sacrifice and then to accept his invitation to become his disciples.

Jesus really does not expect a no from us. He wants us to take up the challenge. He expects us to continue his work on earth. He first tells us to come to him; but his last word to the apostles before he ascended to heaven was "Go." Jesus never ceases to amaze. He challenges us with a paradox: Come in order to go.

The Lord's people, his church, is missionary. A missionary is one who is sent to carry out a specific task. On Easter Sunday Jesus commissioned his apostles,

"As the Father sent me,
so I am sending you" (Jn 20:21).

Our mission is threefold: to be the herald, the sign and the servant of the gospel. We herald the good news when we proclaim the gospel of Jesus Christ. We are a sign of the gospel when we faithfully live the gospel. We serve the gospel when we witness to the message of God's saving love for the world. We do this best when we minister to people in need.

113

This chapter will take up this third aspect of our Christian mission, the social mission of the church. It will deal with the principles behind church teaching and practice concerning social justice issues, while the next chapter will deal with some specific issues.

What Is Social Justice?

The social doctrine of the Catholic church deals with the attitudes individuals should have toward society and treats the problems of social justice. The church's social doctrine is that

> "set of principles for reflection, criteria for judgment and directives for action" proposed by the Church's teaching (Pope John Paul II, *Sollicitudo Rei Socialis*, 41).

Social justice deals with the obligations of individuals and groups to apply the gospel to the systems, structures and institutions of society. This is an important aspect of Catholic teaching because all human relationships take place within the framework of these systems, structures and institutions.

Pope John Paul II reminds Catholics that "the characteristic principle of Christian social doctrine" is that "the goods of this world are *originally meant for all*" (*Sollicitudo Rei Socialis*, 42).

What Role Has the Church Played in Justice Issues?

Throughout its history the church has attempted to show the link between the gospel and the plight of the poor. The history of western civilization shows that the Catholic church has often pioneered efforts on behalf of the poor and the powerless: home and foreign missions, hospitals and medical clinics, disaster relief agencies, orphanages, homes for unwed mothers, services for the elderly, agencies for young people, a massive educational apostolate.

There are those, however, who have criticized the church for not taking a more active role in promoting peace and justice. Karl Marx, for example, claimed that religion drugged people with promises of a future life and was too little concerned about their suffering in this world. Marx's charge was not entirely unfounded. History shows that sometimes church leaders did neglect the social dimension of the gospel while preaching quiet acceptance of their misery to the poor and oppressed. This sometimes happened when the church became too closely allied with various governments which were interested in maintaining the status quo and were uninterested in bettering the lot of the poor. Other times neglect in the area of the social gospel resulted from a false belief which held that things of this world shouldn't concern us because we are destined for a supernatural world. In our day the church has taken a leading role in the promotion of justice:

> Action on behalf of justice and participation in the transformation of the world fully appear to us as a constitutive dimension of the preaching of the Gospel, or in other words, of the Church's mission of the redemption of the human race and its liberation from every oppressive situation (Introduction to *Justice in the World*).

This important document makes it clear that working for justice in the world ranks with the celebration of the sacraments and the preaching of the gospel as an essential ministry in the church.

What Are the Basics of the Church's Social Teaching?

Christian faith reveals that our human life is fulfilled in knowing and loving the living God in union with other people. This faith vision is based on a scriptural view of the human person. Several key, fundamental themes undergird this biblical vision and form the basis of the Catholic church's social justice teaching. First, the church assumes the dignity of the individual person. Second, the church recognizes that human beings are by nature social. Third, the church operates out of the knowledge that human beings are all part of one family, God's family. Fourth, the church recognizes that there are certain basic human rights with their corresponding duties. Finally, the church must follow Jesus in going beyond justice to gospel love, especially love which extends to "the least of these."

What Is Meant by "the Dignity of the Individual"?

The social teaching of the Catholic church rests on the *inherent dignity of each human person*. Our basic dignity flows from our being made in the image of God with a capacity to know and love our Creator. Human dignity means we have freedom to shape our lives and our communities, and that we have the capacity for love and friendship. God has appointed us master of all earthly creatures so that we might use them to God's glory (*Church in the Modern World*, No. 12). As the Psalmist put it:

> Yet you have made him little less than a god,
> you have crowned him with glory and beauty,
> made him lord of the work of your hands,
> put all things under his feet (Ps 8:5-6).

Humans have dignity by the way God made us. But when God became human in the person of Jesus Christ, human nature was "raised in us also to a dignity beyond compare" (*Redemptor Hominis*,

No. 8). Our Lord became our way to the Father; he saved every human being. Jesus Christ, the full revelation of the Father and the perfect human being, shows us who we really are and brings to light our vocation and identity as children of God.

In What Way Are Humans Social Beings?

When God created us, he made us members of the human family. We are by nature *social*. From the beginning God created us for companionship, "male and female he created them" (Gn 1:27). By our very nature we are social beings who need to relate to others both in order to live and to develop our potential.

When we reflect on the relationship between the individual and the social groups to which he or she belongs, we can see that the progress of the human person and the advance of society are interdependent. The three communities to which we belong are like three concentric circles; the individual lives in the circle of the family, which is part of a larger circle, the nation, which is part of the largest circle, the world. We cannot help but relate to all three communities because we belong to all three. These are the communities which are most often discussed in the church's social teaching.

Biblical revelation also underscores the fact that God formed us as a people. The people of Israel—our ancestors in the faith—were formed, saved and instructed by God as a covenant people. The Hebrew God is known as a God who loves and delights in justice and demands justice of his people. Jesus, too, forms a *community* of disciples, a people who are enlivened with his vision and charged with extending his message of peace and justice to all.

What Is the Call to Human Solidarity?

When we reflect on our social nature, it becomes evident that we live in a network of human relationships. Society and the individual person are engaged in reciprocal relationships. The individual is responsible for the well-being of society, and society has duties to the individual.

> The exercise of solidarity *within each society* is valid when its members recognize one another as persons. Those who are more influential, because they have a greater share of goods and common services, should feel *responsible* for the weaker and be ready to share with them all they possess (Pope John Paul II, *Sollicitudo Rei Socialis*, 39).

We cannot escape the call of others, especially the weak. Love of God is united to love of neighbor. We are one human family, dependent on one another, and have the Christ-given call to be one. Jesus himself prayed for human solidarity:

> "May they all be one,
> just as, Father, you are in me and I am in
>   you" (Jn 17:21).

Because we are one, Jesus commands us to love our neighbor as ourselves. This double command to love self and neighbor is illustrated in the parable of the Good Samaritan. The Samaritan realized that when one person suffers everyone suffers because we are fundamentally brothers and sisters. Not to recognize and respect the dignity of a single person, especially one who is suffering, is to deny the Son of Man who came to teach us that we are one with him and with one another.

What Are Our Rights and Duties?

Justice demands that a society be organized in a way that guarantees everyone the ability to participate in the political, cultural and economic life of the society. Basic human rights are prerequisites to living a life of dignity in community. A right is a moral claim a person can make on other persons and on society in general. The following is a list of major human rights which have been discussed and defended in a number of church documents. Some will be discussed in more detail in the following chapter.

Economic rights
- right to life: food, shelter, clothing
- right to work
- right to a just wage
- right to property
- right to rest
- right to medical care

Political rights
- right to participate in government
- right to judicial protection

Religious rights
- right to worship

Social rights
- right to assembly
- right of free association

Cultural rights
- right to a basic education
- right to freedom of speech

Other rights
- right to emigrate/immigrate
- right to development
- right to social security: in the event of sickness, unemployment, old age, loss of support (e.g., death of parents of minors)

Every right has a corresponding duty for others to respect, foster and fulfill the right. Furthermore, the person has a duty corresponding to his or her right. For example, the right to a just wage corresponds to the duty to do an honest day's work. The right to participate in government carries the duty to cast an informed vote in elections. The right of free speech demands honesty and kindness in exercising it.

How Are Social Justice and Gospel Love Related?

Social justice deals with the application of the gospel to the structures, systems and institutions of society. All human relationships—personal, cultural, political and economic—take place in these social frameworks. What is the relationship between justice and love? As stated in *Justice in the World*, "love implies an absolute demand for justice, usually a recognition of the dignity and rights of one's neighbors." We cannot say we love if we do not respect and respond to the rights and basic needs of our neighbors. True love of God and neighbor are united. As St. John reminds us:

> Anyone who says "I love God"
> and hates his brother,
> is a liar,
> since whoever does not love the brother whom
>   he can see
> cannot love God whom he has not seen.
> Indeed this is the commandment we have
>   received from him,
> that whoever loves God, must also love
>   his brother (1 Jn 4:20-21).

To love means to give oneself to another. It is impossible to love without sharing with others what is due them in justice. Love can go beyond justice, however. Justice is simply the *minimal* human and Christian response to others. Love, if we are serious about becoming like Christ, requires going beyond justice.

What Are the Social Documents of the Church?

Papal encyclicals are important letters addressed to Catholics (and often other Christians and men and women of good will). They represent the ordinary teaching of the church, which is an excellent guide for Catholics in the formation of their consciences. Papal addresses and letters from groups of bishops also reiterate significant church teaching. A council document (like *Gaudium et Spes*) is a highly authoritative writing.

The following key church documents treat social justice:

Latin Title	Year	English Title	Author	Topics Treated
Rerum Novarum (papal encyclical)	1891	*On the Condition of the Working Man*	Leo XIII	Unjust wage system in the economic order
Quadragesimo Anno (papal encyclical)	1931	*On the Fortieth Anniversary of Rerum Novarum*	Pius XI	Rights and duties of capital and labor in light of the gospel
_____	1940 –1957	Christmas addresses of Pius XII	Pius XII	Various social issues
Mater et Magistra (papal encyclical)	1961	*Mother and Teacher*	John XXIII	Rights and duties involved in the economic growth and development within a country
Pacem in Terris (papal encyclical)	1963	*Peace on Earth*	John XXIII	Responsibilities of rich nations toward poor nations; the urgency of nuclear disarmament; racial discrimination
Gaudium et Spes (Vatican II council document)	1965	*Pastoral Constitution on the Church in the Modern World*	Paul VI and the Council Fathers	The church's mission to the contemporary world
Populorum Progressio (papal encyclical)	1967	*On the Development of Peoples*	Paul VI	The structures of international economic systems
Octogesima Adveniens (papal encyclical)	1971	*On the Occasion of the Eightieth Anniversary of Rerum Novarum*	Paul VI	Recent patterns of socioeconomic organization; a call to action
Justitia in Mundo (statement of worldwide bishops' meeting)	1971	*Justice in the World*	Second Synod of Bishops	A critique of international economic systems especially in the light of *Populorum Progressio*

_____ (statement of a national conference of bishops)	1976 *To Live in Christ Jesus*	American Conference of Catholic Bishops	Principles of moral life and their application to the family, nation, and community of nations
Laborem Exercens (papal encyclical)	1981 *On Human Work*	John Paul II	A philosophy and theology of work
_____ (statement of a national conference of bishops)	1983 *Challenge of Peace: God's Promise and Our Response*	American Conference of Catholic Bishops	Principles of peace and justice applied to the great moral questions of our day
_____ (statement of a national conference of bishops)	1986 *Economic Justice for All*	American Conference of Catholic Bishops	Catholic Social teaching applied to the United States economy
Sollicitudo Rei Socialis (papal encyclical)	1986 *On Social Concern*	John Paul II	Critique of super-powers' ideologies that work against application of *Populorum Progressio* to modern scene

CONCLUDING REFLECTIONS _____

Today's Christian community is increasingly aware that to follow Jesus Christ means that we must have a "preferential option for the poor." Jesus strongly identified himself with those who had a marginal role in society. He bids his followers to respond in a special way to those whose dignity is threatened because of their position in society. The justice of a society is measured by its treatment of the poor. The measure of our commitment to Jesus is how well we imitate the Lord who came to serve rather than be served.

Christian teaching recognizes that each person has basic human rights and that respect is due each person as a child of God, created in his image to live in community. God loves everyone; Jesus died so that every person can be saved.

Jesus challenges us as individuals and as a Christian community to work for justice. We do this when we speak out for the defenseless. We take up his challenge when we see and judge things from the vantage point of the poor. We respond to the Lord's mandate when we help people experience the good news of God's liberating salvation. Finally, and perhaps most important, we take Jesus' command to heart when we empty ourselves, both individually and as a church, so that we can experience God's power in the midst of poverty and vulnerability.

PRAYER REFLECTION

You have already been told what is right
and what Yahweh wants of you.
Only this, to do what is right,
to love loyalty
and to walk humbly with your God (Mi 6:8).
But alas for you who are rich: you are having
your consolation now.
Alas for you who have plenty to eat now: you
shall go hungry.
Alas for you who are laughing now; you shall
mourn and weep (Lk 6:24-25).

FOR DISCUSSION

1. Which beatitude speaks most clearly to you about social justice?
2. What does it mean to say that social justice is a *constitutive dimension* of preaching the gospel? In what sense is this true?
3. Is it immoral not to vote on local or national issues that affect the welfare of others? Explain.

FURTHER READING

Amos 5-6 (a prophetic cry for repentance and justice)
Matthew 25:31-46

11

Social Justice: Building on the Foundations

Rain down, you heavens, from above,
and let the clouds pour down saving justice,
let the earth open up and blossom
   with salvation,
and let justice sprout up with it;
I, Yahweh, have created it!

—Isaiah 45:8

Catholic moral teaching is interested in social justice because social justice applies the gospel command to respect and love others to the concrete reality of everyday life. The Christian gospel is not meant to be a vague, idealistic statement with no connection to how people live their lives. Rather, the good news of Jesus demands application to the social settings in which we find ourselves. This chapter will look at three networks of relationships in which we all live—the family, the society and the world community—and present some specific teachings of the church on how we ought to live in light of Jesus' message.

What Does the Church Teach About the Family?

The bedrock unit of any society is the family. Its special value lies in its willingness to affirm and to love individuals not for what they can accomplish or the possessions they own but simply for who they are. Married couples in a Christian, sacramental union model Christ's own love for the church. His love is enduring and self-giving.

The encyclical *Populorum Progressio* underscores the importance of the family:

123

The natural family, stable and monogamous—as fashioned by God and sanctified by Christianity—in which different generations live together, helping each other to acquire greater wisdom and to harmonize personal rights with other social needs, is the basis of society (No. 36).

Children are the greatest gift of a marriage. Parents cooperate with the love of the Creator when they regard as their proper mission the transmitting of human life and the education of their children (*Gaudium et Spes*, No. 50). Parents have the right to choose responsibly—in accordance with God's plan—the number of children they will have, but selfishness can never be the determining factor. Thus, marriage is both love-sharing between the couple and life-giving. The twin values of life and love provide a strong foundation for the larger society.

The elderly also deserve special consideration. In justice and in love the elderly should be respected for their wisdom, their knowledge and experience; too often they are neglected. When possible, the aged should be welcomed into their own families.

Anyone who does not look after his own relations, especially if they are living with him, has rejected the faith and is worse than an unbeliever (1 Tm 5:8).

Society, furthermore, has an obligation to care for the aged who cannot take care of themselves.

What Undergirds Teaching on National Concerns?

Two themes dominate church teaching as it applies to larger societies, namely, the *common good* and the *principle of subsidiarity*.

The common good can be defined as all the spiritual, social and material conditions needed in society for the individual to achieve full human dignity. It is "the sum of those conditions of social life which allow not only groups but also their individual members to achieve their own fulfillment more fully and more readily" than they could on their own (*Gaudium et Spes*, No. 26).

The whole society—individuals, organizations, public authorities and the like—has a duty to work for the common good. The state (government), however, has a unique role in preserving public order and, as a last resort, intervening to bring about justice.

The common good that authority in the state serves is brought to full realization only when all the citizens are sure of their rights (*Redemptor Hominis*, No. 17).

The principle of subsidiarity holds that decisions in the social order should be made at the lowest reasonable level in order to enlarge freedom and broaden participation in responsible action. Only when an individual or smaller social unit cannot properly fulfill a task should the task be taken up by the larger society. For example, parents have the primary responsibility of caring for their children. But, perhaps, some parents cannot adequately take care of their children because of extraordinary circumstances. Then the larger society should step in and offer its help.

> Of its very nature the true aim of all social activity should be to help members of the social body, but never to destroy or absorb them (*Mater et Magistra*, No. 53).

What Are Some Current National Concerns?

All nations must be concerned about social issues, problems and rights in order to foster the common good. The topics discussed below—respect for the unborn, women in society, respect for racial and ethnic groups, employment and poverty—take up some of the concerns outlined in *To Live in Christ Jesus*, a 1976 statement by the American Conference of Catholic Bishops, and their more recent important pastoral letter on the economy, *Economic Justice for All* (1986).

What Is the Church's Stance Regarding the Unborn?

Jesus taught in the strongest of terms the need to care for the weak and the helpless. In too many nations today, innocent human life is snuffed out without ever seeing the light of day. For the sake of the common good, the fundamental right to life itself must be first recognized and then protected by law. Efforts to correct legal decisions which permit abortion on demand, for example, are one means to remedy the assault on human life which permits over 1,500,000 abortions annually in the United States of America.

Furthermore, society needs to offer help and assistance to those women who feel that the only way out of their current problem is through abortion. The church, especially because of its pro-life stance, should be in the forefront in supporting women with problems during or after pregnancy and thus bear strong witness to its belief in human dignity.

Respect and reverence for human life arise from the basic dignity of the human person made in God's image and likeness. Life is a most precious gift from God. Abortion is gravely wrong, as is any direct attack on human life like infanticide, euthanasia and certain kinds of fetal experiments.

What Is the Church's Stance Regarding Women?

Jesus recognized the equality and dignity of women. In fact, his free association with women in public often upset the establishment of his day. The church praises those efforts which win recognition that women have the same dignity and fundamental rights as men.

> With respect to the fundamental rights of the person, every type of discrimination, whether social or cultural, whether based on sex, race, color or social condition, language, or religion, is to be overcome and eradicated as contrary to God's intent (*The Church in the Modern World*, No. 29).

However, the church also cautions against views which would ignore or deny significant differences between the sexes, undermine marriage, or erode family life.

What Is the Church's Stand on Race, Ethnic Groups?

All racial and ethnic groups are of incomparable worth because of their dignity as human beings. Yet individuals and the structures of society often discriminate to the disadvantage of innocent people. It is true that laws cannot change attitudes, but they can foster justice by protecting minority groups, by deterring those who might otherwise violate the rights of others, and by educating people to know right from wrong.

> Within a country which belongs to each one, all should be equal before the law, find equal admittance to economic, cultural, civic and social life and benefit from a fair share of the nation's riches (*Octogesima Adveniens*, No. 16).

Racial justice must be fostered especially in regard to housing, education, health care, employment and the administration of justice. In many countries racial injustice is a major problem. Concerned Christians will become informed and do their part in fostering the brotherhood and sisterhood of all peoples.

What Is the Church's Stance on Employment?

The Catholic church has spoken loudly and clearly on the rights of workers:

> Every [person] has the right to work, to a chance to develop his qualities and his personality in the exercise of his profession, to

equitable remuneration which will enable him and his family "to lead a worthy life on the material, social, cultural and spiritual level" and to assistance in case of need arising from sickness or age (*Octogesima Adveniens*, No. 14).

In his encyclical *Laborem Exercens*, Pope John Paul II defends the rights of workers to unionize, "that is, to form associations for the purpose of defending the vital interests of those employed in the various professions" (No. 20). Furthermore, he teaches that workers have the right to strike. At the same time the pope reminds us that a strike is a last resort.

Work is very much a spiritual activity when we respond to God's command to subject the earth and all things it contains. Pope John Paul II recognizes that women have the right to work and that this right should be protected by law. But he also stresses the invaluable contribution mothers at home make to the common good:

> But it is fitting that they [women] should be able to fulfill their tasks in accordance with their own nature, without being discriminated against and without being excluded from jobs for which they are capable, but also without lack of respect for their family aspirations and for their specific role in contributing, together with men, to the good of society. The true advancement of women requires that labor should be structured in such a way that women do not have to pay for their advancement by abandoning what is specific to them and at the expense of the family, in which women as mothers have an irreplaceable role (*Laborem Exercens*, No. 19).

This quotation underscores the church's concern to protect the family. The pope even advocates that society grant a family allowance or direct grants to mothers. This is in response to the need for a just wage "for the work of an adult who is responsible for a family," a just "remuneration which will suffice for establishing and properly maintaining a family and for providing security for its future."

What Does the Church Teach About Poverty?

The American bishops define poverty as "the lack of sufficient material resources required for a decent life" (*Economic Justice for All*, No. 173). Children, female-headed households and members of racial minorities are victimized by poverty to a greater degree than other groups.

The economy of the United States is marked by a very uneven distribution of wealth and income. Catholic social justice teaching does not require absolute equality in the distribution of income and wealth. But it does demand evaluation of the economic structure in light of meeting the basic needs of the poor and increasing the level of participation of all members of society in the nation's economy. Catholic church teaching establishes a strong presumption against extreme inequality of wealth and income as long as there are poor, hungry and homeless people.

The American bishops' pastoral letter on the economy entitled *Economic Justice for All* makes a number of concrete recommendations on how the plight of the poor can be helped. These include raising the minimum wage, adjustment in the tax system to better meet the needs of the poor, a major commitment to education and the eradication of illiteracy, better support of the family so that mothers of young children are not forced to seek employment outside the home, and a thorough reform of the welfare system. But the bishops make a special plea that can help all people of good will reexamine their commitment to the poor:

> We ask everyone to refrain from actions, words or attitudes that stigmatize the poor, that exaggerate the benefits received by the poor, and that inflate the amount of fraud in welfare payments. These are symptoms of a punitive attitude towards the poor (*Economic Justice for All*, No. 194).

What Are Some Other National Problems?

Crime and criminals. People have the right and need to live in peace and to be protected from criminals. Societies should work not only at stricter law enforcement but should also strive to root out the sources of much crime—poverty, injustice and materialism.

Prisoners, too, have rights: They have the right to protection from assault; the right to proper food, health care and recreation; and the right to pursue other human goals such as education.

Migrant workers. *Justice in the World* especially laments the condition of migrant workers who are frequently the victims of discriminatory attitudes and are often obliged to live insecure lives. Emigrating to find work is sometimes a necessary evil, but "migration in search of work must in no way become an opportunity for financial or social exploitation" (*Laborem Exercens*, No. 23).

Prisoners of War. *Justice in the World* reminds us that prisoners of war deserve humane treatment. The basic needs of food, shelter, adequate clothing and health care must be provided. Nor may prisoners of war be subjected to treatment or experimentation that violates their dignity as human beings.

Communications. Pope Paul VI called for public authorities to watch carefully the growing power and influence of the media on social communications. The people who control media have a "grave responsibility with respect to the truth of the information they spread, the needs and the reactions they generate and the values they put forward" (*Octogesima Adveniens*, No. 20).

In this regard the American bishops suggest that the government can help create more wholesome societies by taking "constitutional steps to stem the flood of pornography, violence and immorality in the entertainment media" (*To Live in Christ Jesus*, p. 30).

Environment. When God entrusted the human race with the development of the created world, he made us stewards of all of his magnificent creation (Gn 1:28-30). This is a tremendous responsibility. Yet today we have become more aware that we have exploited nature, and that we risk destroying it. Pollution, refuse, scarcity of vital natural resources and new illnesses result from an unchecked technology fueled by human selfishness and greed. Responsibility demands careful planning, conservation and an unselfish respect for the goods of this world. God's will for us is that we "should communicate with nature as an intelligent and noble 'master' and 'guardian,' and not as a heedless 'exploiter' and 'destroyer'" (*Redemptor Hominis*, No. 15).

What Does the Church Teach on World Problems?

Our concern for the rights of others does not stop with the family or with our own nation. To follow Jesus means to love all people. The Christian in today's world must also show concern for the international community. Christian love and justice prompt us to extend care beyond our national borders. In addition, the intelligent person will look at the scope and seriousness of worldwide problems and conclude that it is foolish not to get involved in the furthering of the rights of all humans.

The world is in dire need of help. Some of the problems which loom on the horizon include hunger, environmental pollution, population growth, disparity of wealth and resources and the persistent danger of war.

Hunger

Thousands of people die of starvation each day, and the situation is getting worse. Yet a publication of the Catholic Relief Services has observed that there is currently enough food produced on our planet to give everyone a minimum but adequate diet. One of the great problems in today's interdependent world is the unjust distribution of resources to purchase or produce food.

Environmental Pollution and Wastefulness

Industrial waste, deforestation, pollution resulting from a consumer society, and other abuses that affect our environment know no national borders. The factories in America's Midwest cause the acid rain that affects Canada's lakes. The deforestation of the jungles of Brazil has global consequences.

The spaceship earth has become the new image of a community of nations whose destinies are inexorably linked. Some social scientists, though, claim that the earth's resources will be depleted within the next 50 years or so. The urgent question is whether the passengers on the spaceship will work together to avert the crisis.

These are issues which must transcend national self-interest.

Population Growth and Glaring Disparities of Wealth

The gap between rich nations and poor nations continues to grow. Half the world's people, nearly 2.5 billion, live in countries with a per capita income of $400 or less. A half billion people are always hungry, while 800 million live in absolute poverty.

Hunger is linked to population growth. But the church notes that family size is dependent on levels of economic development, education, respect for women, availability of health care, and the cultural traditions of communities. The American bishops advise that in dealing with population growth we should also be addressing these other social and economic conditions.

> Population policies must be designed as part of an overall strategy of integral human development. They must respect the freedom of parents and avoid coercion. . . . Where the inalienable right to marriage and procreation is lacking, human dignity has ceased to exist (*Economic Justice for All*, No. 287).

Political Causes of World Problems, Nuclear War

In his encyclical *Sollicitudo Rei Socialis,* Pope John Paul II analyzes the political causes of many worldwide problems. They are rooted in the opposing ideological conflicts between East and West, between liberal capitalism and Marxist collectivism. These conflicting *political* ideologies result in different, opposing economic strategies that have evolved into dangerous *military* opposition.

Both systems threaten humanity and have slowed the true development of poor nations and have led to a dangerous arms race. They both manifest an all-consuming desire for profit and a thirst for power. Thus, it is safe to say that these conflicting ideologies result in a kind of imperialism which is given to the idolatry of money, ideology, class, or technology. When decisions are made on the basis of these criteria, the poor and marginated inevitably suffer. (See *Sollicitudo Rei Socialis,* 14-25, 36-37).

In the judgment of many thinking people, the nuclear arms race is the most serious moral issue of our day, dwarfing all other problems. Pope John Paul II, in a 1981 address to a group of scientists and scholars at the United Nations University in Hiroshima, Japan, emphasized the seriousness of the issue:

> Now it is the whole planet that has come under threat. This fact should finally compel everyone to face a basic moral consideration: from now on it is only through a conscious choice and through a deliberate policy that humanity can survive. . . .
>
> Our future on this planet, exposed as it is to nuclear annihilation, depends upon one single factor: humanity must make a moral about-face.

What Is the Church's Response to Global Issues?

These problems, and many others, are enough to make the fainthearted despair. But regardless of their seriousness, Christians are still fundamentally optimistic because we know that with Christ we can do all things. Our mission in the world focuses on what we can do, not on what we cannot do. And what we can do is significantly more than we are doing now.

Pope John Paul II calls on individuals, leaders, societies and nations to convert and turn away from greed and consumerism and to make a wholehearted commitment to work for the development of every human being. He reminds all people that true development begins with the love of God and love of neighbor and that this love manifests itself in respect for all God's creatures which make up our natural world.

Of major concern to the church in our day has been the right of nations to develop and become liberated from oppressive practices and situations which keep the poor in their dependent and often hopeless conditions. In *Populorum Progressio* Pope Paul VI pointed to the example of already developed nations and tried to show that if poor nations too can develop, then several of the problems listed above could be alleviated. Development brings the kind of wealth that enables nations to have a better chance at self-sufficiency.

A constant theme in papal teaching concerning developing nations has been the right of those nations and peoples to control and direct their own process of development, even though foreign money and technical assistance are included in the process. Thus, the right to develop includes economic growth *and* political, social and economic participation in the process of development.

Sollicitudo Rei Socialis (#43-45) outlines some of the steps necessary to help poor nations develop. They include the reform of the existing international trade system, which unfairly discriminates against the products of young industries of the developing nations; reform of the world monetary and financial system, which is marked by excessive fluctuation in exchange and interest rates to the detriment of the poorer countries; the sharing and proper use of technological resources with the developing nations; and the review and possible correction of the operating methods, operating costs and the effectiveness of existing international organizations. The encyclical encourages the formation of new regional organizations among the developing nations in a given geographical area based on equality, freedom and participation in the community of nations.

Both *Populorum Progressio* and *Economic Justice for All* outline the steps necessary to help poor nations develop. They include more direct development assistance, rectification of trade relationships, improved financing through a funding agency that will help provide low-interest loans, more foreign private investment, and recourse to a strong international organization like the United Nations to help bring about more harmonious international relations.

What Does the Church Say About War and Peace?

The Second Vatican Council, Pope John Paul II and the American bishops in their important pastoral letter *The Challenge of Peace: God's Promise and Our Response* all remind us that to be disciples of Jesus Christ means to be passionately devoted to peace. Peace is not merely the absence of war. It is an enterprise of justice and must be built up ceaselessly.

> Peace cannot be obtained on earth unless personal values are safeguarded and men freely and trustingly share with one another the riches of their inner spirits and their talents. A firm determination to respect other men and peoples and their dignity, as well as the studied practice of brotherhood are absolutely necessary for the establishment of peace. Hence peace is likewise the fruit of love, which goes beyond what justice can provide (*Gaudium et Spes*, No. 78).

Can There Be a Just War?

Catholic teaching begins in every case with a presumption against war; it advocates the peaceful settlement of disputes. In extreme cases, though, some uses of force are permitted. For example, every nation has the right and duty to defend itself against unjust aggression. The principles of the just-war tradition permit war if *all* the following conditions are met.

• There must be a real and certain danger. If a situation threatens the life of innocent people, if basic human rights are violated, or if there is an imminent need for self-defense, then there would be just cause.

• The right to declare a war of defense belongs to those who have the legitimate responsibility to represent the people and are entrusted with the common good.

• The rights and values in the conflict must be so important that they justify killing.

• To be just, a war must be waged for the best of reasons and with a commitment to postwar reconciliation with the enemy. Needless destruction, cruelty to prisoners and other harsh measures cannot be tolerated.

• War must be a last resort, justifiable only if all peaceful efforts have been tried and there are no alternatives.

• The odds of success should be weighed against the human cost of the war. The purpose of this criterion is to prevent irrational use of force or hopeless resistance when either will prove futile anyway.

• The damage to be inflicted and the cost incurred by the war must be proportionate to the good expected. For example, if a large number of people would be destroyed over a dispute that only slightly affects the two countries, the decision to go to war would violate proportionality.

Even if all the above criteria are met and war is declared, the principles of proportionality and discrimination must govern the conduct of the war. The principle of discrimination requires that the combatants in a war make a distinction between aggressors and innocent people.

Mass Extermination

The principles of proportionality and discrimination indicate that any attempt to exterminate an entire people, nation or ethnic minority is unjust. Furthermore, any act of war aimed indiscriminately at entire cities or extensive areas and their populations is a crime against God and humanity. Both actions merit total condemnation.

Because nuclear weapons have great potential for widespread and indiscriminate destruction, the American bishops have spoken out clearly against nuclear war. There are major problems in trying to apply the just-war criteria to any kind of nuclear war. The bishops do not perceive any situation in which the first-use of nuclear weapons could be justified. And they question whether there can be such a thing as a limited nuclear war. They argue that one of the criteria of the just-war teaching is that there must be reasonable hope of success in bringing about peace and justice. They question whether there can be this reasonable hope once nuclear weapons have been used. The American bishops also argue that good ends (defending one's country, protecting freedom) cannot justify immoral means (the use of weapons which kill indiscriminately and threaten whole societies).

The Arms Race

The arms race can never be a safe way to peace. It is to be condemned as dangerous and an act of aggression against the poor. The incredible amount of money spent on weapons is a scandal to the starving in our midst.

> In current conditions "deterrence" based on balance, certainly not as an end in itself but as a step on the way toward progressive disarmament, may still be judged morally acceptable. Nonetheless, in order to ensure peace, it is indispensable not to be satisfied with this minimum which is always susceptible to the real danger of explosion (John Paul II, Message to a Special Session of the United Nations on Disarmament, June 1982).

What Is the Role of Personal Conscience?

The decision to fight in a just war or to be a nonviolent witness to peace, a pacifist, is a difficult one. The church respects the personal conscience of those who enter the military service out of loyalty to their country. They "should look upon themselves as the custodians of the security and freedom of their fellow countrymen." When they carry out their duties in a proper manner, "they are contributing to the maintenance of peace" (*Gaudium et Spes*, No. 79).

By the same token, the church also respects those "who forego the use of violence to vindicate their rights and resort to other means of defense which are available to weaker parties, provided it can be done without harm to the rights and duties of others and of the community" (*Gaudium et Spes*, No. 78).

Furthermore, the church supports laws which would make humane provision for conscientious objectors who refuse to bear arms, ''provided they accept some other form of community service'' (*Gaudium et Spes*, No. 79).

CONCLUDING REFLECTIONS

''Blessed are those who hunger and thirst for justice,'' says Jesus. ''Blessed are the peacemakers.'' These two beatitudes summarize the challenge before every disciple of Jesus: to commit ourselves to the cause of justice for the poor and dispossessed and to work for world peace.

Catholic teaching on social justice ranges over a host of issues and problems. The church is interested in all issues which affect the quality of human life because human life is sacred. Everyone God made is precious to him; everyone is his child. Catholic teaching on social justice ultimately is based on the fact that we are one human family.

What can we do to work for justice and peace? On a personal level we can be just in our dealings with others. We can respect all life, since true peace flows from awareness of the worth and dignity of each human person. We can learn to forgive and ask for forgiveness. We can work to solve our own problems in a nonviolent way. We can be informed on the issues and express our opinions. We can select one issue and act upon it. We can pray for world peace. We can perform works of penance to help us put on the attitudes of Jesus himself.

PRAYER REFLECTION

Lord, make me an instrument of your peace:
    where there is hatred, let me sow love;
    where there is injury, pardon;
    where there is doubt, faith;
    where there is despair, hope;
    where there is darkness, light;
    and where there is sadness, joy.
O Divine Master, grant that I may not so much seek
    to be consoled as to console,
    to be understood as to understand,
    to be loved as to love.
For it is in giving that we receive,
    it is in pardoning that we are pardoned,
    and it is in dying that we are born to eternal life.
        —Attributed to St. Francis Assisi

FOR DISCUSSION _____

1. What do you see as the most pressing social justice issue in today's society? How might Christians address it?
2. What is *consumerism*? How does it contribute to an unjust society? Is there anything a Christian can do about it?
3. What can and should you be doing in the cause of world peace?

FURTHER READING _____

Locate and read one of the major church documents on social justice.

Section 3

12

Sacraments: A Life of Grace

Whatever was visible in Our Redeemer has passed over into the Sacraments.

—St. Leo the Great

What is more valuable than love? Love is precious, but it is also fragile. When we've had a bad day, when people misjudge us, when tragedy strikes or setbacks come our way, we are tempted to forget that we are loved. At such times we need to be reminded. A smile, a humorous card, a hug, a sympathetic word—these symbols of love remind us that we are special, loved and cared for.

We need symbols because we are body-people. We need concrete signs to express mysteries like love. We need to say and to hear loving words, to give and receive gifts, to kiss and be kissed, to shake hands, to write and receive notes of appreciation. This is true in our relationships with other people; it is also true in our relationship with God.

This chapter discusses the sacraments as symbols of God's love, signs of his grace. Sacraments and a sacramental life are absolutely central to Catholic identity and belief. To reflect on their meaning and to appreciate what they represent—God's presence to us in our ordinary life—is to grow in an understanding of what Catholics hold to be very precious. In a real sense, the sacraments are an embodiment of the good news of God's love.

What is a sacrament?

In a previous chapter we saw how Vatican II described the church as a kind of sacrament of God's unity with his people. *Sacrament* is defined as "an efficacious symbol," that is, a special kind of symbol that causes what it points to, that is what it represents.

This definition fits both Jesus and his church. Jesus not only signifies God's love for us, he *is* God's love. His teaching, his healings and other miracles, and his sacrifice on the cross all symbolize the love God has for us. But Jesus is more than just a sign of God's love; he is God-made-man, Love-made-flesh. He is the living proof of God's care for his people.

The church is also a sacrament. It is an effective sign of salvation. The Holy Spirit gives life to the church. The risen Lord lives and works in the community of salvation which serves the cause of God's kingdom. Through the church we can meet Jesus. We can see him serving us in and through the church. We can hear him speak to us today when his word is proclaimed.

Christians are called to be sacrament-people. Jesus invites us to be light to the world, beacons whose faithful lives of service point the way to him and his Father.

With this rich definition of sacrament in mind, we can see how the seven sacraments are special actions of Christ working in the church. They are effective, symbolic actions which not only point to God's life but actually convey it to the members of the church. They bring about what they point to. For example, the symbolic actions connected with baptism not only represent new life, they actually bring about a new life in union with our loving God. The Eucharist not only signifies the sharing of a common meal, but actually and really brings about union with the risen Lord.

What Are These Symbols of God's Love for Us?

The Catholic church recognizes seven sacraments. The number 7 is symbolic of perfection or wholeness. We believe that the Lord has left the Christian community with these seven signs of love which touch us during the key moments of our lives. When we begin life, *baptism* unites us with the risen Lord and all our fellow Christians. As we mature and begin to more fully accept and live the Christian life, *confirmation* showers us with the strength of the Holy Spirit to live faithfully for the Lord. The *Eucharist*, the sacred meal which commemorates and re-enacts the Lord's sacrifice on the cross for our salvation, symbolizes and brings about our union with God.

When we are guilty of sin and in need of reconciliation and forgiveness, we experience the Lord's forgiving love in the sacrament of *reconciliation*. And in times of serious illness, the *sacrament of the sick* gives us God's mercy, forgiveness, courage and hope.

Jesus is with us as we live out our life's vocation. Those who are called to serve God's people as deacons, priests or bishops are supported through the sacrament of *holy orders*. And the sacrament of *matrimony* is an ongoing sign of God's love as it appears in the union of a couple who are committed to loving each other until death. Their union and their fidelity are signs of the Lord's union with us and his faithfulness to his church.

What Does a Sacrament Do?

A sacrament makes visible the mystery of God's love for us. It is easy to see how this definition applies to Jesus Christ. He is the primary visible sign of invisible grace. In Christ Jesus, God has reconciled the world. The Father has spoken his Word in the visible form of Jesus. The incarnation of Jesus Christ is the primary sacrament of our salvation. His death on the cross made visible for all people the love God has for us.

In a similar way the church is sacramental because it continues Jesus' work of salvation. By announcing the good news of salvation, by building up a strong community of believers bound in love and service to others, the church makes visible the Lord who sacrificed his life so that people can have eternal life. The church is made up of individual Christians who are called by the Lord to witness to him and to his message, to live a grace-filled life that attracts others to the gospel. They, too, have a sacramental vocation to be authentic signs of God's love.

The seven sacraments renew the mystery of God's love. As the council fathers taught:

> [Their purpose] is to sanctify men, to build up the body of Christ, and finally, to give worship to God. Because they are signs, they also instruct. They not only presuppose faith, but by words and objects they also nourish, strengthen, and express it (*Constitution on the Sacred Liturgy*, No. 59).

What Is the Traditional Definition of *Sacrament*?

For years Catholics have learned the following definition of a sacrament: A sacrament is an outward sign instituted by Christ to give grace.

Outward sign. Through words and actions we can sense, experience and come to believe spiritual realities that exist beyond our senses. We can see water poured over an infant's head, feel the anointing of holy oils, taste the consecrated bread and wine, and hear the words of God's forgiveness or the exchange of marriage vows. We know that something important is happening behind these outward signs. We are celebrating Christ's presence; God's friendship with this people is entering our lives.

Instituted by Christ. Jesus came to preach the good news and establish his Father's kingdom. He remains active through the church which continues his work in the world. With the guidance and power of the Holy Spirit, the church has developed the seven sacraments as special, unique signs whose purpose is to build up the kingdom of God.

To give grace. The purpose of the sacraments is to convey grace. Grace is a traditional Catholic term which refers to our participating in God's life. Grace is God's free gift of friendship.

Sacraments are not magical rituals. They presuppose openness, faith and cooperation on our part. Through them, our Lord guarantees his friendship and help. We must respond to them and live the gift of God's life which he offers to us.

What Is Sanctifying Grace?

Sanctifying grace makes us holy and pleasing to God. When we speak of sanctifying grace, we are referring to being adopted into God's family, to being temples of the Holy Spirit and heirs of eternal life. The sacrament of baptism brings us into God's family, and the sacrament of reconciliation restores God's life in those who have broken off their relationship with him. The other sacraments increase and intensify our friendship relationship with God.

What Is Actual Grace?

Actual grace is God's help to do good and avoid evil. One of the major benefits of the sacraments is to help us live virtuous lives and avoid the temptations that come our way.

What Are the Scriptural Roots of the Sacraments?

Each of the seven sacraments meets us in a key moment of our life. Each renews a key value from the life and ministry of Jesus. The following chart provides New Testament references which teach important insights about the seven sacraments and the values each sacrament contains.

SACRAMENT	CENTRAL VALUE	SCRIPTURE REFERENCE
Baptism	new life; celebration of Christian community	Mt 28:19; Rom 6:3-11

Confirmation	strength and growth; celebration of gifts	Lk 24:49; Acts 8:14-17; Acts 19:1-6; 1 Cor 12:4-11
Eucharist	ongoing nourishment; celebration of unity	Lk 22:19-20; 1 Cor 11:17-34
Reconciliation	forgiveness; reunion	Lk 15; Jn 20:21-23; 2 Cor 2:5-11
Healing	physical, emotional and spiritual health	Mk 1:32-34; Mk 6:13; Jas 5:14-15
Matrimony	love; family life	Jn 2:1-12; Mt 19:6; Mk 10:11; Eph 5:21-33
Holy orders	service	2 Tm 1:6; Ti 1:5-9

What Is Liturgy?

People who believe in God are drawn to worship him, that is, to praise him, to thank him, to ask his forgiveness, to bring their petitions to him. Believers can and do worship God alone, but the Christian community values communal worship because Jesus said, "For where two or three meet in my name, I am there among them" (Mt 18:20). Worshipping God in Christian community is a celebration of who we are as a people and what God has done for us.

Public worship of God is known as *liturgy*. Christian liturgy uses words, actions and symbols to celebrate the presence of God in our midst. It reminds us of who we are and what we are in relation to our loving Father. It tells the story of salvation. The seven sacraments are liturgical celebrations of the church.

What Is Ritual?

Liturgy is organized into *ritual*. All rituals bring a recognizable order to certain words, actions and symbols in order to create a meaningful celebration for a particular group. Thanksgiving meals, Independence Day celebrations and sports rallies are examples of rituals. They use words (greetings, memorable songs, cheers), gestures (flag waving, parades, hugs or handshakes) and symbols (team mascot, flag, special menu, flowers) to communicate and celebrate. The seven sacraments are important rituals of the Catholic church.

How Are Liturgy and Ritual Related in the Sacraments?

The Christian liturgy is a special kind of ritual that retells the story of Jesus Christ and his victory over death. For example, the eucharistic liturgy employs the *words* of scripture to tell us of God's steadfast love. It uses *music* to help us express our prayers with feeling and to free us to lift our hearts joyfully to God. Through the miracle of God's love, ordinary *food*—bread and wine—is transformed into the body and blood of the Lord himself, a Lord we can receive and take into the world to other people. The Eucharist also contains *gestures* like the sign of the cross to remind us of the love of the Trinity, genuflection to show respect for the Lord's divine presence, and the handshake of peace to share Christian fellowship.

Liturgy is a real celebration because the guest present in our midst is none other than Jesus the Lord. Liturgy—the ritual re-enactment and retelling of the Christian story—should be joyful because our risen Lord chooses to join us when we come together to remember him and his good news. All seven sacraments are ritual celebrations of the Lord's presence at key moments of our lives.

What Are Sacramentals?

Sacramentals are those objects, actions, prayers and the like which help us become aware of Christ's presence in our lives. Sacramentals prepare us for the all-important signs of Christ's grace, the sacraments. The spiritual value of the sacramentals depends on the faith and devotion of the users. The church recognizes many of these sacred signs:

Objects: candles, holy water, statues and icons, holy pictures, rosaries, relics, incense, beads, vestments, church buildings, crosses, medals, blessed ashes, palms.

Actions: blessings, genuflection, exchange of the sign of peace, bowing the head at the name of Jesus, sign of the cross.

Places: the Holy Land, Rome, Fatima, Lourdes.

Practices: fasting, abstaining.

Prayers: the Liturgy of the Hours (Divine Office), which is the public prayer of the church for the sanctifying of the day through praise of God.

Sacred Time: the liturgical year with its five major divisions (Advent, Christmas season, Lent, Easter season, Ordinary Time), holy days, feasts of the saints.

CONCLUDING REFLECTIONS _____

The seven sacraments celebrate the mystery of God's presence and love in our midst. To appreciate them fully, we should remind ourselves that we are also a true sign of God's love.

We need faith and sensitivity to see God working through ordinary things like water, bread and wine. It also takes faith to realize that God works through us. He has chosen us—ordinary people—to continue his work, to be his presence in the world.

Sacraments build up the Christian community. As signs of God's love, we too have our part to play. Each of us is an important child of God who has been given special gifts to share with our brothers and sisters on their journey to the Father.

Because Jesus acts through and is present in the sacraments, we can truly call them celebrations. Because the Lord lives in and works through us, we should fundamentally be joyful people. His promise to be with us through the Holy Spirit can help us see life as an adventure, as a journey where we are called to see God in everyone and do our part to spread the joy of the gospel.

Sacraments are not magic; they demand openness, faith and cooperation on our part. For us as individuals to be effective signs of God's love in the world, we too must be open to serving others. The proof that we are open is when we are willing to share our gifts, talents, time and resources to help others, especially the needy.

Sacraments meet us in the major moments of our lives and strengthen us as we live out our Christian vocation. The Christian life is a journey that requires close contact with our living Lord, our trustworthy companion.

PRAYER REFLECTION

Every sincere disciple of Jesus strives to be his living symbol for others. A major theme of our prayer should be asking our Lord to teach us the way to serving him better. Perhaps the words of these two saints reflect the sentiments of our own heart.

> What have I done for Christ?
> What am I doing for Christ?
> What ought I do for Christ?
>
> —St. Ignatius of Loyola

> Day by day,
> day by day,
> O dear Lord,
>   three things I pray:
>   to see thee more clearly,
>   love thee more dearly,
>   follow thee more nearly,
>   day by day.
>
> —St. Richard of Chicester

FOR DISCUSSION

1. In what ways are you a sacrament of God's grace?
2. How do the seven sacraments continue Christ's presence and work on earth?
3. What are the principal signs of God's love in your life?

FURTHER READING

Read the New Testament references given on page 144-145.

13

The Sacraments of Initiation

"Go, therefore, make disciples of all nations; baptise them in the name of the Father and of the Son and of the Holy Spirit, and teach them to observe all the commands I gave you."

—Matthew 28:19

"Lord, send out your Spirit, and renew the face of the earth."

—from Psalm 104

A church exists for the double purpose of gathering in and sending out. This description aptly fits the Christian community, a community called together by the Lord himself to continue his work in the world. Sacraments celebrate Christian community. But they also remind us that because we are Christians we have work to do.

This chapter looks at the sacraments of initiation. By their very nature the sacraments of initiation help "gather in" God's people, incorporating them into the Body of Christ, the Christian community which is the church. But like all sacraments, they powerfully commission God's chosen ones to be Christ for those in the world. These sacraments confer the life of Jesus, they bestow the gift of the Spirit on the people of God so that they can continue the Lord's mission in word and deed to a world that is hungering for meaning and love.

What Are the Sacraments of Initiation?

The sacraments of baptism, confirmation and Eucharist are known as the sacraments of initiation. Most American Catholics were baptized as infants, received first communion in second grade, and were confirmed either in junior high school or senior high school. The history of the sacraments shows that the age for receiving the various

149

sacraments of initiation has changed over the centuries. When Christianity started, of course, most converts were adults and thus received the sacraments of initiation all at the same time.

How Did the Early Church Prepare for Initiation?

To become a Christian in the early church literally meant to begin a new life in Jesus Christ. It meant that a person had to renounce his or her former life, a life of sin. In a time when being a Christian might lead to death, to enter the Christian community was very serious business.

Most converts to Christianity in the first century were adults. Thus it made sense to have a rather lengthy period of preparation—typically three years—before a person was fully initiated into the Christian community. To turn from a life of sin and embrace the life of love commanded by Jesus took sober thought, reflection and formation.

This period of preparation was tied up with the paschal mystery of Jesus' death and resurrection. Candidates gradually entered into this paschal mystery. They had sponsors and entered a period of preparation called the *catechumenate*. During this time the *catechumens* learned about the Christian faith and became disciplined to the Christian way of life through prayer, fasting and self-denial. The key emphasis was on conversion to Christ.

The sacraments of initiation themselves were celebrated on Holy Saturday after a 40-day period of prayer and formal instruction in the faith. During this proximate period of preparation, the candidate learned the creed and the Lord's Prayer, the privileged prayer of those who have been invited by Jesus to call God *Abba*.

How Were the Sacraments of Initiation Celebrated?

The initiation rite itself consisted of the sacraments we recognize today as baptism, confirmation and Eucharist. Both the candidates and the Christian community prayed and fasted to prepare spiritually for this occasion. The bishop was the main celebrant of the sacraments. He questioned the candidates to see if they were ready to live out the Christian commitment. The candidates demonstrated their assent by renouncing Satan and a life of sin. The bishop then sealed the candidates with oil before they entered the water.

Assisted by deacons or deaconesses, the candidates were stripped of their clothes, entered the water and were immersed three times. After each immersion they were asked the trinitarian questions: "Do you believe in the Father? Do you believe in the Son? Do you believe in the Holy Spirit?"

After emerging from the water, the five senses of the candidates were anointed with chrism and the Holy Spirit was invoked to fill the new Christians with his power. (Today we recognize this second anointing as the sacrament of confirmation.) Candidates were given new white garments to signify the new life of Christ; they were also handed candles which were lit from the Easter candle to symbolize their vocation to be the light of Christ. After the new Christians were introduced to the assembly, common prayers were recited, a sign of peace was exchanged, and the Eucharist was celebrated. At this eucharistic celebration the new Christians received their first holy communion.

This ancient way of initiating adults into the Christian community has been revived in our own day through the *Rite of Christian Initiation of Adults (RCIA)*.

What Is the *Rite of Christian Initiation of Adults?*

The four periods and three stages of the *RCIA* process are outlined and briefly described below.

Period 1: Precatechumenate. The journey to Christian initiation begins with a period of inquiry. Attracted by God to examine the Christian faith community, the inquirers share life experiences with Catholics, reflect on the scriptural word of God, seek knowledge about the Catholic religion and its relationship to Christianity, and have the opportunity to learn about Jesus Christ, at least in a preliminary way.

Stage 1: Rite of the Catechumenate. Through a rite of welcome, the seekers ask for acceptance into the Catholic faith community, and they are joyfully accepted into the church as candidates for Christian initiation. They become known as *catechumens*, persons who promise to take instructions in the Catholic faith and live a Christian life.

Period 2: Catechumenate. After the initial celebration of welcoming in which the catechumens renounce sin and take on a new Christian name, they study the Christian faith more deeply (sometimes under the guidance of a Christian sponsor, a caring role model for how a Christian lives). During this period, which may last for months or even years, the catechumens grow familiar with the Christian way of life, study the Christian scriptures and participate fully in the Liturgy of the Word, and begin to take an active role in the life of the church community. Through study, community participation, service and prayer, the catechumens can properly be called "Christians-on-the-way" toward a full commitment to Jesus Christ and his body, the church.

Stage 2: Rite of Election. After the lengthy period of instruction and testing of the catechumens' resolve to follow the way to Jesus, the church calls them forward to a deeper stage of spiritual preparation. On the first Sunday of Lent the "elect" gather at their parish and are called forward to take the final steps toward Christian initiation. Later in the day they travel to the cathedral where all the catechumens from around the diocese are enrolled as the elect who will be baptized on Holy Saturday and fully received into the Christian community.

Period 3: Enlightenment. When the bishop enrolls the elect, he challenges them to prepare themselves for baptism and full reception into the community by prayer and fasting during the Lenten season. This period of proximate preparation for full initiation into the church is known as the Enlightenment. It coincides with Lent, that time in the liturgical year when all believers are to prepare themselves in a special way for the celebration of Christ's paschal mystery.

During the Sundays of Lent there are special rituals and prayers for the elect. Reflection on the Sunday readings, especially from John's gospel, helps the baptismal candidates choose Jesus and his kingdom over the way of Satan and darkness. The elect also learn the Christian creed and the Lord's Prayer, the basic summary of Christian beliefs and the prayer of all those who follow Christ.

Stage 3: Rite of Initiation. The rite of initiation typically takes place during the Easter vigil liturgy. At this service the elect are baptized, confirmed and take holy communion for the first time as full members of Christ's body. The rite of baptism includes a special litany, the blessing of water, the baptism itself, clothing in a white garment, and the presentation of a candle lit from the paschal candle. Confirmation includes simple words of prayer, the imposition of hands, and the anointing with the blessed oils known as chrism. We can easily see how the *RCIA* parallels the practice of the early church.

Period 4: Mystagogia. During the weeks following Easter, the new Christians meet to reflect on the meaning of the recent events in their lives as Christians. They are supported by the community through a postbaptismal catechesis, that is, a deeper study into the mysteries of the faith. The term *mysteries* refers to those signs of God's love which are present in the church's sacramental life and in the lives of Christians who are united to the Lord.

Pentecost Sunday concludes the catechumenate and begins the lifelong pilgrimage of a fully initiated Christian. By this time the new members of the church have selected some service activity which will contribute to the building of Christ's body. They now have the full responsibility of a follower of Jesus.

What Is Baptism?

Baptism, a sacrament of initiation, is a principal sign of God's love for us. Through this sacrament we enter into and celebrate a new life in union with Jesus Christ and the Christian community. This new life is accomplished by symbolically entering into the mystery of

Christ's death and resurrection. The sacrament forgives sin. It also calls us to live a life worthy of a child who is invited to partake of God's kingdom. Thus, we are challenged to die to sin and accept the new life of redemption in Christ Jesus. Through baptism God makes a covenant of love with us, his adopted children; it enables us to live the law of love in union with and supported by our Christian brothers and sisters.

How Is Baptism of a Child Administered?

The *RCIA* teaches that the initiation of adults is the concern of all the faithful. The community must always be ready to give help to those who need Christ (*Rite of Christian Initiation of Adults*, No. 41). This same general principle applies for children who are baptized in the faith of the church. When parents present their children for baptism, they profess that they are willing to raise their children with gospel values. The godparents (one of whom must be an active, fully initiated Catholic) and fellow parishioners promise to support the parents in their commitment.

Baptism is ideally celebrated at the Easter vigil, but also on other Sundays because Sunday is the Lord's day, the day on which the church assembles to proclaim the paschal mystery of God's love. It is quite appropriate to celebrate baptism at a Sunday liturgy. But it should always be celebrated in an assembly of Christian believers.

The ceremony begins with a greeting from the ordained minister (deacon or priest), the ordinary minister of the sacrament of baptism. He reminds the parents and godparents of their duty to raise the child in a Christian home.

The minister then welcomes the child by making the sign of the cross on its forehead, inviting parents and godparents to do the same. He anoints the child with oil, proclaiming that the child is joined to Christ, the Anointed One. He then blesses the baptismal water and leads the parents, godparents and the Christians assembled to profess their faith and renew their baptismal vows on their own behalf and on behalf of the child.

The parents and godparents affirm that they desire baptism for their child. The minister pours water on the head of the child (or immerses the child in water) and pronounces the words:

> I baptize you in the name of the Father,
> and of the Son,
> and of the Holy Spirit.

Following the baptism the child's forehead is anointed with oil, a white garment is placed on the child, and a candle lit from the paschal candle is held by one of the parents. The celebrant touches the ears and mouth of the child and prays that the child will hear the gospel and proclaim his word. All assembled recite the Our Father after which the celebrant concludes the ceremony by blessing the mother, then the father, and finally the entire congregation.

What Do the Principal Symbols of Baptism Signify?

Water. Baptism means "washing." In the early church the person was immersed in a pool of water. While that is an option today, it is more common for the priest to pour water over the forehead of the person while he recites the formula for baptism. Besides cleansing, water symbolizes destruction and death. Baptismal water means the death of an old life to sin. Water also means life; without it, we would die. Jesus reminded Nicodemus that he was living water, the source of all life. In baptism we are reborn into a new life with Jesus Christ. Original sin is washed away, and we inherit eternal life as adopted children of God. We must strive continually to live our baptism.

Oil. Oil heals and protects. It was also used to anoint kings and queens. The anointing with oil in baptism reminds us that the Lord extends salvation to us and sends his Spirit to protect and strengthen us. The root meaning of *Christ* is "anointed one." The oil of baptism (known as chrism) symbolizes that we have been "Christ-ed," that we share in the life of Jesus Christ. We become his followers, a kingly people. We become the anointed of the Anointed One. The new identity brings new responsibilities. Adopted daughters and sons of a loving Father share in Jesus' mission of preaching the good news of God's kingdom and in the healing ministry of serving others and working toward the unity of a wounded human community.

White garment. In the early church Christians customarily put on new white robes when they emerged from the baptismal pool. Today a white cloth serves the same symbolic function. By putting on a symbol of purity, festivity and a new identity, the newly baptized person shows a willingness to live a new life in union with the Lord.

What Happens to the Unbaptized?

The church teaches that some form of baptism in Jesus Christ is necessary for salvation. This teaching is rooted in Jesus' response to the Pharisee Nicodemus:

> "In all truth I tell you,
> no one can enter the kingdom of God
> without being born through water
>   and the Spirit" (Jn 3:5).

Traditionally the Catholic church has taught that there are three forms of baptism: baptism by water (through the sacrament of baptism), baptism by blood (the death of martyrs), and baptism by desire. Baptism by desire refers to those who were not granted the gift of faith; their lives show that they would have accepted Jesus Christ had they been given the chance to know him.

In the Middle Ages theologians confronted the question of unbaptized children who die without reaching the age of reason. Certainly they would not go to hell or purgatory since they were not guilty of any personal sin. Yet they apparently did not have the chance to have baptism by desire. St. Thomas Aquinas and other theologians taught that these infants go to a place called *limbo*, a state of eternal natural happiness but without the vision of God.

The Catholic church never formally defined the doctrine of limbo. Today many theologians suggest that in God's infinite and mysterious mercy he gives every person a chance to accept or reject him. God's ways are not our ways. But divine revelation is silent on this question of unbaptized infants. Thus the church teaches that parents should take care to baptize their babies into the Catholic faith without unnecessary delay. Total union with God in heaven is such a great gift that we should do everything within our power to share it with our loved ones.

What Is Confirmation?

Confirmation is a sacrament of initiation. Along with baptism and Eucharist, confirmation brings to completion the making of a Christian. It is the seal of baptism, a celebration of the gift of the Holy Spirit and a confirming of the baptismal gifts given by the Spirit. Adults are confirmed at the Easter vigil liturgy immediately after their baptism; children who were baptized as infants are usually confirmed some years afterward. The bishop or his delegate is the usual celebrant of this sacrament. His presiding over the confirmation liturgy underscores the unity of Christians. Our Christian mission of responsible service is lifelong and worldwide.

How Has Confirmation Changed Through the Ages?

As we have seen above, in the early church baptism and confirmation were part of the adult initiation process that climaxed at the Easter vigil liturgy. After the lengthy period of preparation the candidate was baptized, anointed by the bishop (confirmed), and received the Eucharist for the first time. Scholars conclude that in these early years children probably joined their parents in the initiation process. Whole households became Christian together.

A pivotal event in the history of Christianity was the legalization of Christianity in the fourth century. By the fifth century Christianity was the official religion of the Roman Empire. Great numbers of people were baptized. As the church grew, it became increasingly difficult for the bishop to be present at every baptism in every parish of his diocese. Permission was given for the priests to baptize, but the bishop wished to retain some role in the initiation process.

Thus, in the Western church, there gradually grew the custom of the bishop anointing, laying on hands, praying for the power of the Spirit, and "confirming" the baptismal commitment of Christians baptized as infants. Because of the size of his diocese and the numbers involved, this confirmation ceremony took place at some later, more convenient time. By the 13th century church leaders saw a need for youngsters to learn about their baptismal commitment. Confirmation became the logical event for catechetical instructions in the faith.

Until and including recent times, then, the confirmation of those baptized as infants was administered to young people at some time after the age of reason had been reached.

What Are the Emphases in Confirmation Today?

Today confirmation is frequently spoken of as the sacrament of maturity. It gives us the opportunity to say yes to the commitment our parents made for us at baptism. The growing practice of confirming sometime during the years of adolescence underscores the special strength and help of the Holy Spirit needed as we enter adulthood. Confirmation is a sign of God's special love as he showers on us the gifts of the Holy Spirit. These gifts fortify us to live mature, responsible Christian lives.

At confirmation the bishop makes the sign of the cross on our forehead and says, "Be sealed with the gift of the Holy Spirit." To be "sealed" means to become stamped as belonging to someone. At confirmation we become official ambassadors of Jesus Christ, empowered by the Holy Spirit.

In this sacrament, the effects of which are lifelong, we recommit ourselves to the Christian vocation which most of us were invited to live from our earliest years. Confirmation celebrates the seven gifts of the Holy Spirit: knowledge, wisdom, understanding, right judgment, courage, reverence and fear of the Lord (see Is 11:2). These gifts are to take root in us and grow as we mature into Christian adults. Their purpose is to help us witness to the Lord. Works of witness to which all mature, responsible Christians are called include working for peace and social justice, speaking out for innocent life, acting honestly, studying and sharing our faith with others. Through acts of kindness and love we live out our Christian vocation and put into practice the gifts of the Holy Spirit which have been given to us to use on behalf of others.

What Is the Eucharist?

The Eucharist is the greatest sacrament of the church, the prime symbol of love. It expresses the love present among Christians who gather to remember what Jesus has accomplished for us and to thank the Father for all he has given us. This sacred meal calls us together to re-enact the Lord's sacrifice on the cross and to celebrate his glorious resurrection. It empowers us to live the life of love Jesus has demonstrated to us.

The Eucharist helps us remember what Jesus did through his death and resurrection. It reminds us—and we humans need constant reminders—that to follow Jesus we must live as Jesus did. We have to die to our selfishness and sin, and in the Eucharist we receive the strength and courage to do so. Furthermore, the Eucharist commissions us to go out into the world and share ourselves and the Lord we have received. It empowers us to serve others.

The Liturgy of the Word opens us up to the Holy Spirit who teaches us how to live the Christian life in today's world. The Liturgy of the Eucharist helps us join our lives to Jesus and to offer them in praise and love to the Father. In the offering of ourselves, we thank God as a people for his many blessings on us as individuals and as a Christian community.

When we share the body and blood of Jesus Christ, mysteriously and sacramentally made present to us in the Eucharist, we demonstrate our faith in the reality of Christian unity. We declare that we are one with the Lord and with one another. And we promise that we will live as people who are concerned about our brothers and sisters.

The next chapter is completely devoted to a study of the Eucharist.

CONCLUDING REFLECTIONS

Baptism and confirmation are sacramentally received only once, though we live our baptism and confirmation every day when we choose to live like Jesus Christ. The Eucharist, however, is celebrated daily around the world because it is the principal symbol of Christian life. The Lord's life, death and resurrection are commemorated many thousands of times daily. Christians worldwide are gathered in to worship and praise their God through Jesus Christ our Lord.

Catholics are called to celebrate this central act of worship weekly. We need to remember. We need to thank God. We need to gain the strength of the Lord to live his life in service of others. The Eucharist initiates us into the Christian life every time we celebrate and receive the Lord. The body and blood of our Lord is the spiritual food we need to live the baptismal and confirmation commitments to be other Christs in the world.

PRAYER REFLECTION

The sacraments of initiation celebrate the life of becoming a Christian. Reflect on the scriptural passages which teach of our common Christian vocation.

Baptism: Who we are—persons who share the *identity* of Jesus Christ (members of his body, the church).

> But now that faith has come we are no longer under a slave looking after us; for all of you are the children of God, through faith, in Christ Jesus, since every one of you that has been baptised has been clothed in Christ. There can be neither Jew nor Greek, there can be neither slave nor freeman, there can be neither male nor female—for you are all one in Christ Jesus (Gal 3:25-28).

Confirmation: What we do—persons who are empowered by the Holy Spirit to share the *mission* of Jesus Christ.

> "But I say this to you who are listening: Love your enemies, do good to those who hate you, bless those who curse you, pray for those who treat you badly. . . .
> "Be compassionate just as your Father is compassionate. Do not judge, and you will not be judged; do not condemn, and you will not be condemned; forgive and you will be forgiven. Give, and there will be gifts for you" (Lk 6:27-28;36-38).

Eucharist: Where we are going—persons sharing the *destiny* of Jesus Christ, our Lord and Savior.

> "Anyone who does eat my flesh and
> drink my blood
> has eternal life,
> and I shall raise that person up
> on the last day.
> For my flesh is real food
> and my blood is real drink.
> Whoever eats my flesh and drinks
> my blood
> lives in me
> and I live in that person.

As the living Father sent me
and I draw life from the Father,
so whoever eats me will also draw
    life from me'' (Jn 6:54-57).

FOR DISCUSSION_____

1. Explain how the baptism of infants can be a meaningful event for the adult Christian community.
2. What does it mean when we say that Christians are initiated into the death and resurrection of Jesus? How can Christians live this mystery in a practical way?
3. At what age do you think those who were baptized as infants should be confirmed?
4. Discuss evidences of the presence of the Holy Spirit in your own life. For example, when have you put into action one of the seven gifts of the Holy Spirit?

FURTHER READING_____

Ezekiel 36:24-28 (clean water, new heart)
Isaiah 61:1-9 (the Spirit of the Lord)
John 3:1-6 (Jesus with Nicodemus)
John 4:5-14 (waters of eternal life)
Galatians 5:16-25 (life in the Spirit)

14

Sacraments: The Eucharist

"In all truth I tell you
if you do not eat the flesh of the Son
    of man
and drink his blood,
you have no life in you.
Anyone who does eat my flesh and
    drink my blood
has eternal life,
and I shall raise that person up
    on the last day."

—John 6:53-54

What does it mean to be a Catholic? What is central to the Catholic identity? Some might respond that Catholics have a common vision of the gospel and try to live out that vision by sharing it in word and action with others. Others might add that belief and participation in a sacramental life are central to being a Catholic. While both of these statements are true, it is in our belief about and attitude toward the Eucharist that the gospel vision, the call to action and service, and the sacramental life all come together. The Eucharist is the *central* act of worship in the liturgical life of the Catholic church.

Liturgy is the official public worship of the church. It includes the sacraments, recitation of the Divine Office, benedictions and novenas, official blessings, and the like. But the Eucharist—the celebration of the holy sacrifice of the Mass—is the best expression of the church's worship of God.

The liturgy is the summit toward which the activity of the Church is directed; at the same time it is the fountain from which all her power flows (*Constitution on the Sacred Liturgy*, No. 10).

161

Eucharist means "thanksgiving." It is the sublime means Christians have of thanking God the Father for the gift of his Son, Jesus Christ. Like all the sacraments, the Eucharist is a mystery, a sign of love. We can never totally fathom its rich meaning and significance for us.

When we partake of the eucharistic bread and wine, we are united to the Lord Jesus, to the Father and to one another by the power of the Holy Spirit. The Lord's life within us—his love and his healing power—helps cure us of our sinful dispositions and hateful attitudes. Jesus alluded to this when he taught:

> "I am the vine,
> you are the branches.
> Whoever remains in me, with me in him,
> bears fruit in plenty;
> for cut off from me you can do
>   nothing" (Jn 15:5).

What Is Meant by the "Real Presence"?

Christian churches offer different answers to this question. Some Christian denominations say Christ is only present in the faith of the people who worship; others say he is present only symbolically or in the act of communicating.

Catholics hold that Jesus is truly present in the community assembled for worship. We also believe that he is present in the priest who presides over the Eucharist in his name, and in the proclamation of the word. But in addition, we believe that Jesus is present in a special way in the sacred species of bread and wine.

Exactly how Jesus is present in the consecrated bread and wine is a mystery. The church has used the word *transubstantiation* to express that at the consecration of the Mass the reality (the substance) of the bread and wine changes into the reality of Jesus—his risen, glorified body and blood. To receive Jesus in the "species" of the bread or the "species" of the wine is to receive the whole Christ since he is totally present in both species.

Catholics believe that it is a singular privilege to receive our Lord in holy communion. We cannot be more closely united to Christ and to one another than in our reception of the Eucharist.

Catholics also believe that our Lord's presence endures in the sacred species of the Blessed Sacrament. In Catholic churches the Blessed Sacrament is reserved in the tabernacle, a safe-like secure receptacle usually located in a chapel or a side altar. A traditional devotion to our Lord is visiting him in the Blessed Sacrament.

How Is the Eucharist Also a Symbol?

The Eucharist is also a special kind of symbol. It is an outward sign instituted by Jesus Christ which symbolizes what it brings about and brings about what it symbolizes. Among other things, the Eucharist as symbol represents and brings about the following: spiritual life and nourishment; Christian community and unity; the sacrifice of love which sanctifies; the presence of Jesus Christ in the life of the individual and the Christian community; the paschal mystery which brings eternal life.

The eucharistic liturgy is filled with special signs that help to convey those spiritual realities. These signs include the word, the bread and the wine.

What Does the Word Symbolize?

The symbol of the word is used in various scripture readings, prayers, responses and the like. It is a powerful symbol which helps open us up to the word of God speaking to us in our lives.

Ordinary words help make us human; they enable us to participate in life and make sense out of it. The word of God spoken in the eucharistic celebration also helps form us into a human community. It announces the good news of salvation; it teaches us how to live as God's children; it reminds us of the salvation Jesus has won for us.

Words also help us express to God our deepest feelings of praise and thanksgiving. They help us petition God for our needs and ask God's forgiveness for sins we have committed.

What Does the Bread Symbolize?

Bread is a symbol of life. It is the ordinary food of vast numbers of human beings. Consecrated bread at the Eucharist, transformed mysteriously into the body of the Lord Jesus, is life itself. Without the Lord, we are spiritually dead.

The use of *unleavened bread* at Mass carries rich meaning. First, we use unleavened bread in imitation of Jesus who blessed and broke unleavened bread when he instituted the Eucharist at his Last Supper with the apostles.

Second, in the context of the Passover meal that Jesus was celebrating with his disciples, unleavened bread was a reminder of the haste with which the Jews had escaped from Egypt in the time of Moses. They didn't even have time to let the bread rise. After that, the Jews used unleavened bread in their celebration of the Passover event to remind themselves of their absolute need for God because he alone was able to rescue them from slavery.

Third, we use unleavened bread to remind us that we are a pilgrim people. We have not yet arrived at our heavenly kingdom. We are utterly dependent on God's help, love and nourishment for the journey. We need the bread of life, Jesus. Further, Christians should be the yeast or leaven which will spread the influence of Christ into the world and help bring people to God the Father.

What Does the Wine Symbolize?

In many cultures, wine is the ordinary drink at meals. It has a joyous, community quality about it. To make wine the grapes must undergo *fermentation* which can be defined as the "rapid growth of a community of minute organisms." The connection here with the Eucharist is plain: The Lord in the Eucharist helps bring about Christian community.

Consecrated wine is the Lord's blood. Blood in the scriptures is often a sign of life uniting God with his people. In the sacrificial ritual, blood that was dashed or poured at the base of the altar represented life that was symbolically offered to God who was represented by the altar. Moses, for example, sprinkled the blood of the sacrificial animal on the altar and on the people to represent the consecration of the Jewish people to Yahweh their liberator. The lamb's blood smeared on the door saved the firstborn son from death at the time of the Exodus. Moses sprinkled the blood of the sacrificial victim on the altar and on the people. Jesus offered his blood as a sign of the New Covenant between God and his people.

How Is the Eucharist a Celebration?

When we celebrate we observe a day or event with ceremonies of respect, festivity or rejoicing. These descriptions apply to the Eucharist. We celebrate many things at Mass, but especially we celebrate the paschal mystery, that is, the passion, death, resurrection and glorification of Jesus Christ. These events summarize the salvation and eternal life Jesus has won for us.

At Mass the assembled community rejoices in our Lord's risen presence and the power of his love which binds all people together. We show respect at this celebration when we praise God the Father for accomplishing our salvation through his Son, Jesus, and for his healing presence in the Christian community by the power of the Holy Spirit.

The Eucharist is a celebration of praise, worship and thanksgiving to our God. Sin and death have been conquered through the great act of love and obedience of our Lord Jesus Christ. The fruits of the Lord's love are present to us today.

How Is the Eucharist a Sacrifice?

Sacrifice comes from a Latin word which means "to make holy" or "to do something holy." Holiness refers to sharing God's life, his being and his love. Only God himself can make us holy; only God can offer his holiness to us.

Catholics believe that the Mass is a sacrifice instituted by our Lord at the Last Supper. It represents the sacrifice of Christ on the cross. The shedding of the Lord's blood at Calvary was the supreme sign of the love he has for us. It is the action that makes us holy, that makes us pleasing to God. This supreme act of love is mystically made present to us in an unbloody manner each time we celebrate the Mass. In this sacrifice—this act of self-giving love—Jesus Christ is both the priest and the victim who offers himself through the celebrant and the assembled Christian community in praise, thanksgiving, petition and atonement.

What Is the Meaning of the Eucharistic Sacrifice?

In the person of Jesus Christ, both God and humanity are joined. Jesus Christ is both God and man. Through him, God the Father offers us the great sacrament (visible sign) of his love. Jesus is God's love incarnate. But Jesus is also the perfect human being, our representative before God. Through him, humanity both receives and responds to the offer of God's love. The human Jesus was totally open, receptive, obedient and responsive to his heavenly Father—even to death. Unlike the first representative of the human race, Adam, Jesus Christ allowed himself to be put totally in the hands of his Father. By surrendering himself in total obedience to his Father's will, Jesus sacrificed for us. He made us holy; he made it possible for us to share God's life. He did this when he loved us totally, pouring out his blood for our sake.

When we offer the sacrifice of the Mass, we continue to be made holy by accepting and living the example of our brother and Savior Jesus Christ. His freely accepted death shows us that love is the way to holiness. When we remember, re-enact and attempt to live his sacrifice—his way of love—we ourselves are changed by God into more loving people.

By re-enacting the sacrifice of Calvary, we commemorate the death and the resurrection of Jesus. The sacrifice of Jesus on the cross leads to the eternal life of the resurrection. When we imitate Jesus' sacrifice of love, we too are promised eternal life.

At the Last Supper Jesus broke bread and gave it to his disciples and commanded us to do likewise. We obey Jesus when we break bread in his name, when we celebrate the sacrifice of the Mass. Through the

Mass Jesus reminds us to break ourselves for others in imitation of his sacrifice. He tells us that sacrifice is the way to love, holiness and true life—the life of Jesus and union with his Father.

What Does the Cross Symbolize?

The cross is the symbol of our Lord's act of loving sacrifice. In human terms it is the symbol of a defeated man, a criminal. Yet in faith we see it as a sublime sign of victory, of death's defeat, of love's victory. The cross is an apparent contradiction. It symbolizes life's greatest mystery: Self-sacrificing love leads to life united with God and all our fellow humans. It is Jesus himself who calls us to the cross:

> "If anyone wants to be a follower of mine, let him renounce himself and take up his cross every day and follow me" (Lk 9:23).

How Is the Eucharist a Meal?

The Eucharist is a commemorative meal which recalls the Last Supper Jesus celebrated with his apostles. A meal has an intimate quality about it. Those who share the joy of companionship gather and partake of the same food. The word *companionship* means "breaking bread together." A shared meal is a universal symbol of friendship. It signifies oneness of heart, peace and companionship. A meal celebrates and creates unity among friends.

Jesus was aware of the deep meaning associated with meals when he instituted the Eucharist at a traditional Jewish Passover. The Passover meal reminded the Jewish people of God's goodness and fidelity to his promise in rescuing them from Egypt. It served as a festive occasion to thank God for all he did and also to help the Jews solidify their identity as God's people. Jesus changed the meaning of this meal at the Last Supper. He was the paschal lamb which would be sacrificed for all people. His death and resurrection would be the signs of the new covenant.

At the Eucharist we come not just to eat but to savor and enjoy the risen Lord and his life in our fellow Christians. We come to share the bread of life, Jesus. It is no accident that our Lord presents himself in the form of food and drink. Food and drink are necessary for human survival; they remind us that without their ultimate source, God, we would surely die. So, too, without the sharing of our brother and savior Jesus Christ, we would spiritually die.

The Eucharist foreshadows our spiritual inheritance, the heavenly banquet where we will be united totally with God and with our brothers and sisters. Such a union will bring with it untold joy and contentment.

How Did the Early Christians Understand Eucharist?

An early name for the Eucharist was *agape* which means "love feast." Early Christians were trying to emphasize that when they broke bread together they were celebrating the presence of the risen Lord Jesus who created in them a community of love.

Not all Christians in the early church, though, understood the true meaning of the "love feast." St. Paul had to criticize certain abuses which had crept into the eucharistic celebrations in Corinth. Apparently some Corinthians came to the meal, but refused to share the food they brought with the poor. Others hurried to get done, and still others glutted themselves on food or drink. Paul admonished very strongly those who failed to recognize Jesus' presence in the breaking of the bread and the sharing of the cup or in their fellow Christians who had come to celebrate fellowship with them:

> Whenever you eat this bread, then, and drink this cup, you are proclaiming the Lord's death until he comes. Therefore anyone who eats the bread or drinks the cup of the Lord unworthily is answerable for the body and blood of the Lord.
> Everyone is to examine himself and only then eat of the bread or drink from the cup, because a person who eats and drinks without recognizing the body is eating and drinking his own condemnation (1 Cor 11:26-29).

How Does the Mass Relate to the Christian Vocation?

The term Mass is derived from the Latin words recited at the dismissal, *"Ite missa est"* which mean "Go, you are sent." This reminds us of our duty to love and serve the Lord in all the people we meet. The meal symbolism also recalls our duty to feed the hungry, to share some of the bountiful material goods with which we have been blessed. Surely St. Paul would admonish those of us today who do not share with the poor in our midst. Receiving the Lord in the Eucharist should prompt us to see the Lord in everyone we meet, and perhaps especially in the needy.

> Thus the Lord *unites us with himself* through the Eucharist—Sacrament and sacrifice—and he *unites us with himself and with one another* by a bond stronger than any natural union; and thus united, *he sends us* into the whole world to bear witness, through faith and works, to God's love (Pope John Paul II, *Sollicitudo Rei Socialis*, 48).

The Mass eloquently reminds us that communal worship must never be turned in on itself. When we "break bread" in the name of Jesus, we are celebrating our brotherhood and sisterhood and receiving the source of our life, the Lord Jesus. In this sacred meal, he reminds us to take him out into the world, a world that desperately needs his love. We must be broken for others just as he was broken for us. Christian worship that does not translate into service for others is not true worship. Jesus said:

> "It is not anyone who says to me, 'Lord, Lord,' who will enter the kingdom of Heaven, but the person who does the will of my Father in heaven" (Mt 7:21).

The Eucharist reminds us that because we have received the body of Christ we must *become* the body of Christ. We are the Lord's hands that touch and care for the sick, old and infirm; his feet that walk to meet and befriend the lonely; his understanding eyes that reveal compassion to the hurting and lost in our midst; his voice of power and righteousness to speak out on behalf of the marginated in the cause of justice.

"Go, you are sent" mandates that we must serve others. When we celebrate the Eucharist we are reenacting the paschal mystery, a mystery that shows us that the way to life is the way of love. At the Last Supper Jesus washed feet. We cannot celebrate the Eucharist honestly and with a clear conscience without imitating the Lord himself. Christian service and a commitment to work for justice are the true tests of fruitful Christian worship.

How Is the Eucharist a Ritual?

Rituals play an important part in our lives. Rituals always follow a pattern; they are well-organized. For example, we may know exactly what to expect at a family Thanksgiving Day—the greeting, the table setting, the blessing of the food, the eating of the delicious meal, the cleanup after the meal, the ways of relaxing after dinner, the eating of leftovers later at night.

The liturgy of the Mass is also a ritual. It is a renewal of the New Covenant in Jesus Christ. It enables us to enter into the events we celebrate. The ritual of the Eucharist is a patterned remembering of the events Jesus enacted for our salvation. The liturgy of the Eucharist does three things: 1) It celebrates, recalls and re-enacts the *past* of our salvation, the life, death and resurrection of Jesus; 2) it celebrates the paschal mystery which is happening *right now* in our midst; and 3) it looks to the *future* of the church and the ultimate human destiny of a risen life with the Lord in heaven.

What Do the Gestures Used in the Mass Symbolize?

The ritual of the Mass involves many symbolic gestures. The priest marches in procession to indicate that we are pilgrim people moving in the present to a glorious future. We stand to show our basic dignity as children of the Father. We kneel to show our reverence and thanksgiving and to humbly adore our Lord. We eat and drink from the table of the Lord to show we are a community. We pray together. We sing in celebration and praise of the Lord.

What Are the Parts of the Mass?

The Mass consists of the Introductory Rites, the Liturgy of the Word and the Liturgy of the Eucharist. In the Liturgy of the Word we hear the word of God and derive nourishment from it. We are challenged to make it part of our lives and to respond to it. In the Liturgy of the Eucharist we celebrate the death and resurrection of Jesus. We fully participate in the Eucharist when we receive the Lord under the forms of bread and wine.

Introductory Rites

Entrance: The Mass begins with the singing or recitation of a song.

Greeting: The priest and people make the Sign of the Cross. The priest greets the people, and they respond.

Penitential Rite: The priest and people acknowledge their sinfulness and ask God's forgiveness.

Hymn of Praise (not always part of the Mass): The "Glory to God" is sung or recited.

Opening Prayer: The priest offers a prayer of petition on behalf of the worshipping community.

Liturgy of the Word

Readings: The first reading is from the Old Testament; the second from the latter part of the New Testament; the third from one of the gospels. Psalm verses are recited between the readings and alleluias are sung before the gospel.

Homily: The celebrant or deacon relates the readings to everyday life.

Profession of Faith (not always part of the Mass): Together the people acknowledge their common beliefs.

General Intercessions: The community's petitions for the needs of the church, the world, public authorities, individuals and the local community are presented.

Liturgy of the Eucharist

Preparation of the Altar and Gifts: The gifts of bread and wine are brought forward in procession, the altar is prepared, and a prayer is said over the gifts.

Eucharistic Prayer (Canon): There are several Eucharistic Prayers that are used on different occasions. The Eucharistic Prayer includes the words Jesus said at the Last Supper, the memorial acclamation, and concludes with the doxology, praise to the Trinity sung or recited by the celebrant.

Communion Rite: This part of the Mass includes the Lord's Prayer, the prayer for deliverance, the prayer for peace (after which the sign of peace is exchanged), and the breaking of the bread while the Lamb of God is sung or recited. After reception of communion, the priest offers a prayer of petition on behalf of the community.

Concluding Rite: Announcements and dismissal.

Those parts of the Mass which change with the feast or liturgical season are called the *Proper of the Mass*. Those parts of the liturgy which remain the same are called the *Ordinary of the Mass*.

What is the "Sunday Obligation"?

A common question asked about the Mass centers on the Sunday obligation. In the early church celebrating the Eucharist was a privilege. But as the centuries progressed, the church had to pass a law to remind Catholics of their obligation to worship the Lord weekly in the Eucharist. This law of Sunday observance became universal in the 11th century. It is based on Jesus' own mandate to break bread in his name. Weekly attendance at Sunday or Saturday evening Mass is now a fundamental aspect of Catholic life. But to see why this is so we must avoid the mentality which considers attendance at the Eucharist as simply another obligation.

Some people question the weekly obligation. They argue that they don't get anything out of going to Mass. The purpose of the law, however, is to remind us of our responsibility to join ourselves to our brother and savior Jesus and to one another in worship of the Father. By looking to get something out of it, we are approaching the liturgy from the wrong perspective. A better attitude might be to ask what we can bring to the liturgy, that is, to God and to our fellow Christians who have gathered to worship. *Liturgy* means "the people's work." Going to Mass, even when it is difficult to do so or when we simply do not feel like going, is to show love to God and to our fellow pilgrims. We add nothing to the community by our absence; we give by attending. We share ourselves and publicly proclaim that we want to worship and thank God for everything he has given to us, especially our salvation through his Son Jesus.

Other people see the congregation as separate individuals, not a community at all. They say the celebration is artificial. "Most Christians seem to leave their religion in the parking lot anyway; they are a bunch of hypocrites." There is some truth in this criticism. But the real issue is that we are all hypocrites. We profess high ideals, but we very often fall short of them. We sin and we are phonies—at times. The point is this: Jesus wants to get involved in our lives. He comes to us as we are—weak, fallen, ordinary, hypocritical. Our religion is not for the elite; it is for everyone. Jesus associated with all kinds of people during his ministry; the ones he seemed to have the least patience with were those who thought they were better than everyone else.

CONCLUDING REFLECTIONS

The Eucharist is at the heart of Catholic life and worship. This ritual is a celebration of the paschal mystery of God's love. It re-enacts, in the context of a meal, Jesus' sacrifice which has won salvation for us. It brings into our midst the risen Lord who chooses to be intimately and really present to us. It symbolizes a profound message: Death to self is self-sacrificing love which leads to superabundant life.

The Lord comes to us in communion so that we can be united to him, to our Christian brothers and sisters, and to all of his friends. Jesus genuinely wants to live in us so that we might be signs of his love to other people who are so desperately searching for meaning. He invites us to his love-feast so that we can be the bread of love needed for survival in today's world. He invites us to thank his Father for the great gifts we have been given. He shows us the way to be a living prayer of thanksgiving when he challenges us with the words *Ite missa est*, "Go, you are sent." We are sent to serve the Lord. It is a privilege to celebrate the profound good news of the Eucharist. The mystery of this sacrament challenges us to live out the implications of this sacred banquet.

PRAYER REFLECTION

"I am the bread of life,
No one who comes to me will ever hunger;
no one who believes in me will ever thirst."

> "I am the living bread which has come down
>   from heaven.
> Anyone who eats this bread will live for ever;
> and the bread that I shall give
> is my flesh, for the life of the world"
>   (Jn 6:35,51).

FOR DISCUSSION

1. A friend has told you that she stopped going to Mass because she was bored with the repetitious ritual. What could you say to her to help her reconsider joining her Christian brothers and sisters at the Lord's table?

2. "The Eucharist both creates and celebrates Christian community." Explain.

3. How does the Eucharist challenge you to greater Christian responsibility?

FURTHER READING

Exodus 16 (Yahweh saves Israel by sending manna)
Luke 22:14-20 (institution of the Eucharist)
1 Corinthians 11:17-34 (proper celebration of the Eucharist)

15

The Sacraments of Healing: Reconciliation and Anointing of the Sick

> The prayer of faith will save the sick person and the Lord will raise him up again; and if he has committed any sins, he will be forgiven.
>
> —James 5:15

Someone once said that life is not to live, but to be well. In our scientific age, with all of its modern advances in medicine, this advice makes sense. It makes even more sense to the person sick in body, mind or spirit. To live means to be well. With mental and spiritual health in mind, the Christian might even add, "To live means to be good."

Sometimes we are not good, though. We sin. Our spiritual health suffers. We become alienated from God, others and ourselves. At other times we are not physically well. Our bodies are sick with disease, the aches and pains of old age, the inevitable decline toward death.

Our Lord Jesus has left with us two powerful signs of his love. He knows both our spiritual and physical sicknesses, and he has come to restore us to health. He is the Divine Physician.

> "It is not those that are well who need the doctor, but the sick. I have come to call not the upright but sinners to repentance" (Lk 5:31-32).

The Lord continues his work of healing today in the sacraments of reconciliation and the anointing of the sick.

This chapter will discuss these two sacraments. In addition, it will touch on several important topics central to the Christian life and to full appreciation of the sacrament of reconciliation: conscience, conscience formation and sin.

What Is the Scriptural Basis for Reconciliation?

Jesus came to forgive sin and to heal people of the wounded relationships which sin causes. He empowered his church to continue his ministry of healing and reconciliation when he commanded his disciples to forgive sin in his name:

> "Receive the Holy Spirit.
> If you forgive anyone's sins,
> they are forgiven;
> if you retain anyone's sins,
> they are retained" (Jn 20:23).

Has the Sacrament of Reconciliation Changed?

The sacrament of reconciliation has a rich history in the church. In the early centuries it was received only once in a person's lifetime and only for the most serious of sins. It involved a long period of penance so that the sinner experienced the seriousness of being alienated from God and the Christian community. Over time, a second way of receiving this sacrament developed and became standard: repeated, private, individual, devotional confession to a priest.

What Are Some Key Elements in Today's Practice?

In our day the sacrament of reconciliation has undergone a further development. Some of the key elements of today's practice include the following: proclamation of the word of God, contrition, confession and penance.

Today's rite includes *reading from scripture* to remind us of our need for true *contrition* and to announce the good news of God's love for the sinner. When we sin we cut ourselves off from God and from our fellow Christians; we are even alienated from ourselves. When we are honest with ourselves, we know that we have done wrong and we suffer guilt. The rite of reconciliation stresses how much God loves us and wants us to be made whole again. The proclamation of the scripture—the good news of God's forgiving love—helps the sacrament to be a true celebration.

The church obliges the Catholic who has committed serious sin to *confess* privately and individually to a priest at least once a year. We have the option of doing so either anonymously or face to face. Why confess our sins to another human? Simply because it is a concrete sign on our part that we have admitted our guilt and we are sorry for our sin. It keeps us honest. It shows that we are ready to do something about our sinfulness.

The sacrament of reconciliation has always included *penance*, that is, the performance of some charitable act or some sacrifice or the recitation of some prayers. Performing a penance has two purposes. First, it shows that we are willing to help heal the harm we have caused to our Christian brothers and sisters by our sin. Every sin hurts the Body of Christ; a sorrowful person is concerned about this hurt and tries to do something to help heal it. Second, by doing penance we are allowing the Lord to change our lives. The priest helps the penitent choose a penance that is a meaningful sign of reconciliation and love.

What Is the Role of the Priest in the Sacrament?

The priest serves as the Lord's representative and announces the words of *absolution* on behalf of the church. When the priest holds his hands over the penitent's head and recites the words, "I absolve you from your sins in the name of the Father, and of the Son, and of the Holy Spirit," Christ himself is giving us the sign we as humans need to know that we are forgiven. Jesus loves us as individuals; as unique individuals we need to hear the Lord speaking directly to us.

How Does a Catholic Prepare for a Good Confession?

The best preparation for the celebration of the sacrament of reconciliation is a prayerful examination of conscience in light of the teaching of Jesus Christ and his church. With the help of the Holy Spirit, an honest examination of conscience will disclose the presence of sin in our lives and will move us to want to seek forgiveness and repair any harm we have caused by our sin.

What Is a Christian Conscience?

Conscience is a practical judgment concerning whether an action or attitude is good or sinful. It is an ability to discover God's will for us. It is there that we are alone with God whose voice echoes in our hearts.

Another way to view conscience is that within us there is an inner dialogue with God who calls us to be the persons we are intended to be—his children.

There are two key principles to keep in mind when dealing with judging right and wrong. First, we must properly form our consciences. Second, we must follow our consciences.

> In the depths of his conscience, man detects a law which he does not impose upon himself, but which holds him to obedience. Always summoning him to love good and do it and to avoid evil, the voice of conscience can when necessary speak to his heart more specifically:

do this, shun that. For man has in his heart a law written by God. *To obey it is the very dignity of man: according to it he will be judged* (*Pastoral Constitution on the Church in the Modern World*, No. 16).

How Do We Properly Form Our Conscience?

The duty to obey our conscience underscores the necessity of properly forming it. This is because all of us can make mistakes when we are left to ourselves. Many factors can help cloud a conscience and make it difficult to distinguish right from wrong.

Ignorance, simply not knowing or being told the right thing to do or the wrong thing to avoid, can cause us to make false judgments. *Emotions* can cloud our conscience. We may be tempted to do things because they feel good, but feeling good does not necessarily mean the actions are right. *Conformity* to what others are doing can also muddy our decisions. Just because everyone else is doing something does not make it right.

A sincere Christian will take steps to find out the right thing to do, to clear up doubts before making a decision, and to correct a badly formed conscience. He or she will also avoid those situations where experience has taught that strong emotions have a tendency to destroy the freedom to choose the good thing. Finally, the mature Christian knows that doing the right thing often means standing against the crowd.

What Are the Steps in Conscience Formation?

1. *Find the facts.* *What* is the issue? *Who* is involved? *Where? When? How?*
2. *Examine your motives.* *Why* do you want to do this? Pure intentions were very important in the teaching of Jesus.
3. *Think of the possible effects.* How will this action (or non-action) affect you? others? society as a whole? What if everyone did this?
4. *Consider alternatives.* Is there another way to act? Use your imagination to find alternatives.
5. *What does the law have to say?* Law is not opposed to conscience. As a matter of fact, it greatly helps to form it. Conscience is the subjective norm of morality; law is the objective norm. The kinds of laws which need to be considered are:

     Natural Law: God's law written into the nature of things, the way things are made. Prohibitions against murder, the recognition of the dignity of the individual, and honesty in dealing with others are examples of the natural law.

     Civil Law: Particular applications of natural law for a given society. In the United States, everyone drives on the right side of the road (civil law) in order to avoid killing (natural law). In

England, motorists drive on the left side of the road. There the civil law differs. But in both cases the civil law is meant to apply the natural law for the protection of human life.

Divine Law: Law revealed by God. The Sermon on the Mount and the Ten Commandments are classic examples of divine law, especially the law to love.

Church Law:[1] Particular applications of divine law for the Christian community. The church teaches that we must worship God weekly at the Sunday liturgy, for example. This law is a particular application of the third commandment—Remember keep holy the Sabbath—for Catholics.

6. *What is the reasonable thing to do?* Because we are people with minds, we must use them in figuring out the right thing to do. Ask yourself what the reasonable decision is.

7. *What does your own experience and that of other people say about the issue?* Because we are social beings with a history, we must check out other responses to similar problems. If possible, seek out the wisdom of others.

8. *What would Jesus have done?* How does this action measure up to Jesus' yardstick of love? What does the New Testament have to say? Jesus is the absolute norm of Christian morality. He is the one perfect human response to God. Seek out his will and his example before making a decision.

9. *What is the teaching of the church?* We believe that the Holy Spirit resides in the church and helps guide us in right behavior. Jesus continues to teach through the pope and the bishops united with him. Thus, sincere Catholics consider it a serious obligation to consult magisterial teaching on moral issues as well as to learn from competent theologians and other teachers in the church.

10. *Pray for guidance.* The Lord will help you if you ask.

11. *Admit that you sometimes sin and might be wrong.* As St. Paul said, one of the effects of original sin is that we don't always do the good we wish to do and we do do the evil we wish to avoid.

12. *After all of this, follow your conscience.* It is *always* wrong to go against your conscience. "Everyone who knows what is the right thing to do and does not do it commits a sin" (Jas 4:17).

What Is Sin?

Sin is a failure to love ourselves, others and God. It is a breakdown in covenant love. Without a healthy concept of sin, people tend to see little need for Jesus, the one who frees us from sin. Christians do not

---

[1]The precepts of the church are listed in the Appendix, pp. 259–260.

harp on sin out of a morbid attraction to evil; bad news is not what our message is about. Rather, we talk of sin to stress the good news that God forgives us and in the person of Jesus has rescued us from its effects.

There are two basic categories of sin: original sin and personal sin.

What Is Original Sin?

Original sin refers to that condition of disharmony into which all humans are born. This condition is inherited.

> It is human nature so fallen, stripped of the grace that clothed it, injured in its own natural powers and subjected to the dominion of death (Pope Paul VI, *Credo of the People of God*, No. 16).

Universal human experience confirms the Catholic teaching that we are born into a sinful state. The evil we see around us, the anger we have within us toward others and ourselves, the good resolutions we so often break are all evidence of the sin which is part of humanity's condition.

What Is Personal Sin?

Personal or actual sin is any free and deliberate action, word, thought or desire which turns us away from God's law of love. It can be seen as a weakening or killing of our loving relationship with the Father. There are two kinds of personal sin: venial and mortal.

What Is Venial Sin?

Traditionally, venial sin refers to those acts and attitudes which fail to help us grow in our loving relationship with God or weaken the relationship. People sometimes glibly speak of *only* a venial sin. This is false thinking because any weakening of a love relationship is something to be concerned about. Our goal is total union with God; our direction should be one of growing closer to him each day.

Venial sin involves less serious matter than mortal sin, or happens when a person does not fully reflect on or consent to what he or she is doing. An example would be failing to pray on a regular basis. This is a sin of *omission*, a failure to do the good thing. Petty pilfering, perhaps taking pens, note pads and other small supplies from work, might also be a venial sin. This is an act of *commission*, a choice to act in an immoral way. In this case the person has taken something of value which does not belong to him or her.

All sin has social consequences; others are affected by what we do. By claiming credit for someone else's work, for example, the sinner affects himself or herself, the other employees, management and perhaps all the other people the person will contact in the future. Repeated acts of dishonesty can make the person dishonest. This is so because sin tends to make us "rebellious" and "unruly," thus affecting all our relationships (Jer 5:23). Dishonesty weakens the love relationship between God and the sinner because it weakens the love relationship built on trust between the sinner and others with whom Jesus identifies himself.

What Is Mortal Sin?

Mortal sin is the harboring of a serious attitude or the commission of some serious action that kills the relationship of love between God and the sinner. The Father's love is always there; he does not kill the relationship. Rather, the sinner kills the relationship by completely turning away from God's love and saying no to the relationship. Knowing the nature of love and being in a loving relationship, we realize that it takes a particularly rebellious attitude to commit a mortal sin. But saying it is difficult to commit serious sin is not to say it is impossible to do so.

What Are the Three Conditions for a Sin to Be Mortal?

There are three conditions that must be met before a person sins mortally. First, *the action or attitude itself must be serious.* Murder, for example, is serious because it seriously affects human relationships. Adultery, too, is a serious breach of covenant love within a marriage. Rape seriously exploits another person. Attitudes of deep hatred toward minority groups are often fatally destructive of love between people and may lead to violence.

Second, *the person must know that what he or she is doing is sinful.* We are not blameworthy for something we do not know. However, we have a continual obligation to learn, to clarify questions, and to grow in love and knowledge of the Lord.

The third condition for mortal sin is that *the person must freely consent to the evil.* Modern psychology tells us there are a number of forces and drives that limit our freedom; for example, overwhelming fear might keep a person from helping the dying victim of an assault on the street (serious matter). Or blinding rage might cause a person to lose control and do something harmful. However, humans do have some freedom and are capable of serious and deliberate wrongdoing. Proof of this is the violence, hatred, callousness and neglect we see in our world today. Our obligation is to avoid those situations which might limit our freedom and keep us from doing the right thing.

What Is the Role of Reconciliation?

Traditionally, we speak of a person who has turned completely away from God's love and is no longer in relationship as being in "the state of mortal sin." To correct this situation the sinner must repent, that is, turn back to God, admit his or her wrongdoing and acknowledge the need for forgiveness. The Father always offers the grace, the invitation, to accept his love again.

Catholics celebrate the sacrament of reconciliation in which God's healing love is presented to us as a sign which reassures us of his love. The point of Jesus' parable of the Prodigal Son (Lk 15:11-31) is that no matter what we do or how often we do it, God's love is always there for us. We need but turn to him and accept his love. God is not out to get us the minute we slip up and step out of the relationship. Rather, God continually loves and lets his light shine on the good person—and the evil person. In essence, Christian morality is saying yes to this love, letting it shine on us, and then living a life of light that shines out to others.

Where Is the Sacrament of the Sick in Scripture?

Jesus Christ is a healer. The gospel stories abound with examples of his making people whole again; for example, curing the blind, making lame people walk, cleansing the lepers, bringing the dead back to life. Through his healings Jesus showed special love to the suffering by curing their spiritual, psychological and physical hurts. Jesus saw the hurting people in his midst and responded to them holistically—to both their bodies and their spirits. He was specially responsive to people who exhibited faith in him as the sign of God's love.

Jesus' healing ministry went hand in hand with his teaching ministry. Healing was a principal sign of the advent of God's kingdom. It demonstrated the power of the Son of God over sin and evil. Jesus answered once and for all the argument that a person who is sick must have sinned. Illness should not be seen as a punishment for past sins; there is no necessary connection between a person's sickness and guilt for personal sin. But Jesus clearly saw that sin and sickness are related. Sickness and human suffering are effects of original sin, the general human condition that needs healing, saving, redeeming. Jesus' healing ministry should be seen in the context of his forgiving sin and his proclamation of God's kingdom and the need for repentance.

Jesus charged his disciples to continue his message and mission. Thus, the early church celebrated and proclaimed the good news of salvation by continuing Jesus' healing ministry. The letter of James provides the scriptural basis for the sacrament of anointing, the symbol of love:

> Any one of you who is ill should send for the elders of the church, and they must anoint the sick person with oil in the name of the Lord and pray over him. The prayer of faith will save the sick person and the Lord will raise him up again; and if he has committed any sins, he will be forgiven. So confess your sins to one another, and pray for one another to be cured (Jas 5:14-16).

What Is the History of This Sacrament?

There is evidence that anointing the sick was commonplace in the early church. The blessed oils could be used either internally or externally. Further, church historians indicate that laymen and women could confer this sacrament, for example, by anointing sick members of the family with the consecrated oil taken home for such a purpose.

By the ninth century, however, the clergy became the ordinary ministers of this sacrament. Furthermore, by the Middle Ages the sacramental action of anointing was reserved, for all practical purposes, for those who were dying. By this time the sacrament was typically called *extreme unction*, that is, the last anointing before death. This last anointing was typically preceded by penance and the reception of a final Eucharist (known as *viaticum*—"food for the way"). The medieval practice of anointing only those near death continued until recent times.

What Are the Emphases in Today's Rite?

Today's renewal of the sacrament has returned to a more biblical understanding. The sacrament is administered not only to the dying but also to those who are sick. It is referred to as the sacrament of the sick. Today, the celebration of this sacrament attempts to include the prayerful support of the Christian community (the family, friends and parish community of the sick person). Communal anointings of the sick during the Mass, for example, sensitize the parish community to the needs of the hurting in its midst and remind it to respond in a loving way to their needs.

Today's rite also underscores the need for the sick person to overcome the alienation caused by sickness and suffering. It helps and challenges the sick person to grow to wholeness through the illness, to identify with the sufferings of Jesus Christ and enter more fully into the paschal mystery. Today's rite also urges the person to assume a more active role, for example, by requesting the sacrament himself or herself rather than having someone else do it.

What Are the Effects of the Sacrament of the Sick?

Pain and suffering can make us miserable and can weaken our faith in a loving, caring God. Sickness can lead us to question the very meaning of life. Through this sacrament the Lord, acting through the Christian community, assures us of his care and concern. He extends his forgiveness and strengthens the sick person. Through this sign of love, the Lord also invites us to integrate our sickness, even a mortal one, into the mystery of his own suffering, death and resurrection—the paschal mystery that has won for us eternal salvation. The sacrament reminds the community, too, that it must stand by and love its Christian brothers and sisters in time of need.

Anointing of the sick is typically united to the other sacrament of healing—reconciliation. Thus, God's presence to the sick person in this sacrament brings forgiveness and spiritual healing which enable the person to accept the suffering sent into his or her life. This spiritual healing brings peace and empowers the person to offer his or her suffering to Jesus whose own sufferings brought about our salvation. Sometimes God also chooses to physically heal a person by means of this sacrament. The sacrament of the anointing of the sick is a marvelous sign of God's love when we need it the most.

How Is the Sacrament of the Sick Celebrated?

Typically the sacrament of the anointing of the sick is celebrated individually during a serious illness or before a serious operation. Family and friends should be present. As noted above, though, there is a growing trend toward a communal celebration of the sacrament within the context of the Eucharist.

The rite itself begins with a greeting, sprinkling with holy water, a penitential rite, and the Liturgy of the Word which recalls the Lord's healing power.

All present then join in a litany of prayers for the sick. After he lays his hands on the person to be anointed, the priest blesses the oil and then anoints the forehead and hands. He prays:

> Through this holy anointing may the Lord in his love and mercy help you with the grace of the Holy Spirit. Amen. May the Lord who frees you from sin save you and raise you up. Amen.

Another prayer and the Lord's Prayer follow. Holy communion may then be given before the final blessing which concludes the service.

CONCLUDING REFLECTIONS _____

Some years ago there was a popular movie entitled "Love Story." Its most famous line of dialogue was "Love is never having to say you're sorry." This observation is simply not true. To express sorrow verbally to a loved one is often the catalyst for healing relationships. We need to say we are sorry when we have sinned against someone.

We also need to hear, "You are forgiven." These words speak of true love. This is why the sacrament of reconciliation is truly a sign of the good news of God's love. This sacrament affords us the opportunity to express our sorrow and, more important, to be assured of God's forgiveness and love.

The Lord continues his healing ministry in the sacrament of reconciliation and the sacrament of the sick. Through both of these signs, the Lord also challenges us—we who are forgiven and healed by his love—to be signs of reconciliation and healing to others.

Sacraments are not magic. Rather, they are actions of the Lord working through his body, the church. We are the church. The Lord taught us best. We must infect others with the good news of salvation. Because we have been forgiven, we have the duty to be signs of forgiveness to others. "Forgive us our trespasses as we forgive those who trespass against us."

PRAYER REFLECTION _____

Place yourself in the presence of God. Feel his love for you. Ask the Holy Spirit to help you review your day. What good things happened to you? Where and when were you a true sign of God's love?

Then turn to those times when you might have missed the mark. What words, thoughts and actions were self-centered? What attitudes were unworthy of a child of God? What did you fail to do that you should have done?

When finished with your examination of conscience, turn to the Lord and recite prayerfully, over and over,

> Lord, Jesus Christ,
> Son of the Living God,
> have mercy on me, a sinner.

FOR DISCUSSION _____

1. What steps do you take to examine your conscience?
2. Why is it so important to forgive ourselves?
3. Explain how reconciliation is related to the forgiveness of sin.

4. How can you personally contribute to the healing ministry of Jesus
   Christ?

FURTHER READING

   Ezekiel 18:20-32 (the converted sinner finds life)
   Joel 2:12-19 (a call to repent)
   Luke 7:36-50 (Jesus and a repentant sinner)
   Matthew 9:9-13 (Jesus and sinners)

16

Christian Marriage: The Sacrament of Friendship

"This is why a man leaves his father and mother and becomes attached to his wife, and the two become one flesh."

—Matthew 19:5

A sage philosopher once defined friendship as "a single soul dwelling in two bodies." If we are fortunate enough to have even one true friend, we know how wise this saying is. Friends are of one mind and heart; they think of themselves as spiritually one. But another wise person changed this saying around in the case of friends who are married: "Two souls dwelling in one body." There is truth to this observation, too. However we look at it, marriage is a celebration of friendship, a communion of love.

Christian marriage, celebrated in the sacrament of matrimony, is truly the sacrament of friendship. All sacraments are signs of God's friendship and love; they are celebrations of his ongoing presence to us in our ordinary lives. So, too, Christians who marry in the Lord are a living sign of God's love in human relationships, in friendship, in life-giving procreation, in family living.

We who have been made in God's image and likeness mirror him best when we love. God comes to us in love because he is Love. We discover God when we love. Marriage is a sacrament because it celebrates love.

What Is the Sacrament of Marriage?

In the sacrament of matrimony a baptized man and woman vow their love in an exclusive, permanent, sexual partnership. This union is marked by love, respect, care and concern, and a commitment to share

185

responsibility in the raising of a family if God should bless them with children.

Christian marriage is an extraordinary sign of God working through and in the ordinary. A good marriage is not simply a civil contract between two persons; rather, it is a holy covenant involving three persons. The couple is joined on their life's journey by Jesus Christ who promises to bless, sustain and rejoice in their union.

The church teaches us that the sacrament of marriage mirrors God's covenant of love with his people. By giving us his Son, the Father loved us freely and faithfully kept his promises. Jesus—the greatest sign of God's love—draws us into community, showers us with unexpected gifts, relates to us as unique individuals, and invites us to grow in love by serving others.

In the covenant of Christian marriage, a husband and wife freely bind themselves together for life. Theirs is an open-ended commitment to love exclusively. No time conditions or any other conditions are put on their relationship. In sickness or health, in poverty or wealth, in good times and in bad times, the couple promises to be faithful. A covenant commitment mirrors God's unconditional love for his people. If a man and woman insist on certain conditions, they are simply engaged in a legal contract.

In Christian marriage love is freely given and faithfully weathers the trials that come its way. Christian marriage is life-giving because through it God gives the married couple the privilege of procreating life. It is full of surprises, providing countless opportunities to grow in holiness. It is a concrete way to live the Christian life of love and service in the context of family living.

What Do the Hebrew Scriptures Say About Marriage?

There has been a gradual growth in understanding of the meaning of marriage. In early times polygamy was tolerated; husbands could freely divorce their wives (who were often treated as property); and a married man could have sexual relations with an unmarried woman and not be accused of adultery. By the time the book of Genesis was written, however, God revealed to the Jewish people two profound truths about the *purposes* of marriage. First, marriage is a share in God's creative act of bringing new life into the world. Second, marriage is meant to enhance, celebrate and increase the love between the wife and husband.

The first reading from Genesis tells us that Yahweh established marriage and sex and declared that they are good and are meant for the procreation of human life.

> God created man in the image
> of himself,
> in the image of God he created
> him,
> male and female he created them.
> God blessed them, saying to them, "Be fruitful,
> multiply, fill the earth and subdue it."...
> ...God saw all that he had made, and indeed it
> was very good (Gn 1:27-28, 31).

The second reading from Genesis reveals the other major purpose of marriage: companionship between friends who share the same life and love:

> This one at last is bone of my bones
> and flesh of my flesh!
> She is to be called Woman,
> because she was taken from Man.
> That is why a man leaves his father and mother
> and becomes attached to his wife, and they be-
> come one flesh (Gn 2:23-24).

God fully intends a permanent, exclusive, monogamous relationship between man and woman who have been created in his image.

How Does Marriage Mirror God's Love for his People?

The prophets use marriage as an image to describe Yahweh's great love for his people, Israel.

> I shall betroth you to myself for ever,
> I shall betroth you in uprightness and justice,
> and faithful love and tenderness (Hos 2:21).

The prophet Malachi forcefully states the ideal:

> Yahweh stands as witness between you and the wife of your youth,
> with whom you have broken faith, even though she was your partner
> and your wife by covenant. Did he not create a single being, having
> flesh and the breath of life? (Mal 2:14-15).

Proverbs paints a picture of an ideal wife: "She is clothed in strength and dignity" (Prov 31:25). In a collection of beautiful, passionate poems, the Song of Songs describes the love between a bride and her bridegroom. Because God has blessed marriage, affectionate, erotic love between a man and a woman is something good and holy and joyful.

What Does the New Testament Reveal About Marriage?

The New Testament reveals further important insights into the nature of marriage. Jesus' attendance at the wedding feast of Cana implicitly underscores the goodness and naturalness of marriage. When Jesus explicitly teaches about marriage, he reaffirms the original intention of his Father—that marriage should be a permanent, exclusive love relationship:

> "Everyone who divorces his wife and marries another is guilty of adultery, and the man who marries a woman divorced by her husband commits adultery" (Lk 16:18).

Jesus shows his profound respect for human dignity when he teaches that looking at a woman lustfully is the equivalent of committing adultery (Mt 5:27-28). Motives and interior attitudes are important to him.

The early church also regarded marriage highly. St. Paul, for example, supplies a key teaching on marriage:

> In the same way, husbands must love their wives as they love their own bodies; for a man to love his wife is for him to love himself. A man never hates his own body, but he feeds it and looks after it; and that is the way Christ treats the Church, because we are parts of his Body. . . . This mystery has great significance, but I am applying it to Christ and the Church (Eph 5:28-32).

The union of a husband and wife is like the union of Christ with his church. St. Paul calls this reality a *mystery* (a word translated by St. Augustine as "sacrament"); Christian marriage is an external sign of Christ's love. Marriage is a covenant, a total lifelong commitment that mirrors Christ's love for his church.

What Is the Proximate Preparation for Marriage?

Preparation for a Christian marriage in most dioceses includes a policy that the engaged couple attend marriage preparation conferences. These church-sponsored classes give the couple an opportunity to learn about the sacramental commitment from a priest and learn many practical details about married life from a doctor and other experts on marriage, including couples who are living the sacrament. During the period of preparation, a priest or other parish minister will continue to meet with the couple to prepare them for the serious commitment they are about to make. Topics examined include love and communication, the raising of a family, the role of a faith life in marriage, and the plans for the actual ceremony.

In the case of a Catholic marrying a non-Catholic (a mixed marriage), a dispensation must be granted. The Catholic partner promises to continue to live his or her Catholic faith and share it with his or her children. The non-Catholic partner is made aware of this pledge, but he or she is not required to make any promises.

The banns (announcement) of marriage are usually printed in the parish bulletin for three consecutive weeks before the wedding ceremony. The publication and reading of the banns has two purposes: first, to inform the Christian community of the impending celebration; and second, to give informed parties the opportunity to come forward if they know any reason why the sacrament of marriage should not take place.

What Is the Long-Range Preparation for Marriage?

The long-range preparation for this sacrament includes learning how to be a good friend. After all, Christian marriage is a celebration of lifelong friendship between a man and a woman and between a couple and their Lord Jesus Christ.

Being a friend includes some of the following:
- Communicate openly, sharing ideas and feelings.
- Enjoy doing things together.
- Be willing to change.
- Respect each other by accepting the other's uniqueness.
- Openly and honestly discuss attitudes toward children and raising a family.
- Cultivate patience.
- Learn to say "I am sorry" and "You are forgiven."
- Celebrate the sacrament of reconciliation.
- Practice self-control—marriage demands sacrifice.
- Learn from the example of good, happily married couples.
- Forget trifling annoyances; no one is perfect and life is too short anyway.
- Trust each other.
- Plan financial affairs together, but remember that the love of money is the root of evil.
- Celebrate the Eucharist together.
- Develop an active prayer life with the Lord; he's the best friend a marriage can have.

What Are the Requirements for a Valid Marriage?

To celebrate the sacrament of marriage validly, the couple must be of mature age, unmarried, not closely related by blood or marriage, and freely desire to marry. They must intend to commit themselves to a lifelong covenant of love. Furthermore, they must be capable of sharing sexually since sexual intercourse is a sign of mutual love and union, the full expression of the mutual love between husband and wife. Finally, the couple must be open to the possibility of raising a family if God blesses the marriage with children.

The celebrants of the sacrament of Christian marriage are the bride and bridegroom themselves. Today's church law requires that a Catholic couple exchange their vows before a priest and two other witnesses. When one of the parties is not Catholic, special permission can be obtained from the local bishop and pastor for a minister of another faith to participate in the marriage ceremony. In extraordinary circumstances a dispensation might be given for a minister of another faith to witness the exchange of vows.

How Is the Sacrament of Marriage Celebrated?

Ordinarily the sacrament of Christian marriage takes place during a eucharistic celebration. There is an entrance procession, greeting, prayers, readings and homily. After this, the priest questions the couple concerning their freedom in choosing marriage, their desire to be faithful, and their willingness to have and rear children. The bridal couple then exchanges vows in the presence of the priest, two witnesses and the assembled Christian community. The traditional words used are:

> I call upon these persons here present to witness
> that I, N._____,
> do take thee, N._____,
> to be my lawful wedded wife/husband
> to have and to hold from this day forward,
> for better for worse, for richer for poorer,
> in sickness and in health,
> to love and to cherish
> till death do us part.

As the church's official witness, the priest blesses the rings and asks the couple to exchange them as symbols of fidelity and unending love. The Liturgy of the Eucharist proceeds as usual with the nuptial blessing given after the Lord's Prayer.

To make the wedding ceremony even more meaningful to them, their family and friends, the couple is encouraged to select favorite hymns and scripture readings, to engage in certain rituals like drinking from a common cup, and to write their own petitions.

The celebration of the wedding ceremony is only one important element in the sacrament. When a man and a woman exchange their vows, the church witnesses and blesses their covenant promises. The Christian community celebrates with the new bride and groom. But the sacrament of marriage is not just a one-day affair; it unfolds over the years as the husband and wife live out their mutual relationship with each other and the Lord. The risen Lord promises to be with the couple to sustain them on their life journey. He sanctifies sexual love, a most powerful sign of total, exclusive, intimate sharing. He sustains the couple in the ordinary give-and-take of family life. He empowers them to be signs of love to each other, their children, and to all their friends and acquaintances. Through their daily love and fidelity, they will meet the Lord who lives within them by the power of the Holy Spirit. The celebration of Christian marriage is ''till death do us part.''

Why Is Christian Marriage Forever?

Christian marriage is a serious commitment because it is a prime way to bring Christ into the world for other people. This is certainly true for the children who result from the marriage. Children first encounter the love and knowledge of God from their parents. They, in fact, are living symbols of their parents' love. They need the stable, reassuring love of a solid marriage to develop healthy attitudes to life and to God.

But a faithful marriage is a powerful sign to others as well. Just as God's love is forever and has no strings attached to it, so the Christian husband and wife point to the mystery of God's love at work in ordinary life. Their fidelity and exclusive love is an extraordinary sign to the world of God's fidelity and undying love for his people.

Jesus himself underscored the permanence of the marriage bond:

> ''Have you not read that the Creator from the beginning *made them male and female* and that he said: *This is why a man leaves his father and mother and becomes attached to his wife, and the two become one flesh?* They are no longer two, therefore, but one flesh. So then, what God has united, human beings must not divide'' (Mt 19:4-6).

Thus the Catholic church does not permit divorce and remarriage because Jesus forbade it. The covenant made between two validly married Catholics can only be dissolved by the death of one of the partners. In extraordinary circumstances a couple may separate for the good of the children and the individuals involved. Though the civil authority may dissolve the legal aspects of a valid marriage (called in civil law a divorce), the state has no authority to dissolve a true Christian marriage—its true sacramental nature.

According to Catholic church teaching, a legally separated Catholic (divorced under civil law) may not remarry while his or her spouse is alive. This teaching is consistent with the Lord's teaching, "Everyone who divorces his wife and marries another is guilty of adultery" (Lk 16:18). Christ calls his disciples to high standards. The church encourages a person who is suffering from a broken marriage to continue to celebrate the sacraments and remain close to the Christian community. The Lord promises in a special way to bless those who suffer most. Fellow Christians should support hurting brothers and sisters, pray for them, and follow the teaching of the Lord by not judging them.

More than at any time in history, thoughtful, prayerful preparation for Christian marriage is essential to its future success.

What Is an Annulment?

An annulment is an official declaration of the Catholic church that what appeared to be a valid Christian marriage in fact was not. A couple may have entered the marriage psychologically immature or lacking true understanding of the demands a Christian marriage covenant makes. One or both partners might not have given free, true consent to the marriage. Perhaps one or both partners intended never to have children. Possibly one or both partners were incapable of sexual relations.

A "failed" marriage may not have been a true Christian marriage to begin with. In these cases the couple should submit their situation to the diocesan marriage tribunal (court) for examination and judgment. If it can be shown that the marriage was not valid from the beginning, then the individuals involved are free to enter a true Christian marriage in the future.

What Does the Church Say About Family Living?

In the past, churchmen had mixed feelings about marriage and family life. However the church today clearly considers Christian marriage and family living a primary means to holiness.

> The Christian family, which springs from marriage as a reflection of the loving covenant uniting Christ with the Church, and as a participation in that covenant, will manifest to all men the Savior's living presence in the world, and the genuine nature of the Church. This the family will do by the mutual love of the spouses, by their generous fruitfulness, their solidarity and faithfulness, and by the loving way in which all members of the family work together (*Constitution on the Church in the Modern World*, No. 48).

These lofty ideals require a Catholic couple to make their family the number one priority in their lives. Married couples know from experience that they have to construct their marriage on trust, forgiveness and a genuine desire to make it a real sign of love. They take seriously their commitment to remain faithful until death separates them. Because of the stresses in our fast-paced, materialistic society, wise couples know the value of prayer, developing a personal relationship with the Lord, and staying close to him in the Eucharist. Today's church supports marriages through various retreat programs like Marriage Encounter, parish renewals, enrichment programs and seminars.

What Are the Building Blocks of a Strong Family Life?

Parents build a strong family when they provide their children not only with food, shelter and clothing but with spiritual values as well. Some of the building blocks for a strong family life include: a couple's good example of trying to live honest, upright lives; both nonverbal and verbal expression of their love for each other and for their children; a Christian, prayer-filled home environment; a religious education rooted in Catholic faith and practice; modeling and teaching their children self-denial; and family goals which include a commitment to justice in the family and in the larger community.

What Does the Church Teach About Sexual Sharing?

The Catholic community praises married love as a great gift from God. Sexual intercourse is a profound means of love and commitment between a man and a woman. Its purpose in God's plan is twofold: *unitive*, that is, to bond a man and woman together as partners for life; and *procreative*, that is, to share in God's creative activity of bringing new life into the world.

As a deep symbol of love between a man and a woman, sexual intercourse (and all acts leading up to it) expresses a total, unreserved commitment of love. We believe this can take place only when a couple has declared lifelong devotion to each other, that is, in a marriage. Sexual sharing in a marriage, then, is an authentic sign of the total gift of the husband to the wife and the wife to the husband. It mirrors the Lord's unconditional commitment to his body, the church.

What Does the Church Teach About Adultery?

Sexual intimacy signifies a total giving and a total receiving. To engage in sexual relations outside of marriage is to misuse this profound sign of human love. Thus adultery—sexual intimacy engaged in by a married person with another who is not his or her spouse—is a serious breach in the covenant love of Christian marriage. When a husband and wife exchange marriage vows, they promise before God to be faithful exclusively to each other. Adultery is a failure to honor the fundamental commitment of marriage; it threatens the very stability of the family.

What Does the Church Teach About Fornication?

Fornication is sexual intercourse engaged in by unmarried people. It is also wrong because it often exploits others or is indulged in for selfish motives under the guise of love. God intended intimate sexual sharing to express total love and commitment, the kind of love and commitment that leads to the sharing of life. Fornication seeks pleasure without responsibility. This is sinful because people are using each other by engaging in a profound symbol of love and communication that says "I love you *forever*—with no strings attached." But the state in life of the unmarried is such that they have not said "forever"— with all the responsibility and commitment the word implies.

What Does the Church Teach about Masturbation?

The church also teaches that masturbation—self-induced sexual pleasure—is wrong because it misuses the powers of sex which in God's plan are directed to sexual intimacy with another and with bringing new life into the world. It is difficult to assess a person's culpability for failures in this area of sexual morality because of the potential lack of full consent of the will. This is especially true in the case of adolescents who are searching for sexual identity and are developing the maturity and strength of character to overcome self-indulgent habits. Maturing adults should be concerned about a persistent habit of masturbation because it can be a sign of escapism or a lack of proper integration of sexual identity. A sensitive confessor can be of help in this regard.

What Does the Church Teach About Homosexuality?

The church distinguishes between a homosexual *condition* and homosexual *acts*. Homosexuality as a condition exists when a person's sexual desires are directed to a member of the same sex rather than to a member of the opposite sex. This condition of itself does not mean that a person is necessarily a sinner or is alienated from God. The church teaches that homosexual acts are wrong, however, because they violate God's plan for male/female bonding and are not open to the procreation of life.

The same norms for sexual morality hold for both homosexual and heterosexual people: Sexual intercourse and all acts leading up to it are meant to be exercised within the committed, exclusive, covenant relationship of a marriage between a man and a woman.

How Does the Church Help in the Area of Sexuality?

Many failures in the area of sexuality result from *lust*, one of the so-called deadly sins. Lust is misdirected love. True sexual loving is beautiful, a holy expression of profound love between a man and a woman. Failures in the area of sexual morality are often caused by separating sex and love. The church recognizes that because of original sin we are especially vulnerable to temptation in this area. The church, also known as a compassionate mother, offers her help though the sacraments of reconciliation and the Eucharist, through prayer, through encouragement and love to everyone who faces the difficult struggle of living chastely in a world filled with false sexual values.

The Christian community has the Christ-given duty to remind all people to live virtuously in the area of sex out of self-respect and respect for others. Failures in the area of sexual morality should never be occasions of self-hatred; they are examples of our own weakness and need for continual conversion. The Christian life is a struggle. But we take great comfort in the good news of God's infinite love for us and his acceptance of us in our weakness.

What Does the Church Teach About Family Planning?

Birth control refers to a couple's deliberate limitation of the number of children they will bring into the world. Christian parents are called upon to plan the size of their families in a responsible way. Physical and psychological health, family finances, the population explosion and the current number of children are some of the factors which will help a husband and wife determine the size of their family. The church teaches that for a *legitimate* reason a Catholic couple has the right and duty to practice natural methods of birth control. Selfishness or greed—for example, not wanting a child because of a desire to attain a certain materialistic lifestyle—would indicate sinful motives for practicing birth control.

What Is Natural Birth Control?

Periodic abstinence from sexual relations and natural family planning methods are moral means of birth control because they work in harmony with normal, natural bodily functions. Two popular and effective natural methods of birth control are the sympto-thermal method and the ovulation method, also known as the Billings method. The *Family Life Bureau* of most dioceses sponsors classes to help train couples in these methods.

How Does the Church View Artificial Birth Control?

Church teaching holds that artificial means of contraception are contrary to God's will. Artificial birth control refers to pills or devices (like condoms or diaphragms) that interfere with the conception of a child. The church also teaches that sterilization—making the reproductive organs unfruitful—is also wrong except when the organs are diseased and threaten the health of the whole body.

This teaching rests on the Catholic view that marriage is directed to two aims simultaneously: the procreation (and rearing) of children, and the mutual love and affection of the couple. Thus sexual relations which are selfishly engaged in by one partner without taking note of the feelings and desires of the other partner are wrong because one of the aims of marriage—mutual love—is destroyed. Likewise official church teaching maintains that any artificial means used to frustrate the natural processes of procreation go against the very nature of marriage. Christian marriage is a sacrament, an effective sign of mutual love and openness to life. To rule out either of these purposes unnaturally or selfishly is to frustrate God's intent which is built into the very nature of marriage.

The classic statement of official church teaching in this regard is found in Pope Paul VI's encyclical entitled *Humanae Vitae* (*Of Human Life*):

> The church calling men back to the observance of the norms of the natural law, as interpreted by constant doctrine, teaches that each and every marriage act must remain open to the transmission of life (No. 11).

In striving to live the ideal, sometimes people fall short. Thus the pope and the bishops encourage married couples to frequent the sacraments of reconciliation and the Eucharist to gain strength from the Lord. The bishops advise us not to judge the consciences of those couples who fall short of the church's teaching. This moral judgment is God's to make. Couples must follow their consciences in this moral issue and all moral issues. It is well to remember, though, that a Christian conscience is formed in light of authentic church teaching; its proper role is to apply the principles of morality, not to judge something right because "it feels good" or wrong because "it's too hard."

What Does the Church Teach About Abortion?

Abortion—the direct killing of a fetus or embryo or causing it to be ejected before it is viable—is forbidden. Certain pills or devices have as their purpose the aborting of a fertilized egg by preventing implantation in the womb. In the Catholic view, abortion is the taking of an innocent human life. Individual human life begins at the moment of conception, and thus should be given the fundamental right to life. Christians have the grave duty to speak out in defense of human life, especially innocent human life.

CONCLUDING REFLECTIONS

A successful Christian marriage must be built on a firm relationship with God. "Three to get married" is a quite appropriate saying for those who wish to live the sacrament of Christian marriage. Christian marriage is not a contract between two, but a covenant among three. Jesus Christ must be invited to the wedding feast, and there must be a place in the home for him if the marriage is to survive. He promises to help the couple carry their daily crosses and to live the high ideals of Christian love to which he calls them. And if the miracle of wine at Cana is any indication, Jesus will also be there to help enliven the marriage and bring it joy.

PRAYER REFLECTION

Alcoholics Anonymous has a code for its members called "Just for Today." Several of its sayings can also be a tremendous support for a married couple. Perhaps you will want to live one of these. . . just for today.

Just for today I will adjust myself to what is; I will not keep trying to adjust everything else to my own desires.

Just for today I will exercise my soul in three ways: I will do somebody a good turn and not get found out. I will do at least two things I don't want to do—just for exercise. And today, if my feelings are hurt, I will not show it to anyone.

Just for today I will look as good as I can, dress becomingly, talk low, act courteously, criticize not one bit, and not try to improve or regulate anybody except myself.

Love is always patient and kind; love is never jealous; love is not boastful or conceited, it is never rude and never seeks its own advantage, it does not take offence or store up grievances. Love does not rejoice at wrongdoing, but finds its joy in the truth. It is always ready to make allowances, to trust, to hope and to endure whatever comes (1 Cor 13:4-7).

FOR DISCUSSION

1. Explain how the Christian couple and their life together are the sacrament of marriage.

2. What advice would you give a young couple contemplating marriage?
3. Why is fidelity a key virtue in marriage? How does it mirror God's covenant love? How does the church's teaching in regard to sexual morality support this virtue?

FURTHER READING

Song of Songs
1 Peter 3:1-9 (harmonious family living)

17

Christian Ministry: Christian Service and Holy Orders

"You know that among the gentiles those they call their rulers lord it over them, and their great men make their authority felt. Among you this is not to happen. No; anyone who wants to become great among you must be your servant, and anyone who wants to be first among you must be slave to all."

—Mark 10:41-44

A Christian is a disciple. Disciples learn from and strive to imitate their master. Disciples want to be like their teacher. Christian disciples want to be like Jesus. To be like Jesus means simply to serve others in imitation of him.

Jesus epitomizes what it means to be a "person for others."

"For the Son of man himself came not to be served but to serve, and to give his life as a ransom for many" (Mk 10:45).

Jesus served by preaching and teaching the good news of God's kingdom, by healing those suffering from physical, mental and spiritual illnesses, and by simply being with those marginal people who needed the assurance of a friend to tell them that they were loved by God.

Jesus taught the necessity for his chosen ones to imitate his life of service. At the Last Supper, only hours before he freely died on the cross so that all people could attain eternal life, Jesus washed the feet of his disciples. This living parable was intended to drive home to the apostles and all Jesus' disciples that to be great in God's kingdom means to serve others.

"If I, then, the Lord and Master, have washed your feet, you must wash each other's feet. I have given an example so that you may copy what I have done to you" (Jn 13:14-15).

If we bear the name Christian, then we have to serve others. A wise person once said that service is the price we pay for the space we occupy. The Christian would add that service is the price we gladly pay for being privileged members of Christ's body.

Christ has no body now on earth but yours, no hands but yours, no feet but yours; yours are the eyes through which Christ's compassion looks out on the world, yours are the feet with which he is to go about doing good, and yours are the hands with which he is to bless us now (St. Teresa of Avila).

This chapter will briefly discuss the universal Christian vocation of ministry and will focus on the sacrament of service, holy orders, and the ordained ministries within the church.

What Is Ministry?

The common vocation of all Christians is to minister, that is, to serve others in the name of Christ. Minister means "one who serves." Christian ministry means serving others in Christ and because of Christ.

Authors in the Catholic tradition distinguish between and among different kinds of ministry. For example, theologian Yves Congar, O.P., speaks of three levels of ministry. The first is general ministry which is rooted in the gifts of the Holy Spirit and is expressed in occasional, passing service to others. A married couple giving instructions to an engaged couple would be an example of this level of ministry. A second level of ministry is one publicly recognized as relating more directly to the needs and habitual activities of the church; catechists and eucharistic ministers are examples of this level of ministry. A third category is ordained ministries which are public offices in the church; for example, bishops, priests and deacons whose base is sacramental.

Is Every Christian a Minister?

Through the sacraments of baptism and confirmation, every member of the church is called to serve others in imitation of Jesus. This vocation of service is the universal vocation of every disciple of Jesus Christ.

By virtue of baptism, all Christians share in the threefold ministry of Jesus as prophet, priest and king. By definition a priest is an intermediary between God and people. Jesus, of course, is the mediator par excellence. He is the way, the truth, the life—our means of salvation, the gate of heaven. When we are joined to him in baptism we share in his priestly function. The Lord commissions all members of his body to preach the good news of salvation. This is done through prayer, loving service of others, healing and reconciliation, acts of justice and mercy shown to the poor and oppressed, and through any work on behalf of God's kingdom.

Jesus commanded us to serve others. And he empowers us for ministry by sending us the Holy Spirit. The Holy Spirit showers on us the gifts necessary to do God's work. St. Paul lists the gifts which help us to imitate the Lord's life of service:

> There are many different gifts, but it is always the same Spirit; there are many different ways of serving, but it is always the same Lord. There are many different forms of activity, but in everybody it is the same God who is at work in them all. The particular manifestation of the Spirit granted to each one is to be used for the general good. To one is given from the Spirit the gift of utterance expressing wisdom; to another the gift of utterance expressing knowledge, in accordance with the same Spirit; and to another, the gifts of healing, through this one Spirit; to another, the working of miracles; to another, prophecy; to another, the power of distinguishing spirits; to one, the gift of different tongues and to another, the interpretation of tongues. But at work in all these is one and the same Spirit, distributing them at will to each individual (1 Cor 12:4-11).

What Are Some Ways to Minister?

In general, ministry involves many different ways to serve others. The obligation of every baptized Christian is "make holy the marketplace," that is, to bring Christian values to everyday life. For example, the accountant who is honest in his business dealings witnesses to the value of truth. The attorney who takes care in defending her indigent client is working for social justice. The mother who exerts the energy to raise her family in a warm, loving environment contributes greatly toward the common good of the future society. The factory worker who takes pride in his work ensures the making of a product that is safe and dependable. Christ can be found in co-workers, in people we meet on the job, in everyday life. There are countless opportunities to witness to his law of love and his command to serve others.

In a recent encyclical, Pope John Paul II reminds all Christians of their need to identify in solidarity with the poor. The laity, in particular, have a preeminent role in serving the cause of peace and justice in their ordinary life. They do this by the way they live as individuals and as families, by the use of their resources, by their civic activity, by contributing to economic and political decisions and by personal commitment to national and international undertakings (Pope John Paul II, *Sollicitudo Rei Socialis,* 47).

Besides serving others in the world, there are many ways for Catholics to serve fellow Christians in the church itself. For example, the ordained ministries of bishop, presbyter (priest) and deacon are *essential* church ministries for proper order in the church and for the faithful celebration of the sacraments. A post-Vatican II phenomenon, though, has been the growth in opportunities for lay ministry. The following list includes some of the key ministries which the Holy Spirit in our day is inviting God's people to undertake:

- Religious educators, catechists and parochial schoolteachers and personnel
- Eucharistic ministers, lectors, music and art ministers, hospitality ministers
- Ministers to the sick and handicapped
- Parish councilors and financial consultants
- Ministers to the separated and divorced
- Ministers to the poor
- Ministers to youth, young adults and the elderly

What Is the Ordained Ministry?

Although all baptized Christians are called to ministry and share in the priesthood of Jesus Christ, there is a need in the Christian community for certain members of the Lord's body to "minister to the ministers." The Christian community is also an organization; it needs order, fixed structures, clearly defined duties, and visible leaders to organize the massive efforts necessary to carry on Christ's mandate to preach and live the gospel to the very ends of the earth. *Ordained ministers* serve in one of the structured ministries of the church; they are entrusted with leading the church through a special ministry of service to the Christian community and by extension to the whole world.

Vatican II teaches that the priesthood of the faithful and the ministerial priesthood (ordained ministers) are interrelated. Each of them participates in a special way in the Lord's own priesthood.

The ministerial priest, by the sacred power he enjoys, molds and rules the priestly people. Acting in the person of Christ, he brings about the Eucharistic Sacrifice, and offers it to God in the name of all the people. For their part, the faithful join in the offering of the Eucharist by virtue of their royal priesthood. They likewise exercise that priesthood by receiving the sacraments, by prayer and thanksgiving, by the witness of a holy life, and by self-denial and active charity (*Lumen Gentium*, No. 10).

Ordained minsters include bishops, presbyters (priests) and deacons. Their special role is to proclaim God's word to all people, to lead the Christian community in worship, and to model in a special way the universal Christian vocation of service.

What Is Holy Orders?

Holy orders is best described as the sacrament of Christian ministry. Through the laying on of hands by bishops, the sacrament of holy orders confers on certain men a special role of service within the Christian community. The graces of this sacrament help the ordained ministers to fulfill the offices for which they were ordained and strengthen them in their vocation to become special symbols of the ongoing presence of Jesus Christ.

Bishops, priests and deacons are ordained to lead Christ's people and to serve and support their Christian brothers and sisters. They fulfill their vocation when they live virtuous lives, preach the gospel, teach the faith and help God's people learn how to live Christian lives in the modern world. They are called to be living signs of holiness in our midst, constant reminders that Jesus calls us to conversion and holiness. Through the sacrament of holy orders, the Lord promises to be with them as they serve him in a demanding but rewarding ministry of love and service.

Who Were Ordained Ministers in the Early Church?

The story of the development of the ordained ministry is complex. The twelve apostles served as the first formal ministers in the church. As the original Jewish-Christian communities became organized, they adopted models with which they were familiar from the Jewish synagogues: elders, prophets and preachers.

As the church moved out into the Greek and Roman world, other models of ministry were followed, notably that of bishops and deacons.

The *early church* was marked by variety and diversity. *Overseers* (bishops) were men of upright character who led the local churches. *Elders* or *presbyters* (priests) helped the apostles, were appointed to help the mission churches (Acts 14:23) and directed local churches in teaching and prayer. *Deacons* served the early Christian communities in many ways, for example, by ministering to the poor on behalf of the

Christian community, by serving at the Eucharist and by preaching God's word.

How Did Ministry Develop in the First Centuries?

The development of these offices happened differently in the various regions where the church spread. But by the *third century*, it is clear that the church had adopted a hierarchial organization; that is, it became organized in a certain way with clear leadership roles and functions. The term *orders* was borrowed from the Roman world and specifically referred to hierarchial organization. When a person receives holy orders, he is consecrated to a certain *position* in the hierarchial church, a position of service and leadership, a position which confers certain responsibilities.

By this time, the bishop's role was firmly established. He had the high priestly service for the local flock of Christ; he was the symbol of unity. In the early years, apparently only the bishop was ordained. But eventually he needed to share his authority with presbyters (priests) and deacons. This was accomplished through the laying on of hands and a special prayer to the Holy Spirit.

As the church became more formally organized, clearer lines were drawn between the laity and clergy. The church wanted to make sure that its priests were living the kind of spiritual and moral life worthy of those specially called to serve God's people. By around the *fifth century*, ordination was seen as conveying a special ''sacramental character,'' which meant that once ordained a priest, a man remains a priest forever. Holy orders touches the priest's very being. He is permanently designated by God to be a living sign who points to the Lord and his coming at the end of time.

Who Were the Ordained in the Middle Ages?

In the *Middle Ages* the order of diaconate as an active ministry declined. During this period, deacons only assisted at liturgies. Gradually the diaconate was included as only a step on the way to the priesthood. A whole series of ''minor orders'' was commonly recognized: *porters* (who gathered together the worshipping community), *lectors* (who read God's word), *exorcists* (who assisted the bishop and priests in caring for the catechumens), *acolytes* (who served the deacon and the priest at Mass). These minor orders—which had their roots in the early church—were widely regarded as merely ceremonial steps to the priesthood. A fifth order, *subdeacon*, was raised to a major order in medieval times because the obligation of celibacy was also required of subdeacons (as it was in the Western church by this time of bishops, priests and deacons). Today, minor orders are called *ministries* and are open to lay people. Only the ministries of lector (reader) and acolyte have been retained. The practice of ordaining subdeacons has been discontinued.

At the Council of Trent (16th century), in response to Protestant reformers, the church fathers reaffirmed that holy orders is a sacrament. Stress was put on the fact that orders conferred on priests the powers to celebrate the Eucharist and to forgive sin in Christ's name.

How Do We See the Ministerial Priesthood Today?

Today ministerial priesthood is often seen in terms of the images of prophet, priest and king—three roles fulfilled by Jesus the Lord. Ordained ministers have the special vocation to proclaim God's word (prophet), build up and lead the priestly people in worship (priest), and imitate Christ's servanthood by serving God's people and acting as a sign of Christ in the modern world (king). In addition, any talk of ordained ministry today includes the major theme of both clergy and laity sharing in Christ's one priesthood. Laity also have the vocation and obligation to serve. The Christian call to holiness is universal:

> Thus it is evident to everyone that all the faithful of Christ of whatever rank or status are called to the fullness of the Christian life and to the perfection of charity. By this holiness a more human way of life is promoted even in this earthly society (*Lumen Gentium*, No. 40).

What Are the Functions of Bishops, Priests, Deacons?

The ordained ministries are those of bishop, priest and deacon. The bishop is a successor of the apostles. His duties include preaching the word of God, celebrating the sacraments and overseeing the church in a particular region. A priest is ordained to help the bishop carry out his duties of preaching and celebrating the sacraments. A deacon cooperates with the bishop and priests in liturgical celebrations, in preaching, and in the social work of the church, for example, charity for the poor.

The chart below outlines the different functions of the three ordained ministries:

BISHOP	PRIEST	DEACON
Word comes from *episkopoi* which means "overseer"	Word comes from *presbyteroi* who were "elders" in the early church and who presided over the Eucharist	Word comes from *diakonoi* which means "servers"

Successor to the apostles; in union with the pope—the bishop of Rome—and other bishops; is responsible for the welfare of the whole church	Helps the bishop; is his extension into the diocese	Today, a "revived" order which can include married and single men of more mature age as well as celibate young men
Spiritual "father" of the local church/diocese	Presides at Eucharist; leads the people and serves the Lord in representing the sacrifice of the cross	Ordained by a bishop; serves him and the people of God by baptizing, distributing communion, teaching, conducting marriages and funerals, administering "sacramentals," doing works of charity and perhaps doing church administrative work
Minister of all sacraments; the only one who can administer holy orders and is the normal minister of confirmation	Preaches and teaches God's word, calling on his blessing for the people	
	Is an active agent for building the Christian community	

How Is Holy Orders Celebrated?

Holy orders implies ordination to a number of church offices, although today the sacrament of holy orders is celebrated only in the case of the major orders of bishop, priest and deacon.

Ordination is celebrated within a Eucharist presided over by a bishop or bishops. God's people, from whom an ordained minister is called in order to serve the Christian community and all people everywhere, are present at this celebration.

At the ordination of priests, the candidates are called forth by name after the Liturgy of the Word. They are asked whether they wish to serve God's people. Each candidate responds, "I am ready and willing." The bishop elicits confirmation that the candidates are worthy to serve, and the people of God show their approval by applauding and responding "Thanks be to God."

The bishop questions the candidates about their willingness to share in his care for God's people, in celebrating the sacraments, in preaching God's word, and in a life dedicated to God's kingdom. He then asks if they are willing to obey their bishop. Finally, ordination takes place when the bishop and other presbyters present lay their hands on the candidates while the bishop prays for God's help. The hands of the newly ordained priests are anointed and the symbols of their office are conferred (vestments, chalice containing water and wine, a paten on which rests the bread to be consecrated). The sign of peace is exchanged. The liturgy continues with the newly ordained concelebrating with the bishop and his fellow priests.

What Are the Reasons for a Celibate Clergy?

Church law since the 11th century requires priests and bishops of the Western Catholic Church not to marry. This is known as priestly celibacy. Priests undertake this discipline freely to express their whole-hearted commitment in serving both God and his people. The following four reasons are generally offered for this practice.

St. Paul noted that celibacy gives a person more freedom to serve Christ. Not having a family to worry about, a priest is both more free to serve others and more able to attach himself wholeheartedly to the Lord. Second, giving up a family is a concrete witness to the sacrifices in the name of the gospel asked by Jesus of some of his followers:

"And everyone who has left houses, brothers, sisters, father, mother, children or land for the sake of my name will receive a hundred times as much, and also inherit eternal life" (Mt 19:29).

Third, and perhaps most important, by living as a loving celibate person, a priest is in reality pointing to eternal life when there will be no marriage. His life is a witness, in the middle of the ordinary affairs and concerns of the world, that we are all destined for union with God.

Finally, there is the witness of Jesus himself who did not marry so that he could be totally involved in doing God's will in serving others.

What Is a Religious Vocation?

In general, *vocation* means "calling," an invitation by the Lord to a special kind of service. One can be called to serve God as a married person, in the single life, as a priest, or in religious life.

Down through the centuries certain Christian men and women have consecrated themselves to God and the work of his kingdom by taking vows of poverty, chastity and obedience. These Christians ordinarily live a common life in a religious community which typically was founded to engage in a specific work (ministry) to help build up God's kingdom.

By taking the vow of poverty, those living the religious life are attempting to free themselves of the things of this world so that they can be attached to the One who is really important, Jesus Christ. By vowing chastity for the sake of the gospel, religious become a sign to the world that they belong simultaneously to Christ and to all people. Through the vow of obedience, religious commit themselves to serve their community, which in turn is dedicated to serving the Christian community. All three vows are positive ways to liberate those living them to a more active life of prayer and service in God's church.

Sisters (or nuns) are women who take the three vows and belong to a community dedicated to some specific ministry like social work, care of the sick, religious education or parish ministry. Religious orders of brothers also live a communal, vowed life in working for the kingdom. There are also priests who belong to a particular religious community. These ordained religious typically undertake the specific work of their community, for example, teaching, missionary work, preaching.

CONCLUDING REFLECTIONS _____

Christian ministry is the urgent work of the church today. No Catholic can "pass the buck" when it comes to service. Vatican II rightly pointed out that the laity has always had a special vocation of engaging in temporal affairs and ordering them according to God's plan (*Lumen Gentium*, No. 31). General Christian ministry includes work on behalf of peace and justice, resolution of social, political and economic conflicts, work on behalf of the poor, the oppressed, all the "little ones." We serve Christ when we bring the gospel to the marketplace. But Vatican II also reminds us that:

> As sharers in the role of Christ the Priest, the Prophet, and the King, the laity have an active part to play in the life and activity of the Church (*Decree on the Apostolate to the Laity*, No. 10).

New opportunities to serve God's people within the church are open to lay people in today's church. People must examine their gifts in a spirit of prayer to see how God is calling them to use their talents.

God will always have a special call for some to serve his people within the ordained ministry. Those who generously respond to this vocation are a sign to all God's people of the presence of the kingdom. We live in an age when the ordained ministry and the religious life are especially countercultural. All Catholics have the duty to support and encourage our ordained brothers who are carrying on an important service for God's people. Furthermore, we can encourage our young people to consider the possibility that God might be calling them to a life of service as priests, professed sisters or brothers. Praying for religious vocations and for generous hearts among God's people is itself an important ministry in today's church.

PRAYER REFLECTION _____

> Teach us, Lord,
>> to serve you as you
>>> deserve;
>> to give
>>> and not to count the cost;
>> to fight
>>> and not to heed the wounds;
>> to toil
>>> and not to seek for rest;
>> to labor
>>> and not to ask for any reward,
>>>> save that of
>>>> knowing
>>>> that we do your will,
>>>> through Jesus Christ our Lord. Amen.
>>>>> —St. Ignatius of Loyola

FOR DISCUSSION _____

1. What common characteristics would you like to see in all Christian ministers?
2. How is Christian ministry related to holy orders?
3. What can you do in a concrete way to further vocations to the priesthood and religious life and to support those who are serving in the ordained ministry?

FURTHER READING _____

Jeremiah 1 (the call of the prophet)
Acts 9:1-16 (the call of Paul)
Matthew 25:31-46 (Christian service)

Section 4

18

Prayer

"Ask, and it will be given to you; search, and you will find; knock, and the door will be opened to you. Everyone who asks receives; everyone who searches, finds; everyone who knocks will have the door opened."

—Matthew 7:7-8

A contemporary slogan reads, *Dare to be great!* Jesus' version of this same sentiment is *Dare to be holy!* We who follow the Lord are called to holiness, that is, to true union with God in both mind and heart.

"You must therefore set no bounds to your love, just as your heavenly Father sets none to his" (Mt 5:48).

Jesus is the perfect model of holiness. His love was without limit. His union with his Father was total. By the power of the Holy Spirit, the Lord makes it possible for us to imitate him, to be one with him and his Father. At the Last Supper Jesus prayed:

"May they all be one,
just as, Father, you are in me and
I am in you,
so that they also may be in us,
so that the world may believe it
was you who sent me"
(Jn 17:21).

What are the signs that we are growing in holiness, that we are achieving closer union with God? Perhaps the best sign that we are one with the Lord is that we are generous in serving others. Holiness is faith put into action, love translated into deed. Holiness is befriending the Lord Jesus so that we can see him in others.

Growth in holiness is a gift from God. The Spirit never forces his love on us, but he does empower us to freely respond to the many opportunities God gives us.

The opportunities to grow into a closer union with God are many. Our Lord presents himself to us every day in every person we meet, thus giving us countless occasions to respond to him. He encounters us in the Bible, his living word. By taking this word to heart, our minds can be more closely attuned to the mind of our Savior. He meets us in the sacraments, visible signs of the Lord's presence and grace. The Eucharist holds center stage in the lives of Catholics who want to grow close to our Lord.

This chapter will treat another essential way to get closer to God: prayer. There are many different ways to pray in the Catholic tradition. There are different paths to our Lord. Try several in your journey.

What Is Prayer?

Prayer is different things to different people. The traditional Catholic definition of prayer is "the lifting of one's mind and heart to God." This definition stresses a conscious turning to God, directing our thoughts and our love to the God who made us.

A popular contemporary definition states that prayer is "loving conversation with God." This definition underscores that in prayer we both talk and listen to God. There is an active dimension where we take our concerns, worries, petitions to God; there is also a more passive dimension where we pause and allow God to speak to us.

The great spiritual writer Thomas Merton defined prayer as "the consciousness of one's union with God, an awareness of one's inner self." This definition makes sense when we compare it to the prayer Jesus taught us—the Our Father. The Lord's Prayer teaches us to address God as Father. When we pray, we are conscious of ourselves as children of a most loving Father who watches out for us and cares for us.

However we define prayer, there is always a dimension of turning to God and becoming aware of his presence. When we pray we are awake to the marvelous activity of God in our lives. St. Teresa of Avila saw prayer as consciously turning to the invisible friend who walks by our side.

What Are the Purposes of Prayer?

There are many ways to distinguish between and among the different kinds of prayer. One traditional category teaches us the acronym *ACTS*, which helps us remember the four purposes of prayer: *A*doration, *C*ontrition, *T*hanksgiving and *S*upplication. We pray to adore

God, that is, to praise him for his goodness and for all creation. We express sorrow to God for the sins we have committed when we offer prayers of contrition. We thank God for the many gifts he has given to us. Finally, prayers of supplication, also called prayers of petition, are requests for God's help and for personal favors.

How Do Public and Private Prayers Differ?

In the public prayer of the church—and the liturgy is the prime example—Christians come and pray together as members of Christ's family to praise God, seek forgiveness, ask for help or offer thanks.

Private prayer, on the other hand, is prayer engaged in by an individual Christian in personal communication with God. Private prayer, though, can certainly be for others; we can and should pray for our families and friends, members of the church, for leaders, for people in need, for our enemies, indeed for all people.

How Do Formal and Spontaneous Prayers Differ?

When we recite the Hail Mary or read the psalms aloud, we are engaging in formal vocal prayer; we are using prayers already composed according to a certain form. But we are not limited to saying formal prayers. Our prayer can also be spontaneous, that is, in our own words and following no set formula. Examples of spontaneous prayers would be a private conversation you might have with the Lord or a public petition offered at a prayer service for a sick relative.

What Are the Basics of Prayer?

To grow in friendship with the Lord we need to spend time with him. It is good to keep the following points in mind.

Place/Time. You can pray anywhere, but it is good to find a special place where you can slow down, relax and focus your attention. The outdoors, a chapel or your own room are all appropriate places for prayer.

You can also pray at any time, but it is a good idea to select a regular time each day. The biggest excuse most Christians have for not praying is that they can't find the time. The truth is we can all spare 10 or 15 minutes each day to spend with the Lord, but we have to discipline ourselves by finding a special time and staying with it. Prayer is a habit. We learn to pray by praying.

Relaxation. Prayer demands our attention. If we are tired, distracted or edgy we won't be able to pray well. Masters of the spiritual life suggest that we assume a body position that keeps us alert but also helps us relax. Sitting in a chair with our backs in a straight line, lying on the floor, kneeling, sitting in the lotus position are all acceptable prayer positions.

We should also spend some time calming our bodies so that our minds and spirits are free to commune with the Lord. Becoming aware of our various senses, rhythmic breathing, listening intently for the sounds around us, becoming aware of the tensions in our body and consciously allowing them to fade away—all of these can help us get ready for prayer.

Proper Attitude. Prayer requires openness and devotion to God. It is always good to begin our prayer by recalling God's presence, his friendship and the many gifts he has bestowed on us.

How Can We Develop a Positive Attitude to Prayer?

Jesus taught us much about prayer. All of the following points help us develop positive and healthy attitudes toward prayer:

Remember that God is Abba. When the disciples asked Jesus to teach them to pray, he taught them the Our Father. Our God is a loving Father. We need never fear approaching him. He knows our needs and is vitally concerned with our lives. We can trust our Father. Jesus taught us that a major theme of our prayer should be, ''Thy will be done.''

Be persistent. Jesus taught that we should ''pray continually and never lose heart'':

> ''There was a judge in a certain town,'' he said, ''who had neither fear of God nor respect for anyone.'' In the same town there was also a widow who kept on coming to him and saying, ''I want justice from you against my enemy!'' For a long time he refused, but at last he said, ''. . . I must give this widow her just rights since she keeps pestering me. . . .''
>
> And the Lord said, ''You notice what the unjust judge has to say? Now, will not God see justice done to his elect if they keep calling to him day and night even though he still delays to help them? I promise you, he will see justice done to them, and done speedily'' (Lk 18:1-8).

Be confident. Deep faith in God should accompany our persistence in prayer. ''And if you have faith, everything you ask for in prayer, you will receive'' (Mt 21:22).

Be humble. Jesus criticized the hypocrites who prayed publicly to impress others and those who babbled long prayers to get a hearing before God. In contrast, Jesus instructed his disciples to pray simply and humbly. He also taught us there is no need to heap up a lot of words because our heavenly Father already knows our needs. Humility is a true sign of our love for God.

Be forgiving. The God of forgiveness wants us to approach him with forgiveness in our hearts. This is a sign of sincerity and peace that will help make our prayer beneficial for us.

> "And when you stand in prayer, forgive whatever you have against anybody, so that your Father in heaven may forgive your failings too" (Mk 11:25).

What Is Vocal Prayer?

Vocal prayers are prayers that are usually said aloud. They can either follow a prescribed formula or be spontaneous. In the Catholic community, the Eucharist and other sacraments are prime examples. The Liturgy of the Hours—the official daily prayer of the church—is another kind of vocal prayer recited by many Catholics. Formal prayers like the Creed, the Morning Offering, the Act of Contrition, the Hail Mary and the Our Father are vocal prayers many Catholics recite on a regular basis.

Vocal prayers can also be "one-liners" known as ejaculations. An example of this kind of prayer is "Holy Spirit, enlighten me" or "Queen of Peace, pray for us."

We typically recite vocal prayers when we are with others, for example, at Mass. Some Catholics come together—for example, in charismatic prayer groups—to raise their voices in spontaneous praise of the Father. Others participate in special devotions like the Stations of the Cross, Forty Hours, novenas and the Rosary. Singing done at these services is also a form of vocal prayer. It has the positive benefit of helping to foster unity among those praying.

Some prayers are so familiar to us that we forget to reflect on what we are saying. To counteract this tendency, it is helpful to pause before praying, recall God's presence and the reason why we are praying, and then consciously reflect on the individual words and phrases in the prayer. Recite the prayer slowly.

How Do We Pray With Scripture?

St. Jerome was fond of saying that "ignorance of scripture is ignorance of Christ." Christians from the earliest centuries have found reading and reflecting on the Bible as the living word of God a most helpful means to spiritual growth. Any part of the Bible can be read prayerfully, but Christians have traditionally found the psalms and the New Testament especially fruitful for prayer.

To read the Bible prayerfully, select a passage ahead of time. Then find a place where you can quiet down and recall the presence of God both within your heart and in his written word. Ask the Lord to help you see that what you are to read is *his personal word spoken directly to you.* Begin reading slowly and reflectively, pausing frequently to see what the text is saying to you and what meaning it might have for your life. While reading, turn frequently to the Lord and speak to him as to a friend, asking him to make his word take root in your life. After your period of prayer, think back over what you learned and take a key insight with you. Thank the Lord for what he has given you in this prayer session. Then, throughout the day, return to the insight you gained as a way of remembering the Lord's gift of himself to you.

What Is Meditation?

In the past 20 years or so, meditation has grown in popularity in the Western world as a way to quiet down, as a means to focus concentration and as a method to tap into the inner spiritual resources that each of us possesses. But for centuries the Catholic church has had a rich tradition of both meditation and contemplation. Prominent saints like Ignatius of Loyola and Teresa of Avila have promoted these methods of prayer as excellent ways to grow in holiness.

Meditation is "tuning into God," thinking about him and trying to become aware of his presence in our lives. It usually involves active use of the mind and imagination. A person can meditate on anything because God speaks to us wherever he is present—and he is present everywhere.

There are many methods of meditation, some designed for beginners in prayer and others for the more advanced. All of them, though, suggest the following:

1. Find a quiet place to pray, a place where you will not be disturbed.

2. Quiet your body. Let the cares of the day drain away. Breathe slowly. Relax your body so your mind can focus on the meditation. Sit with your spine straight, hands on your lap, with your eyes closed.

3. Now direct your attention to some object of meditation. You may focus on a crucifix, or recall how the Lord met you through other people during the course of your day, or read a passage from the New Testament.

4. Pause periodically to talk intimately to the Lord, to let him speak to you through the reading or picture or the event on which you are meditating.

5. At the end of your prayer time, thank the Lord for his friend-

ship and any spiritual insights he might have given you. Make a resolution to do something with your insights and return to them periodically throughout the day.

What Is Contemplation?

Contemplation, on the other hand, is more passive than meditation. A person doesn't really try to think about anything. Rather, the pray-er puts himself or herself in God's presence and simply enjoys his loving company. Contemplation is wordless prayer. It is expressed well in the sentiment of John Bunyan: "In prayer it is better to have a heart without words, than words without a heart."

Contemplation is a way of praying which leaves behind images and words in order to meet the living God who is beyond human comprehension and understanding. St. John of the Cross and St. Teresa of Avila are two famous Catholic mystics who teach this method of prayer.

What Is the "Jesus Prayer"?

An increasingly popular prayer is the Jesus Prayer. This prayer calls on the saving name of Jesus and helps calm us so that we can be contemplatively present to the Lord.

The Jesus Prayer consists of the words, "Lord Jesus Christ, Son of God, have mercy on me, a sinner." Alternative forms are "Jesus, have mercy on me" or, simply, "Jesus." Rhythmic breathing is often used when reciting this prayer. We imagine the saving, loving presence of Jesus infusing our spirits when we inhale and recite "Lord Jesus Christ, Son of God" and we picture our sinful attitudes and hurts leaving us when we exhale and say "have mercy on me, a sinner."

The purpose of this prayer is to deepen our love of the Lord and to put ourselves in his presence. After reciting it for a time, we might simply stop and enjoy the company of the Lord. If distractions come our way, we can return to the prayer.

How Does Praying Affect Us?

Praying on a regular basis keeps our true goal in life constantly before us. It helps us become more aware of God's presence to us and realize his deep love for us as individuals. This awareness can help make us more loving and patient and more attuned to what is really important. In this fast-paced, pressure-filled world of ours, prayer makes a definite contribution to our happiness.

CONCLUDING REFLECTIONS

Think of your closest relationship. You know how vitally important this person is to you—and you to him or her. You cherish what the person says and who the person is. You like spending time together, laughing, talking, knowing each other more and more deeply. You give meaning to each other's lives.

Friends of the Lord Jesus cherish their friendship with him, too. They know that to deepen their friendship with him, they must make some time for him. Thus, prayer is vitally important in their lives. Prayer—like friendship—demands commitment and fidelity. It means that we take time out of our schedules to spend with the Lord. The question is: Do we want to grow in our relationship with the Lord?

Someone once said that if you are too busy for prayer, you are too busy. Are you too busy?

PRAYER REFLECTION

Apply the method of meditation discussed in this chapter to the following bible meditation. The gospel stories told by Jesus are a rich resource for this kind of prayer. Select one of your favorite stories of Jesus, then ask God's help during your period of prayer. Take time to become relaxed and block out distractions. Breathe deeply. Assume a comfortable position. Read the story and let it come to life. Here are some possible themes for your meditation:

1. Put yourself imaginatively into the story (What is going on here? What is Jesus saying? What do the words mean? What is Jesus like? How does he look? What does he reveal about God? How does this story affect others? What does this story say to me? Am *I* a character in the story?)

2. Determine the theme of the passage (for example, God's love for the sinner) and try to see all the implications of this theme for your life right now.

3. Turn to God and respond to his presence to you. Share with him your deepest feelings and thoughts. Turn over to him your cares and needs. Praise him for his goodness. Ask him to forgive your sins and failings. If distractions come your way, return to the scripture passage. Take your time and enjoy these moments with the Lord.

The following parables are good starting points for meditation:

Laborers in the Vineyard (Mt 20:1-6)
Merciless Official (Mt 18:21-35)
Rich Man and Lazarus (Lk 16:19-31)
Good Samaritan (Lk 10:25-37)
Good Shepherd (Jn 10:1-21)

Prodigal Son (Lk 15:11-32)
Treasure and the Pearl (Mt 13:44-46)
Mustard Seed (Mk 4:30-32)

You can meditate on any gospel passage using the above format. You might want to try this form of meditation on a regular basis and record your thoughts, feelings and resolutions in a prayer journal.

FOR DISCUSSION

1. What is the most meaningful way for you to pray?
2. Based on your own personal experience of prayer, what advice would you give to an adolescent on how and why to pray?
3. "Prayer can change the world." Discuss.

FURTHER READING

Isaiah 52:13—53:12 (the 4th "Suffering Servant Song")
Luke 1:68-79 (Zechariah's Canticle)

19

The Communion of Saints and Our Blessed Mother

Mary said, "You see before you the Lord's servant, let it happen to me as you have said."

—Luke 1:38

I believe in the communion of saints.

—from the Apostles' Creed

The church, the Body of Christ, is a community—or communion—formed in Jesus Christ. The Lord sends the Holy Spirit, the Spirit of love, to endow the members of the body with the necessary gifts to continue Christ's work for the kingdom. Jesus sanctifies the members of this communion through the grace of his friendship and the presence of the Holy Spirit.

Jesus calls all Christians to lives of holiness, that is, to imitate his heavenly Father, to live morally, to worship God and to serve others. Jesus calls us to the vocation of sainthood.

The Acts of the Apostles and the epistles commonly refer to Christians as "the saints." The claim being made was *not* that Christians were already perfect. Rather, the early church writings called Christians saints because the Lord calls us to holiness—the word *saint* means "holy one." Through our baptismal initiation into Jesus' own life of holiness, Christians have been given a privileged vocation: to become saints in imitation of our Lord.

This chapter discusses the Catholic doctrine of the communion of saints and treats the special role Mary plays in the church as the perfect model of Christian holiness.

Who Belongs to the Communion of Saints?

The communion of saints, that is, the communion of the holy, includes all those who are now living on earth (the pilgrim church), those who are being purified in purgatory (the church suffering) and those who are blessed in heaven (the church in glory).

The term *communion* of saints also underscores that the people of God, the church, is a *eucharistic* community. The church is a community of people, a real communion, gathered around the eucharistic table of the risen Lord. This community is called, gathered from around the world, and unified by the Holy Spirit. The risen Lord comes to us in his word proclaimed at the Eucharist and in the consecrated bread and wine. Through the power of the Holy Spirit, the church is united into a communion of love and holiness as it partakes of the gift of the risen Lord, the source of all holiness.

What Is the Basis for Belief in This Doctrine?

The doctrine of the communion of saints flows from our belief that we Christians are closely united in the Spirit of Jesus Christ. The bond of love makes us one. In a certain sense, all of God's people are dependent on one another. Those of us who are still living depend on the prayers and good works of our Christian brothers and sisters who are united to us in the friendship of the Lord. "The heartfelt prayer of someone upright works very powerfully" (Jas 5:16). We also believe in the value of prayer for our departed brothers and sisters who are being purified in purgatory. Finally, we believe that those Christian heroes whom we call saints in heaven are vitally interested in those of us who are still living or in purgatory.

Who Is a Saint?

Every Christian is called to be a saint, that is, every disciple of Jesus is called to be holy. A saint is a good person. Saints are people who always choose the better of two courses open to them. Saints are Christian models of holiness. To believe in Christian heroes and to learn from their lives can inspire us to do heroic deeds of service ourselves on our own journey to holiness.

Under the guidance of the Holy Spirit the Catholic church will sometimes declare that a person who lived a good life and died a death joined to Jesus is a saint. The process leading to adding a person's name to the list of saints (a process known as *canonization*) involves a careful study of that person's life and a sign from God (usually miracles performed in that person's name) that this person is truly a saint and worthy of our imitation. When the church honors a saint, the church is praising God who shares his life of holiness with us, his creatures.

Every person in heaven is truly a saint, whether canonized or not. Some of these saints may be our own deceased friends and relatives. The church honors all these good people on All Saints' Day. In some countries All Saints' Day is celebrated as a holy day, a day of truly celebrating the countless number of people who have lived good, holy lives and are now sharing in God's life and happiness in heaven.

Why Do We Pray to the Saints (The Church in Glory)?

Devotion to the saints is a traditional means to holiness. We venerate, that is, honor these men and women. We do *not* pray to the saints as though they were God. Rather, we petition them to intercede for us with our heavenly Father. They are living a deep, personal and loving relationship with God; they have proven their friendship by the extraordinary goodness of their lives while on earth.

We pray to the saints to befriend us, too, especially those to whom we feel particularly close. We ask these personal heroes to take our petitions to the Father on our behalf. We also ask them to inspire us by the example of their lives. They were flesh-and-blood people who rose to the challenge of the Christian life. They can be a great source of inspiration and can provide us with an example of single-hearted commitment to God's kingdom. Erasmus made a telling observation when he said: "No devotion to the saints is more acceptable and proper than if you strive to express their virtue" (*Enchiridion*).

What Is Mary's Role in the Church?

Mary, foremost among the saints, has a special place in the story of salvation history. The New Testament reports that she was singled out and graced by God for the special and unique privilege of being the mother of the Savior. Not fully understanding how she—an unmarried woman—was to conceive a child, she became the perfect symbol of faith when she said yes to the invitation to bear God's Son. With her husband, Joseph, Mary raised Jesus in a loving, prayer-filled home, taught and cared for him. When Jesus launched his public ministry, Mary faithfully witnessed and supported him. With courage and sorrow in her heart, she stood at the foot of the cross in Jesus' dying moments. Finally, the Bible tells us that Mary was with the apostles praying in the upper room after Jesus' resurrection, expectantly awaiting the descent of the Holy Spirit. The church teaches that Mary is the greatest Christian saint of all, the perfect model of Christian faith.

What Are Some of Mary's Titles?

The church honors Mary with many titles such as Our Lady, Mother of God, Our Lady of the Immaculate Conception, Blessed Mother, Mother of the Church, Ever Virgin, Queen of Heaven and Earth. These titles reflect what the church believes and teaches about her.

What Do We Mean by the Immaculate Conception?

The Catholic church teaches that Mary was conceived without original sin. This means that from the first moment of her existence Mary was full of grace, that is, free of any alienation from God caused by original sin. Because of Mary's special role in God's saving plan, she was graced with this divine favor in anticipation of her son's death and resurrection. In addition, Mary was so attuned to God that she was free of all personal sin. She lived a blameless life. The proclamation of the angel—"Rejoice, you who enjoy God's favor! The Lord is with you" (Lk 1:28)—proclaims that Mary is the most blessed of all humans, for she plays a central part in God's plan of salvation.

What Is the Church's Teaching About Mary's Virginity?

The Apostles' Creed states that Jesus was conceived by the Holy Spirit and born of the virgin Mary. Mary conceived Jesus without a human father, and the church has traditionally taught that she was a virgin "before, in, and after" the birth of the Lord. The theological significance of Mary's virginity is intimately related to the divinity of Jesus. By defending Mary's virginity the Catholic church teaches that God is the unique Father of our Lord and Savior Jesus Christ.

How Is Mary Mother of God, Mother of the Church?

In reflecting on the identity of Jesus, the early church, under the inspiration of the Holy Spirit, taught that Jesus is *one* divine person who has both a human nature and a divine nature. Further, the church taught that Jesus was divine from the very first moment of his conception. Thus, at the Council of Ephesus (A.D. 431) the church solemnly taught that Mary is *theotokos*, that is, "bearer of God." By being the mother of Jesus, Mary is truly the mother of God. It is most appropriate for Christians to address Mary with the lofty title: Mother of God.

But Mary is also our mother, the Mother of the Church. As he hung dying on the cross, Jesus gave his mother to all people everywhere to serve as their spiritual mother. "This is your mother" (Jn 19:27). By giving Mary to us as our mother, the Lord wishes the church to learn what God does for those he loves. The church also has a maternal role. As such she can learn much from Mary, the perfect model of faith, obedience, fidelity, compassion and prayerfulness. Mary is the model of Christian holiness and an image of God's love for his people.

What Is the Assumption?

In 1950 Pope Pius XII officially proclaimed the doctrine of the assumption: "The Immaculate Mother of God, the ever Virgin Mary, having completed the course of her earthly life, was assumed body and soul into heavenly glory." This doctrine, which has its roots in ancient Catholic belief, shows the connection between Mary's unique role as God's mother preserved from original sin and the reality of our final resurrection in Christ. In her assumption, Mary was preserved from the decay of death. Mary, the mother of the Savior, is the first to share in the Lord's resurrection. She is the living model for all people whose future destiny is union with the risen Lord.

Why Do Catholics Have Special Veneration for Mary?

Catholics venerate Mary because she is the mother of God and our mother. By praying to and honoring Mary in a special way, we are led to love her and to imitate her many virtues, especially her total commitment to God's will and her single-hearted faith in God's work. "You see before you the Lord's servant...let it happen to me as you have said" (Lk 1:38). As his mother she is uniquely close to him; she is the perfect model of those who center their lives on Jesus.

Mary draws us closer to her son. Note how good Marian art—the Pieta or any of the famous icons of Mary and Jesus—depicts Mary drawing our attention to her son. The focus of the painting or the statue is Jesus, not Mary. *Mary's role in salvation is to give humanity her Son, to lead us to him, to show us how to live in response to him and to intercede on our behalf.*

Sometimes Catholics are accused of worshipping Mary as though she were a god. True devotion to Mary *honors* Mary; God alone may be worshipped. When we pray in Mary's honor, we are really thanking and praising God for blessing one of our sisters. The doctrine of the communion of saints teaches us that those who are close to God will intercede on our behalf. The New Testament reveals a valuable lesson concerning Mary: Jesus does answer her pleas for others. The miracle of the wine at Cana testifies to this (see Jn 2:1-12).

What Is the Rosary?

There are any number of devotions to Mary, but the most popular is the Rosary. The Rosary is a perfect blend of vocal prayers and meditation. The vocal prayers center on the recitation of a number of decades of Hail Marys, each decade introduced by the Lord's Prayer and concluded by a Glory Be. Introductory prayers to the Rosary include the Apostles' Creed, an initial Our Father, three Hail Marys and a Glory Be. During the recitation of these vocal prayers, we meditate on certain events, or mysteries, from the life of Christ and Mary.

The complete Rosary consists of 15 decades, though we customarily only recite five decades at a time. Rosary beads are used to help count the prayers.

The repetition of the Hail Marys helps to keep our minds from distractions as we meditate on the mysteries. Next to the Lord's Prayer, the Hail Mary is the most popular of all prayers among Catholics. The first part of the Hail Mary is rooted in the New Testament; it combines the greetings of the angel (Lk 1:28) and Mary's cousin Elizabeth (Lk 1:42). The second part of this prayer requests Mary's intercession for us:

> Hail Mary, full of grace, the Lord
>   is with you;
> blessed are you among women and
>   blessed is the fruit of your
>   womb, Jesus.
> Holy Mary, mother of God, pray for
>   us sinners now and at the
>   hour of our death. Amen.

The mysteries of the Rosary are divided into the following three categories:

Joyful Mysteries	*Sorrowful Mysteries*	*Glorious Mysteries*
1. The Annunciation	1. The Agony in the Garden	1. The Resurrection
2. The Visitation of Mary to Elizabeth	2. The Scourging at the Pillar	2. The Ascension
3. The Birth of Jesus	3. The Crowning With Thorns	3. The Descent of the Holy Spirit on the Apostles
4. The Presentation of Jesus in the Temple	4. The Carrying of the Cross	4. The Assumption of Mary Into Heaven
5. The Finding of Jesus in the Temple	5. The Crucifixion	5. The Crowning of Mary Queen of Heaven

What Are Some Other Devotions to Mary?

There have been a number of popular devotions to Mary through Christian history. Among them are the Angelus, the First Saturday devotion, the Litany of the Blessed Mother, and various novenas.

The *Angelus* commemorates the incarnation and is traditionally recited in the morning, at noon and in the evening. It includes three short verses which recall the angel Gabriel's announcing to Mary that she was chosen to be the mother of the Lord and her humble acceptance. Three Hail Marys and a special prayer are also included. The Angelus is included in the Appendix of prayers on pages 267-271 of this book.

The *First Saturday devotion* originated as a result of Mary's appearances to the children at Fatima in Portugal in 1917. The devotion consists of the celebration of the sacrament of reconciliation, receiving holy communion on the first Saturday of five consecutive months, reciting five decades of the Rosary and meditating on the mysteries of the Rosary for 15 minutes. This practice is offered to God for the intention of the conversion of sinners and in reparation for sin.

A *litany* is prayer in the form of petitions with a response. The Litany of the Blessed Mother is found in most prayer books.

A *novena* is a devotion practiced over nine consecutive days (or over a period of nine weeks, with one day a week set aside for the devotion). A novena recalls the nine-day period of prayer spent by the apostles and disciples of Jesus in the upper room before the descent of the Holy Spirit. A popular novena to Mary is the novena in honor of Our Lady of Perpetual Help.

CONCLUDING REFLECTIONS _____

Deep within us is an urgent longing to be loved by others, to be understood and to be accepted as we are. We desire union with others; we fear loneliness and isolation.

The Christian doctrine of the communion of saints teaches that the Christian is never alone. We are spiritually united to all our brothers and sisters in the faith. The power and the love of the Lord bring us into the very unity of the Blessed Trinity. We *are* loved. Our Lord Jesus redeems us and continues to demonstrate his love by inviting us—both those of us alive on this earth and our brothers and sisters who have preceded us in death—into his family, a communion of love united by the power of the Spirit.

PRAYER REFLECTION

The realization that God loves us in an incredibly wonderful way overwhelmed Mary. Her Magnificat is a powerful prayer of praise to a gracious God. All Christians can identify with Mary in this joyous song. God has done great things for us; he has invited us into fellowship with him and his saints.

> My soul proclaims the greatness of
>   the Lord
> and my spirit *rejoices in God my*
>   *Savior;*
> because *he has looked upon the*
>   *humiliation of his servant.*
> Yes, from now onwards all
>   generations will call me
>   blessed,
> for the Almighty has done great
>   things for me.
> *Holy is his name,*
> and *his faithful love extends age*
>   *after age to those who fear*
>   *him* (Lk 1:46-49).

FOR DISCUSSION

1. Who is your favorite saint? What have you learned from his or her life about how to respond to God?
2. What do the teachings about Mary reveal about her son Jesus? about the church?
3. What role does Mary play in your life?

FURTHER READING

Leviticus 19 (the way to holiness)
Romans 6—8 (Christian freedom, holiness and spiritual life)

20

Christian Destiny: The Last Things

> We look for the resurrection of the dead and the life of the world to
> come.
>
> —From the Nicene Creed

> Come, Lord Jesus!
>
> —Revelation 22:20

A famous baseball manager once observed: "It's never over until
it's over." His lesson is simple: Don't give up hope for a victory, even
when the odds seem stacked against you.

One apparent defeat that stares all humans directly in the face is
death. It is inevitable. But death does not have the last word; life
does. St. Bernard of Clairvaux said it well: "Death [is] the gate of
life." The good news of Christianity is that life is never really over.
Jesus taught:

> "I am the resurrection.
> Anyone who believes in me, even though that
>   person dies, will live,
> and whoever lives and believes in me
> will never die" (Jn 11:25-26).

Religion deals with the basic questions of life: Is there a God?
What is the meaning of life? What is the meaning of death? Where
and how will the world end? Is there life after death? This chapter will
examine the church's teachings on these issues, topics in the area of
eschatology.

What Is Eschatology?

Questions of ultimate human destiny are treated in the branch of theology known as *eschatology*. Eschatology (from the Greek word *eschaton*, meaning "the last thing") takes up issues like the kingdom of God, death, judgment, the second coming of Christ, heaven, hell and purgatory.

What Does Our Faith Teach Us About Death?

The Book of Ecclesiastes teaches that it is natural to die: "There is a season for everything. . . . A time for giving birth, a time for dying" (Eccl 3:1-2). Death might be natural, but most people fear it. Divine revelation tells us that death is a penalty for sin. St. Paul writes:

> It was through one man that sin *came into the world,* and through sin death, and thus death has spread through the whole human race because everyone has sinned (Rom 5:12).

If sin had not infected the human race, we would be immune from bodily death.

To make sense out of death and our own personal future death, we must look to Jesus Christ. As a human being, Jesus himself was anxious about his own impending death. When he prayed in the Garden of Gethsemane, he foresaw the terrible death that awaited him, and he petitioned his Father:

> "*Abba* (Father)! For you everything is possible. Take this cup away from me. But let it be as you, not I, would have it" (Mk 14:36).

Jesus' "Let it be as you, not I, would have it" demonstrated his final act of total self-giving to the Father. As his followers, we should imitate him. Even though it is natural to fear dying, in faith we recite with Jesus, "Father, *into your hands I commit my spirit*" (Lk 23:46).

Death is a great mystery. But Christian faith reveals that Jesus Christ, our Savior, has conquered death. Jesus Christ lives. Jesus Christ wants us to befriend him in this life so that we can live joyfully with him in eternity. This is not only the good news of the gospel, this is the greatest news humanity is privileged to know.

> It is in the face of death that the riddle of human existence becomes most acute. . . .
> Although the mystery of death utterly beggars the imagination, the Church has been taught by divine revelation, and herself firmly teaches, that man has been created by God for a blissful purpose beyond the reach of earthly misery. In addition, that bodily death from which man would have been immune had he not sinned will be van-

quished, according to the Christian faith, when man who was ruined by his own doing is restored to wholeness by an almighty and merciful Savior (*The Church in the Modern World*, No. 18).

What Does Our Faith Tell Us About Judgment?

The word *judgment* as used in the Bible has a number of meanings, all rich in imagery. A common meaning of God's judgment in the Hebrew scriptures is that Yahweh comes to bring judgment for his people. This was usually taken in a positive sense; for example, God judged (delivered) David from his enemies, or God judged (defended) the poor, the orphaned and widowed. When the people of God stubbornly refused to live by the terms of the covenant, however, God's judgment would be against them.

The New Testament understanding of judgment has two interrelated meanings which are summarized in the terms "the already" but "not yet." God's kingdom is already here, but it is not yet fully established. We already participate in Christ's resurrection, but we have not yet died physically. Jesus Christ has already come and lives with us, but he has not yet come again. We are already saved, but we are not yet perfect—we still sin.

In *Dictionary of the Bible* John McKenzie writes, "For each man the 'day of judgment' is the day on which he makes a permanent decision to accept Jesus Christ or to reject Him." But McKenzie also notes that the Bible reveals there is to be another judgment at the end of time, a final judgment where there is final victory over evil. As the Apostles' Creed puts it, "Jesus shall come to judge the living and the dead."

What Is the Particular Judgment?

The Bible reveals that judgment is now. If we choose Jesus, then we should live today in response to God's laws and our neighbors' needs. Each day we live we are either deciding for God or against him. We don't know how many days we have, so we should follow the Lord's advice and be constantly prepared to meet him in eternity.

The church teaches that each individual will immediately appear before God after death for a *particular judgment*. This teaching was affirmed by Vatican II in the *Dogmatic Constitution on the Church*:

> For before we reign with the glorious Christ, all of us will be made manifest "before the tribunal of Christ, so that each one may receive what he has won through the body, according to his works, whether good or evil" (2 Cor 5:10).

When we die, our period of trial is over. Those who die in God's friendship and who do not need further purification enter heaven; those who die in God's friendship, yet need some purification enter heaven after that purgation is accomplished. Those who die in the state of mortal sin—cut off from God's grace—enter hell. The particular judgment will reveal us for what we truly are. After death each of us will see his or her life as God sees it: a loving response to him or a self-centered turning away from his love.

The Father of Jesus—our Father—is not a cruel, vindictive God. The Bible shows that God's judgment is essentially *for* us, not against us.

> "In all truth I tell you,
> whoever listens to my words,
> and believes in the one who sent me,
> has eternal life;
> without being brought to judgement
> such a person has passed from
>   death to life" (Jn 5:24).

There won't be any surprises when we stand before our Father's judgment seat. We know well enough if we are God-centered or self-centered. At the particular judgment God will judge us lovingly, mercifully and justly. His judgment will simply be a declaration of what is the truth about our acceptance or rejection of him.

What Is the General Judgment?

St. Matthew tells us that when the Son of man comes in his glory, he will gather all the nations and separate the sheep from the goats. This is the general judgment at which time God will establish the heavenly community. The entire saving plan of God will be evident to everyone who ever lived.

Jesus will serve as judge. His goodness, justice, mercy and peace will establish God's kingdom in all its glory. People will recognize the sealing of their own destinies and their relationship to others. All will acknowledge and marvel at the majesty of the Lord.

And what is the basis of this last or general judgment? Simply, did we love God with our whole heart and our neighbor as ourselves?

> "For I was hungry and you gave me food, I was thirsty and you gave me drink, I was a stranger and you made me welcome, lacking clothes and you clothed me, sick and you visited me, in prison and you came to see me" (Mt 25:35-36).

What Is the Second Coming of Christ?

Jesus came to preach and inaugurate the kingdom of God, that is, to announce the presence of God's peace, justice, reconciliation and love actively working in the world. Jesus embodied the kingdom and helped to usher it in.

Christians believe that God's kingdom is here in our midst, that God's loving grace is freeing people and giving them life. God's people, the church, have the urgent mission to work for the spread of the kingdom. Work on behalf of social justice, for example, is an essential part of the church's mission. By their unending labor on behalf of peace, equal rights and human dignity for everyone, Christians are showing the world that all of God's creation is directed to a common destiny of human community.

Because God's kingdom "is already present in mystery," Christians have the duty to work for human solidarity. But we know that in our world there are many forces opposed to God's saving will. God's kingdom is here, but it has not yet been fully established on earth. All Christians look for the future day when Christ's work will be complete. The day of this glorious future will be the day when human history will come to a definite close, the day when Jesus Christ will come again. On this day the kingdom of God in all its eternal glory will be finally established.

When Will Christ's Second Coming Take Place?

We do not know when the world will end and Jesus will come again in glory. Jesus himself taught:

> "But as for that day or hour, nobody knows it, neither the angels in heaven, nor the Son; no one but the Father" (Mk 13:32).

In the early church Christians fully expected that the Lord would come in their lifetime. They were mistaken.

The gospels (for example, Mark 13, Luke 21 and Matthew 28) and the Book of Revelation use a special symbolic language, *apocalyptic language*, when writing about the end of the world and Jesus' Second Coming. This language should not be interpreted in a literal manner. Some of the passages refer not only to the end of the world, but also to the destruction of Jerusalem in A.D. 70 and to the persecution of the Christians under the Roman emperor. An overly literal interpretation of these passages has led some people to picture a bloodthirsty, vindictive God who comes to punish humanity at the end of the world. On the contrary, Christians look forward to this day as a joyful encounter with the risen Lord, as a time when eternity and its promises of perfect happiness, joy and peace are fulfilled.

What the church believes and teaches about the end of the world is that human history will come to a close at some time in the future. Jesus will come again at the *parousia*, a word which means "presence" or "arrival." When this takes place, at a time known to God alone, everyone who ever lived will recognize Jesus as Lord of all.

What Do We Believe About Bodily Resurrection?

Associated with Christ's coming is the resurrection of the dead.

> He who raised up the Lord Jesus will raise us up with Jesus in our turn, and bring us to himself—and you as well (2 Cor 4:14).

The resurrection of the body means that each person will be completely human—body and soul—for all eternity, sharing in the glorious life of our Lord Jesus Christ.

From the earliest years, Christians have speculated on what our resurrected bodies will be like. Again, it is St. Paul who addressed this question:

> Someone may ask, How are dead people raised, and what sort of body do they have when they come? How foolish! What you sow must die before it is given new life; and what you sow is not the body that is to be, but only a bare grain, of wheat I dare say, or some other kind; it is God who gives it the sort of body that he has chosen for it. . . .
>
> What is sown is perishable but what is raised is imperishable; what is sown is contemptible but what is raised is glorious; what is sown is weak, but what is raised is powerful; what is sown is a natural body, and what is raised is a spiritual body (1 Cor 15:35-37, 42-44).

Related to the resurrection of the body is our belief that material creation will also be transformed in Christ. We simply cannot imagine what God has in store for us, but it would make sense that he would create a suitable environment where our resurrected, glorified bodies would thrive for eternity.

What Is Heaven?

Heaven is the state of eternal life in union with God and all those who share in his life. The church uses the term *beatific vision* to help describe heaven. We will "see" God, and this seeing will bring us happiness (beatitude). God made us to share his life with him; he made us for eternal happiness. Heaven is the final, perfect human fulfillment, that state of being that makes us wholly what we are meant to be, that state which will make us happy.

In heaven we will be united to God and all his creation, but we will retain our individual identities. The love of Jesus will transform us into totally unselfish images of the Father.

We believe firmly in the existence of heaven, and yet it is totally beyond human comprehension:

> It is as scripture says: *What no eye has seen and no ear has heard, what the mind of man cannot visualize; all that God has prepared for those who love him* (1 Cor 2:9).

We can only imagine the degree of happiness in heaven:

> [God] "*will wipe* away all *tears from their* eyes; there will be no more death, and no more mourning or sadness or pain. The world of the past has gone" (Rv 21:4).

Our desires for truth, wisdom, goodness, beauty, peace, justice, companionship, understanding, love—all will be infinitely fulfilled.

What Is Purgatory?

The church teaches the existence of purgatory, that is, a place or state of purification as a preparation for entrance into heaven.

This doctrine makes sense. To see God face to face means that we must be purified of all of our imperfections, our hesitations in committing ourselves totally to God, our unwillingness to love God perfectly. The Book of Revelation teaches that no unclean person can enter heaven.

Purgatory means "purification, cleansing." What we need cleansing of is any venial sin or any punishment due our sin which is present at death. In one sense, for the Christian the process of purification takes place each day as we live and attempt to rid ourselves of sin and attachment to self. Experience teaches us that it is a long and painful process to become other-centered and more loving.

The exact nature of purgatory has never been defined by the church. The church has never officially declared what kind of "place" purgatory is or "how long it lasts." Space and time images are just that—images that attempt to describe the mystery of eternal life.

Perhaps the process of purification involves the pain of letting go of *all* selfish attachments as the deceased passes over to a new life of total union with an all-loving God. Our departed brothers and sisters in purgatory are at peace because they know that they are destined to be united to God in heaven. Along with joy and peace, though, there is a state of suffering. The nature of the suffering has been compared to fire. The person "burns" with remorse because he or she is separated from God who is infinite goodness and joy. This separation, though temporary, is the result of the person's own actions on earth.

The best scriptural basis for this doctrine can be found in 2 Macca-bees 12:41-45 which encourages the living to pray for the dead so they can be released from their sin. The church teaches that the prayers of the living, especially the offering of the Eucharist, can help those ''in'' purgatory. The doctrine of the communion of saints underscores our unity with all our Christian brothers and sisters. Our prayers for them are heard by the Lord.

Some theologians speculate that purgatory might well take place in an instant after death in an encounter with the Lord. They suggest that when we see Christ's loving look, our own sinful infidelities ''burn'' us to the degree that we have failed to respond to God's love. This encounter burns away imperfections and opens the person totally to God. This modern explanation is close to that of the 15th-century mystic, St. Catherine of Genoa. She wrote that God's love burns the soul so that it may be totally and perfectly aflame with the fire of God's love. The pain exists in wanting to be totally united to God, and realiz-ing that our own imperfections are keeping us from it.

What Is Hell?

Hell is eternal separation from God. In the New Testament Jesus clearly stated its existence in a number of places. For example, in Mark's gospel Jesus warns against scandal:

> ''It is better for you to enter into the kingdom of God with one eye, than to have two eyes and be thrown into hell where *their worm will never die nor their fire be put out*'' (Mk 9:47-48).

The church teaches that there is a hell, but that the images em-ployed by scripture to describe it are symbolic. They are attempts to describe the horror of an eternal life alienated from God and his love. This alienation extends to all interpersonal relationships. The person who dies having turned away freely and deliberately from God's re-deeming love has chosen to live a life turned in on self—eternally.

Some people suggest that the doctrine of hell denies the goodness of God. This is not so. God doesn't send an individual to hell; an indi-vidual has chosen this option by the way he or she lived. The Lord al-ways offers his grace and forgiveness and love—repeatedly during our life—but he does not force his love on us.

If love is true, it is freely given and accepted. God respects our freedom. If we decide to mold ourselves into heartless, unloving, self-ish people, then God respects our decision. God does not play games with us; to do so would destroy our freedom as human beings. He won't destroy the person who has chosen self either, that is, he won't annihilate any individual. This would violate the humanity, the very existence, of the person—something the God of life would never do.

The church teaches that the punishment of hell consists both of a sense of loss caused by alienation from God and a suffering of the senses. The church, though, warns us not to speculate too much on the exact nature of the "fires of hell." A satisfying modern image is that the person who is separated from God burns with self-hatred and abject loneliness.

Who Is in Hell?

We know that it is possible to choose self over God and thus merit eternal punishment. But we do not know for sure who is in hell. We simply don't know who—in the depths of their consciences—have definitively rejected God. Jesus tells us not to judge others in order to avoid judgment ourselves.

The person who loves God and translates that love into actions need not obsessively fear hell. The one who loves God knows that God is not out to get us. After all, Jesus died to give us eternal life. However, the existence of hell should cause us to think reflectively. Our actions do have meaning. We shape ourselves and our future destiny by everything we do—right now. God respects our freedom, even if we sin. But we should never forget that he is a God of both justice *and* mercy.

CONCLUDING REFLECTIONS

Anyone who tries to do the right thing, or who struggles to love others, or who sees the wicked of this world getting ahead must sometimes wonder, Is it worth it? Will my efforts to do good and to be good make any difference? Or is life basically meaningless?

Our Christian beliefs about the "last things" make all our attempts to follow Jesus Christ worth the effort. There is life after death. If we fight the good fight, we will enter eternity resurrected in the Lord.

Everything we do—everything we fail to do—has significance. We are important to God; what we do is noticed and rewarded by him. Jesus himself promised those who deny themselves the following:

> "In truth I tell you, there is no one who has left house, brothers, sisters, mother, father, children or land for my sake and for the sake of the gospel who will not receive a hundred times as much, houses, brothers, sisters, mothers, children and land—and persecutions too—now in this present time and, in the world to come, eternal life" (Mk 10:29-30).

PRAYER REFLECTION _____

And after this perishable nature has put on imperishability and this mortal nature has put on immortality, then will the words of scripture come true: *Death is swallowed up in victory. Death, where is your victory? Death, where is your sting?* The sting of death is sin, and the power of sin comes from the Law. Thank God, then, for giving us the victory through Jesus Christ, our Lord.

So, my dear brothers, keep firm and immovable, always abounding in energy for the Lord's work, being sure that in the Lord none of your labours is wasted (1 Cor 15:54-58).

FOR DISCUSSION _____

1. How do the Christian teachings about the "last things" give us hope that this life has ultimate meaning?
2. What poetic image could you use to describe our eternal life with God in heaven?
3. In what sense could this life be considered a kind of purgatory?

FURTHER READING _____

Revelation 21—22 (the vision of a heavenly Jerusalem)

21

Ecumenism: The Church and Other Religions

My dear friends,
let us love each other,
since love is from God
and everyone who loves is a child of
    God and knows God.
Whoever fails to love does not
    know God,
because God is love.

—1 John 4:7-8

As we have seen, pilgrimage is an important image for the spiritual life. Pilgrims are on a journey to a specific destination, but along the way they will encounter many interesting people whose stories make the journey much more fascinating. We can't escape the imagery of travelling through space and time with others because our modern media has made us increasingly aware that we are fellow passengers on "spaceship earth." For example, news of famine in Africa is brought into our homes by television. The political turmoil in Latin America directly affects the economics of the whole world. Natural disasters around the world are reported in our morning newspapers. We are constantly reminded that the human pilgrimage includes the entire human family.

The journey theme is also important for understanding and living our Catholic faith. Jesus reminds us that we do not travel alone. Our Christian brothers and sisters help us make it to our destination; we also have the obligation to sustain them on their journey. Numerically there are many Roman Catholics, fellow travelers who share the same faith, for Catholicism is the largest Christian denomination in the world and the largest branch of any of the world religions. Many Catholics consider it a privilege and an honor to be a member of this religious body, one we believe is guided by none other than the Holy Spirit.

We must be aware, however, that most of the world's population is not Catholic. Millions of people belong to other religions. Yet they are our brothers and sisters too. We share the same gift of God's creation, and our mutual journey has a common destination—union with God. To think that one is superior because he or she belongs to one religious group rather than another is to fall victim to the sin of pride. Worse yet, negative judgments about our fellow travelers can often lead to prejudice. Perhaps this is the worst sin of all, because religious bigotry has permitted so many horrible evils over the course of the centuries.

Today the church's attitude is one of profound respect and reverence toward other religions and those who practice them. Just as the bee gathers honey from thorny rose bushes, so too Christians and Catholics can and should gain much nourishment from respecting and learning about other religious traditions. This chapter briefly treats the topic of *ecumenism* whose aim is mutual understanding among religions.

What Are the Major World Religions?

The major world religions are typically divided into the religions of the West and the religions of the East. The religions of the West include Judaism and its two spiritual descendants: Christianity and Islam. Judaism defines itself as a people of the Covenant: Yahweh formed and sustained the Jewish people in return for their love and worship. Yahweh is their God, and Israel is his people. Christianity professes that Jesus of Nazareth, a Jewish carpenter and teacher, is the Messiah who fulfills all the promises made to Israel. The Moslems share with Judaism and Christianity a strong faith in one God. Though Islam acknowledges Jesus as a prophet and honors Mary his mother, it maintains that Mohammed is Allah's greatest prophet.

The religions of the East include Hinduism and Buddhism which were born on the Indian subcontinent, Taoism in China and the Shinto religions in Japan.

To these major religions we could add the numerous minor religions, sometimes called primitive religions. These include the religions of the American Indians and various aboriginal people, for example, of Australia and Africa.

What Are the Major Christian Religions?

Christianity is numerically the largest major world religion. It is divided into three major sections: Catholic, Orthodox and Protestant.

Catholicism, the largest Christian denomination, includes those Christians who acknowledge the primacy of the pope. Most Catholics are of the Roman or Latin rite, the predominant rite of the Western church. Of the five major Eastern rites, the Byzantine rite is the largest; it includes a number of Catholic groups of diverse ethnic origin. The term *rites* refers to the forms and rules regarding liturgical worship and the various ways of expressing the rich theological, spiritual and disciplinary heritages of the churches of the East and West. These different rites developed over the course of history as the church adapted itself to the various cultures it encountered through time.

The Eastern Orthodox (or Orthodox) are Eastern rite churches (notably the Greek and Russian Orthodox churches) that are in schism from Rome, that is, not in union with the pope. Of all Christian groups, the Orthodox are closest to Roman Catholicism in faith, theology and church structures.

The Reformation of the 16th century resulted in the formation of the mainstream Protestant churches. These denominations share many beliefs in common with Catholics, notably the articles of faith in the Nicene Creed, but they differ on other points of belief and practice.

How Did Division Among Christians Come About?

A long and complex history would have to be told to show how the church of Christ splintered into the various Christian denominations. The first chapter would tell of the *schism* (split) between the Western and Eastern churches. Both political and church differences arose due in some measure to the rivalry between the two capitals of the Roman empire—Rome and Constantinople. Various cultural, sociological and theological differences finally led to the great schism of 1054. These differences focus on the role of papal authority. This schism has divided the Roman Catholic and the Eastern Orthodox churches ever since.

The second chapter in this history would tell of the *Protestant Reformation* and its aftermath. The 16th-century church was indeed in need of reform. Men like Martin Luther and John Calvin protested against the corruption they found in the church and eventually separated themselves and their followers from the Roman Catholic Church.

In a short time a number of Protestant churches came into existence. These churches varied considerably in their beliefs and practices. The most prominent today are the Lutheran, Presbyterian, Methodist,

Baptist and United Churches of Christ. The present-day Anglican church, known as the Episcopalian church in America, was begun by King Henry VIII as a result of a conflict with the pope who refused to annul Henry's marriage. It has much of the institutional form of the Roman Catholic Church, but maintains independence from the pope.

Other significant Protestant faiths include the Pentecostal and Holiness groups. Still other groups are described as sects, that is, they are typically small, have become separated from a larger church, and are difficult to classify according to traditional definitions of a Christian church. These groups would include the Mormons (The Church of Jesus Christ of the Latter Day Saints), the Jehovah Witnesses and the Christian Scientists.

What Is Ecumenism?

Ours is an age of ecumenism. *Ecumenism* comes from a Greek word which means "universal." The ecumenical movement generally means two things: (1) It refers to the attempt among all world religions to understand one another better and to overcome needless opposition, and (2) when applied to Christians, the ecumenical movement refers to the efforts of Christian denominations to work for greater unity among themselves and to better understand and improve relations with the other major world religions.

The Christian Ecumenical movement began among Protestants in Edinburgh, Scotland, in 1910. Meetings were held periodically, culminating in 1948 with the founding of the World Council of Churches. The Catholic Church did not officially participate in non-Catholic ecumenical efforts until the Second Vatican Council (1962-1965). The *Decree on Ecumenism* made efforts for Christian unity a top priority for the church and praised efforts on behalf of ecumenism.

Does Ecumenism Mean All Churches Are the Same?

Work on behalf of ecumenism does not mean that the Catholic church denies its unique role in God's plan of salvation. For example, the Catholic church still teaches that the fullness of the truth and grace of Jesus Christ subsists (can be found) in the Roman Catholic Church:

> For it is through Christ's Catholic Church alone, which is the all-embracing means of salvation, that the fullness of the means of salvation can be obtained. It was to the apostolic college alone, of which Peter is the head, that we believe our Lord entrusted all the blessings of the New Covenant, in order to establish on earth the one Body of Christ into which all those should be fully incorporated who already belong in any way to God's people (*Decree on Ecumenism*, No. 3).

Nevertheless, the Catholic church also teaches that the Holy Spirit works in all people of good will in order to build up God's kingdom. Other churches share in the building up of the kingdom to the degree that they are related to the one true church of Jesus Christ, centered primarily in the Roman Catholic Church.

What Is the Goal of Ecumenism?

The goal of Christian ecumenism is a common commitment among Christians to live out the gospel and to be open to the unifying action of the Holy Spirit. Much already unites Christian churches, for example, agreement that the true nature of the church of Christ is to be "salt of the earth" and "light of the world."

How Can the Individual Christian Work Toward Unity?

Every Catholic can work for Christian unity, can be part of the ecumenical movement. Vatican II defined this movement as "those activities and enterprises which . . . are started and organized for the fostering of unity among Christians" (*Decree on Ecumenism*, No. 4).

A primary duty of Catholics in the work for unity is to make sure that the Catholic church itself is living the gospel message in fidelity to Jesus Christ. Catholics must try to live holy lives in order to draw others to Jesus and his church. Furthermore, Catholics can acknowledge the spiritual gifts which our Lord has endowed on our Christian brothers and sisters and remember that their faith, hope and love can inspire us. In addition, we can do the following:

Prayer. The most important thing any of us can do to foster Christian unity is to pray. We can pray *for* Christian unity, asking the Spirit to guide our efforts, and *with* our Christian brothers and sisters.

Study. We have a duty to know our own faith well and to share its truths with others. This is a lifelong quest—to know better the depths of our own faith and to appreciate the meaning of church doctrines so that we can help others to understand them as well. Knowledge of other religions can also be very helpful for mutual understanding.

Communication. Since Vatican II, Catholic theological experts and those of many different religions have engaged in dialogues to better mutual understanding and to arrive at common professions of faith. As individuals we can share our own Catholic beliefs and engage in open exchanges with members of other faiths as occasions arise. The Council encourages us to eliminate prejudicial language from our conversation. We can share points of view in Christian harmony, charitably and with understanding.

Cooperation. The church calls on us to work together with our

Christian brothers and sisters of other communions on projects of social action. Putting the gospel into action in joint efforts of Christian charity can go a long way in bringing Christians together.

What Is the Church's Attitude Toward the Orthodox?

The Catholic church respects the Eastern Orthodox churches. Though there are some differences in belief, the Eastern Orthodox churches keep all the basic beliefs and traditions of the Roman Catholic Church up to the separation of 1054. They celebrate all of the sacraments and have a valid hierarchy and priesthood. The basic difference is over the role of the pope whom they claim does not have jurisdiction over the whole church. Major efforts toward reunion have been made in the years since the Second Vatican Council.

What Is the Church's Attitude Toward Protestants?

The church acknowledges, respects and praises what we have in common with most Protestant churches: faith in God the Father, his Son Jesus Christ and the Holy Spirit; the Bible as the living word of God; a life of prayer and grace; faith, hope and charity and other gifts of the Holy Spirit; baptism; commemoration of the Lord's Supper; work for the kingdom and a looking forward to the day of its glory; concern to live moral lives in accordance with God's revelation.

The church teaches that all Catholics should honor Protestants who are saved by faith and baptism. They "are accepted as brothers by the children of the Catholic Church" (*Decree on Ecumenism*, No. 3).

What Is the Church's Attitude Toward Judaism?

The church in our day speaks out strongly against anti-Semitism, prejudice directed against Jews. The church reminds us that any persecution against the Jews, and any form of discrimination because of race, color, condition of life or religion is contrary to the will of Christ and a direct violation of his call to love.

Through the ages many Christians wrongly blamed the Jews as a people for the death of Christ. What happened in Jesus' passion "cannot be blamed upon all the Jews then living, without distinction, nor upon the Jews of today" (*Declaration on the Relationship of the Church to Non-Christian Religions*, No. 4).

All Christians owe the Jewish faith special reverence and respect. The Christian religion finds its spiritual roots in Judaism. Jesus himself was a pious Jew who loved his religion. Jews have not ceased to be God's chosen people.

The Jews still remain most dear to God because of their fathers, for he does not repent of the gifts He makes nor of the calls He issues (cf. Rom 11:28-29). (*Declaration on the Relationship of the Church to Non-Christian Religions,* No. 4).

The Jewish people witness to the Father of Jesus and revere the books of the Hebrew scriptures (what we call the Old Testament). Furthermore, they live by the same moral code handed down to Moses, the Ten Commandments.

What Is the Church's Attitude Toward the Moslems?

The church also esteems the Moslems who worship the one and merciful God. Moslems do not acknowledge the divinity of Jesus Christ, but they do revere him as a great prophet, and they honor his mother Mary. With Christians they await judgment day and resurrection, prize the moral life and worship God through prayer, almsgiving and fasting.

The Council recognized that the history of Christians and Moslems has seen conflicts and hostilities, but the church now calls for cooperation. All are urged to forget the past and to strive sincerely for mutual understanding. The Council urges Moslems and Christians to work in common for social justice, moral values and the causes of peace and freedom.

How Does the Church View Other Religions?

The church recognizes that in his own mysterious way, God extends his saving love to all people everywhere. Thus, the church,

> rejects nothing which is true and holy in these religions. She looks with sincere respect upon those ways of conduct and life, those rules and teachings which, though differing in many particulars from what she holds and sets forth, nevertheless often reflect a ray of that Truth which enlightens all men (*Declaration on the Relationship of the Church to Non-Christian Religions,* No. 2).

Even those with no professed faith deserve respect as persons. God extends his grace to them and if they strive to live good and loving lives, they are responding to his gift of salvation. Whatever is good or true found among these people is seen as a preparation for the gospel.

> Those also can attain to everlasting salvation who through no fault of their own do not know the gospel of Christ or His Church, yet sincerely seek God and, moved by grace, strive by their deeds to do His will as it is known to them through the dictates of conscience (*Dogmatic Constitution on the Church,* No. 16).

CONCLUDING REFLECTIONS _____

A tragedy of Christian history is that the one church of Jesus Christ is fragmented into many churches. Today there is a wounded unity in the Body of Christ. Undoubtedly this happened because Christians preached their own message instead of heeding the gospel call of the Lord to repentance and service.

More than ever before the members of the human community need to grow closer to one another, if simply for the survival of the species. Human community is fostered by unity. Christians believe that the Lord Jesus through the power of the Holy Spirit—the Spirit of love—can bring about what human efforts cannot. Like a magnet that draws particles of iron to itself, the power of love can attract Christians to Christ and thus unite them one to another. United, Christians stand as a beacon to a world searching for light; divided, Christians fall and scatter the fire of hope.

For love to work its mysterious wonders, Christians must strive to live according to the gospel of Jesus. Mutual respect, a genuine desire to learn from others, shared prayer and humble works of service for those suffering—all these are essential for Christian unity. The religious antagonism of the past has no place in a world struggling against the forces of evil for its mere survival. All people of good will must join hands to help work for God's kingdom. By centering on Jesus and letting go of superior attitudes toward others, Christians place themselves in a much better position of being the light of the world they are called to be.

PRAYER REFLECTION _____

The parable of the Good Samaritan (Lk 10:29-37) has as its central character a man who is travelling. He is waylaid by an anonymous thug, but more important, he is ignored by the established religious figures who were his countrymen. Only the stranger—an enemy—stopped to help him. There are many lessons in this parable, including two that drive home the message of this chapter. First, religious prejudice is ugly and wrong according to the teaching of Jesus. Second, one way to transcend religious differences is through service of one another.

Let us turn to Mother Teresa of Calcutta for a simple yet profound prayer for service to others.

> Make us worthy, Lord,
> to serve our fellow human beings throughout the
>   world who live and die in poverty and
>   hunger.

Give them through our hands this day their daily
   bread.
And by our understanding love,
give peace and joy.

FOR DISCUSSION

1. Think of a person of another faith who seems to really live his or her beliefs. How might Catholics learn from this person?
2. How should today's church reach out to people of other faiths?
3. What can you do in a practical way to work for Christian unity? How do you witness to your faith on a daily basis?

FURTHER READING

Jonah (God proclaims his message to everyone)
1 John 4

22

Being Catholic: Commitment to Life

"You are salt for the earth. But if salt loses its taste, what can make it salty again? It is good for nothing, and can only be thrown out to be trampled under people's feet.

"You are light for the world. A city built on a hill-top cannot be hidden. No one lights a lamp to put it under a tub; they put it on the lamp-stand where it shines for everyone in the house. In the same way your light must shine in people's sight, so that, seeing your good works, they may give praise to your Father in heaven."

—Matthew 5:13-16

In this book we have been looking at what a Catholic is and what Catholics believe and practice. An important part of our individual identity is our Catholic faith. Being a member of the Lord's body is indeed a privilege. But the privilege of being invited in a special way to join God's people brings with it major responsibilities. The Lord has chosen us to do his work. Matthew's gospel reminds us of two very important tasks of every Catholic: to be salt of the earth and to be light for the world.

Salt has both a flavoring and a preservative function. Our lives of service for others in fidelity to the gospel should help to make the journey to our Father less difficult, especially for the poor, the hungry, all the "little ones." The world should "taste" different because Christians have spiced it with their lives. Likewise our commitment to the kingdom of God—especially in furthering the healing mission of Jesus through forgiveness and attention to the needs of others—should model the salvation the Lord wills for all our fellow travelers.

Jesus is the light of the world, the hope everyone has for eternal life and salvation. He calls on his disciples to be beacons of this light. Marked with the sign of the cross, we are commissioned by the Lord to

251

go forth joyfully and proclaim him in worship, in word and in acts of loving service. The Holy Spirit inflames the hearts of Christians so that Jesus can be seen as the way, the truth and the life. Our task is to shed light on the Light of the world who is the way to the Father for all spiritual travelers.

This chapter will review the identity of a Catholic and indicate that a commitment to life is a vital way today to be salt of the earth and light of the world.

Who Is a Catholic?

As we have seen, a Catholic is a Christian who belongs to a certain faith community that shares Jesus' vision and responds to his presence in our midst. A Catholic loves each member of this community and uses his or her unique talents to contribute to it in a positive way.

A Catholic believes in God, who is our loving Father. This loving Father has made us brothers and sisters to everyone who has ever lived. Moreover, he has sent us his Son Jesus Christ who won for us our salvation and gave us eternal life.

A Catholic believes in the presence of the Holy Spirit, accepting and using the many gifts he showers on us. By the power of this Holy Spirit, a Catholic accepts Jesus into his or her life.

A Catholic attempts to live in harmony with Jesus' teaching: loving God above all things; loving neighbor as oneself; forgiving enemies; extending special care to the poor, lonely and the outcast.

A Catholic prays and lives a sacramental life, for example, by recognizing a need for forgiveness through the celebration of the sacrament of reconciliation. Moreover, a Catholic cherishes the Eucharist as a special sign of God's nourishing love, a way to encounter the living Lord Jesus. A Catholic participates fully in the eucharistic celebration every week.

A Catholic reveres and reads the Bible, the word of God.

A Catholic acknowledges the role of proper authority in the church, for example, by seeking guidance for moral decisions from the church's official teachers, the pope and the bishops in communion with him.

A Catholic serves others and shares his or her faith in publicly acknowledging Jesus Christ and his church. He or she is willing to stand up to ridicule and suffering in the service of the gospel truth.

A Catholic is all of the above and more. You might try to summarize in your own words what it means to be a Catholic. More than likely you will add some traits that are very special to you. To the above points, though, we must add that a major distinguishing trait of the

Catholic church in today's world is its fierce stand and work for the preservation of human life.

How Has the Church Led in the Pro-Life Movement?

Cardinal Joseph Bernardin of Chicago delivered a remarkable set of speeches on the church's pro-life stand. Called the "seamless garment" speeches, the cardinal suggested that the "pro-life position of the church must be developed in terms of a comprehensive and consistent ethic of life," that is, the church must be concerned about *all* aspects of the protection of life. These include not only the areas of abortion and euthanasia, but also capital punishment, the nuclear arms race, economic policies that exploit the poor, and the like.

The many pro-life speeches of the pope in his travels around the world, the American bishops' pastoral letters on peace and on the economy and the participation of countless Catholic laity and clergy in pro-life causes testify that the church has taken a leadership role in the defense of human life. In addition, especially since the landmark Supreme Court decision in 1973 establishing the civil legality of abortion in America, the church has spoken clearly for the rights of the unborn.

As a result of their strong stand on life issues, Catholics and others who support the pro-life movement have often been criticized and even ridiculed in the media, especially by the advocates of abortion on demand. These critics argue that a minority religious group has no right to force others to adopt its moral positions.

What Is the Catholic Position on Abortion?

Direct abortion is the expelling of a nonviable human fetus from the mother's womb by surgical or medical means. Certainly abortion, along with the nuclear arms race, is one of the major moral issues of our day. Some pro-life authors have even termed abortion "a silent holocaust," comparing the killing of unborn babies to Nazi Germany's annihilation of millions of innocent Jewish people. In this holocaust the innocent babies cannot speak out for themselves to demand the most fundamental right of all—the right to life.

The basic difference between pro-lifers and those who would permit abortion resides in whether abortion is a medical or moral issue. In its abortion opinions, the Supreme Court asserted that the abortion decision "is inherently and primarily a medical decision, and basic responsibility for it must rest with the physician."

While not denying the medical question, the church teaches that abortion itself is fundamentally a moral question. Genetics, biology and fetology have accumulated enough medical evidence to demonstrate forcefully that each individual human life begins at fertilization, that is, when the female egg and male sperm unite to form a new genetically distinct, human life. *Because we are dealing with a human life, the life of the unborn baby is of value to us.* It is valuable because all human life is a great gift from God.

> For God, the Lord of life, has conferred on men the surpassing ministry of safeguarding life—a ministry which must be fulfilled in a manner which is worthy of man. Therefore from the moment of its conception life must be guarded with the greatest care, while abortion and infanticide are unspeakable crimes (*Pastoral Constitution on the Church in the Modern World*, No. 51).

What Does the Church Teach About Euthanasia?

Euthanasia, which means "good death," most often refers to actions taken to hasten painlessly the death of some suffering person. It is sometimes called mercy killing. Even though the intent is usually to help those suffering from tragic diseases and accidents, in effect euthanasia is a form of murder.

The church fosters respect for human life no matter what the person's physical, mental or emotional condition. Human life is sacred of itself; its worth is not dependent on its productivity. Furthermore, a person is sacred not only because he or she is a person, but because he or she is made to God's image and likeness, saved by our Lord Jesus Christ, and destined for union with the Father in eternity.

Christians, as followers of Jesus, should actively affirm life. We do this when we fight against whatever threatens life—hunger, disease, poverty, the arms race, natural disasters and the like. However, Christians do not deny the reality of death. We are creatures, thus we are mortal. We have to die in order to be fully united with the Lord. Hence, keeping a person alive regardless of the cost is not an absolute value. On the contrary, church teaching holds that we must use ordinary means to prolong life (and thus manifest respect for life), but we are not obligated to use extraordinary means to keep a person alive. A terminally ill patient can be allowed to die in peace. The use of extraordinary means involving complicated medical procedures or grave expenses to the family need not be employed to prolong a life destined for union with the Creator. Mercy killing (euthanasia), however, is clearly not the same thing as the refusal to take extraordinary measures to prolong life.

The Catholic church strongly condemns all *direct* and *intentional* acts which have as their purpose the taking of human life:

> Whatever is opposed to life itself, such as any type of murder, genocide, abortion, euthanasia, or willful self-destruction, whatever vio-

lates the integrity of the human person . . . all these things and others of their like are infamies indeed. They poison human society, but they do more harm to those who practice them than those who suffer from the injury. Moreover, they are a supreme dishonor to the Creator'' (*Pastoral Constitution on the Church in the Modern World*, No. 27).

Proponents of euthanasia ignore the Christian concept of suffering which maintains that suffering is not purely negative. Suffering can purify and make holy if the person accepts it in a spirit of penance and, in resignation to God's will, joins it to the salvific suffering of our Lord Jesus himself.

Finally, we must admit that euthanasia presents many challenging moral questions that have no easy answers. For example, not only our ability to maintain life almost indefinitely in some cases, but also the fact that what is an extraordinary means today will be an ordinary means tomorrow, raises morally complex questions. But the one guiding principle at work in all these problems is the sacredness of human life which forbids us from actively performing any action that directly results in the death of a fellow human being.

What Does the Church Teach on Capital Punishment?

The church has traditionally taught that the state, which has authority to provide for the common good, has the right to defend itself and its members against unjust aggression. This right has permitted the state to use the death penalty in extreme cases to punish criminals who were found guilty of serious crimes against individuals or a just social order. The essential purposes of the death penalty are to punish the criminal—in a permanent way—and to deter crime.

In recent years the American bishops have seriously questioned the morality of the death penalty. The church wishes to present a consistent pro-life stance, and the bishops' key argument is that the use of the death penalty leads to an erosion of respect for life in our society.

The American bishops also oppose capital punishment because of the way it is administered in the United States. They observe that the death penalty has been applied in a discriminatory way in America with respect to the poor, members of racial minorities and other disadvantaged and socially impoverished individuals. Furthermore, they seriously question whether capital punishment actually does deter crime, one of the major arguments advanced by those who support it.

The bishops in no way wish to compare innocent unborn babies to condemned criminals; what they wish to point out is that *all* life must be respected, even the lives of condemned criminals. The bishops certainly do not wish to approve any criminal actions, including the kinds of crimes which have merited the death penalty. What they call for is equal justice under the law for all citizens, a right guaranteed by our Bill of Rights. The laws which permit capital punishment are applied in a grossly unfair way; thus, the bishops' argue, these laws should be abolished.

CONCLUDING REFLECTIONS

Every thinking person knows that life is the greatest gift God has bestowed on us. Every believing person knows that Jesus Christ is the Lord of life; because of his supreme sacrifice we are destined for a superabundant life with his Father. Jesus taught us that every human life is God's plan written in time; it is precious and awe-inspiring and worth dying for.

Contemplating this great gift of life prompts Christians to thank God for our existence. We show our appreciation for the gift of life by passionately protecting and defending all human life, especially innocent human life.

The Christian believes and proclaims that we are so precious in God's eyes that God's Son came to us. This Son, Jesus Christ, taught us how to live. He showed us that to live, really live, means to love. And he demonstrated the truth of this by surrendering his own life for us.

The good news of the Catholic faith is the message of Jesus Christ:

> "I have come
> so that they may have life
> and have it to the full" (Jn 10:10).
>
> "I am the resurrection.
> Anyone who believes in me, even though that
>   person dies, will live,
> and whoever lives and believes in me
> will never die.
> Do you believe this?" (Jn 11:25-26).

What better companion for our life's journey than the Lord, our brother and Savior, Jesus Christ? "Do you believe this?"

PRAYER REFLECTION

Prayerfully examine your Catholic beliefs by reflecting on the following statements:

As a Catholic Christian, do I . . .

- Believe in a loving *Abba* who looks out for each person, all of whom are my brothers and sisters?
- Acknowledge the lordship of Jesus Christ in my own life and

believe that through the paschal mystery he has saved me and won for me eternal life?
- Believe in the active presence of the Holy Spirit in the world, a Spirit who endows me with the gifts of a Christian life, enabling me to respond to the Lord Jesus?
- Believe in the one, holy, catholic and apostolic church, the Body of Christ to which I am personally committed?
- Pray on a regular basis?
- Respect the scriptures as the word of God and try to read and seek guidance from them?
- Acknowledge my sinfulness by celebrating the sacrament of reconciliation?
- Live a sacramental life, especially by participating lovingly in the Sunday celebration of the Eucharist
- Model my life on Jesus Christ by
  - Loving God above all things?
  - Loving my neighbor as myself?
  - Caring in a special way for the poor, rejected, lowly, lonely?
  - Forgiving my enemies?
  - Treating all that I meet as my brothers and sisters and as the Lord himself?
- Consult the teachings of the church before making moral decisions?
- Recognize and respect the Christ-appointed leaders in the church and all proper authority?
- Do something concrete to serve others?
- Share my faith in Jesus with others?
- Honor Mary and the saints?
- Respect and defend human life?

FOR DISCUSSION _____

1. How do you define what it means to be Catholic?
2. What are some other issues to which the ''seamless garment'' argument should apply?
3. Discuss ways today's Christian should be witnessing on behalf of life.

FURTHER READING _____

Acts 7 (the witness of an early Christian)
James (timely counsel for Christians of all ages)

Appendix 1 —————————————————
Church Precepts

Belonging to the Catholic faith community involves certain basic commitments. Like all law, church law is reasonable, given by proper authority, published in a way that people know about it, and directed to the common good. The following are four major precepts for responsible Catholic living in today's church.

1. *To keep holy the day of the Lord's resurrection.* This means primarily to worship God by celebrating the Eucharist every Sunday and holy day of obligation. It also means to reserve Sunday as a day of relaxation, thanksgiving and celebration. We respect this day by avoiding those activities that would hinder personal renewal, for example, by avoiding needless work and business activities and unnecessary shopping.

2. *To lead a sacramental life.* Catholics who are in the state of grace should receive the *Eucharist* frequently. Catholics are obliged to receive holy communion during the Easter season (between the First Sunday of Lent and Trinity Sunday). They approach the sacrament reverently by refraining from food or drink (other than medicine or water) for at least one hour before reception of holy communion.

Good Catholics celebrate the *sacrament of reconciliation* regularly as a means to experience the healing touch of the Lord, to help conquer sinful habits and to grow in holiness. A Catholic is obliged to celebrate this sacrament annually if in the state of mortal sin.

Catholics are obliged to be fully initiated into the faith community by celebrating the *sacrament of confirmation*. To prepare for confirmation Catholics must study church doctrine. After celebrating the sacrament they must commit themselves to lifelong study of the faith and work in some capacity for the advancement of the good news of Jesus Christ.

Catholics are encouraged to celebrate the *anointing of the sick* whenever seriously ill; they may also be anointed in preparation for a major operation. One of the effects of this sacrament may be physical healing, so the sacrament is not meant just for those who are near death. Many parishes have communal celebrations of this sacrament. The last rites, which include *viaticum* (holy communion given to a dying person), are administered to those near death.

Catholics should also observe the *marriage* laws of the Catholic community. A couple intending marriage should contact their local pastor. They should be free to marry, mature enough to give mutual consent, and willing to celebrate marriage as a lifelong covenant of love. Married couples are obligated to provide a religious education for their children. This is done primarily through their own example and teaching as well as using the parochial schools and catechetical programs.

3. *To strengthen and support the church.* As full members of Christ's body, Catholics have an obligation to support the local church community—the parish and its staff, the charities run by the local diocese and the like. Catholics also belong to a worldwide community which has the Lord's own mandate to spread the good news. Thus, they must support the pope and the missionary efforts of the church.

A Catholic recognizes that service of others is not only a major mission of the church as an institution but an obligation of each member. Thus, Catholics will lend their talents and time to the local parish and will dedicate themselves to serve the human family in some way. Service is an obligation of every Christian.

4. *To do penance and strive for holiness.* Catholics take seriously Jesus' command to pick up a cross and follow him. In the Sermon on the Mount (Mt 5-7), Jesus taught three good and mutually enriching paths to holiness: prayer, fasting (and abstaining) and almsgiving (charity to the poor). These traditional means of self-discipline remain excellent ways to follow in the footsteps of Jesus.

Divine Office

The Divine Office, meaning "sacred duty," is known today as the Liturgy of the Hours. It is part of the official, public prayer of the church. Along with the celebration of the sacraments, it helps render constant praise and thanksgiving to God.

The purpose of the Liturgy of the Hours is to sanctify the whole day by continual praise of God. Each service is called an "hour." Most of the prayers are rooted in scripture, especially the psalms. Each day follows a separate pattern of prayer with the themes tied in with the liturgical year and saints' feast days. There are five major divisions:

1. An Hour of Readings
2. Morning Praises
3. Mid-day Prayers
4. Vespers (Evening Prayers)
5. Compline (a short Night Prayer)

Priests, monks and many nuns pray the office daily on behalf of all God's people. Vatican II also encouraged lay people to pray the Liturgy of the Hours. A good way to begin is to pray the Morning Praises and Vespers.

Holy Days

Holy Days are certain feast days the church celebrates throughout the church year. On these days Catholics attend Mass to celebrate the particular feast. In the United States the following are the holy days of obligation:

Immaculate Conception—December 8
Christmas Day—December 25
Solemnity of Mary—January 1
Ascension Thursday—40 days after Easter
Assumption of Mary—August 15
All Saints' Day—November 1

Liturgical Year

Throughout the year the church celebrates the paschal mystery of Jesus Christ. In a special way this happens every *Sunday*, the day of the Lord's resurrection, a day of victory over sin and death. The greatest feast of all is Easter Sunday which celebrates the saving events accomplished in the Passion, death and resurrection of the Lord Jesus.

Additionally, over the course of a year, the church unfolds in its liturgy the various mysteries of our redemption. These include the incarnation of Jesus, his nativity, the major events in his teaching ministry, his ascension, the sending of the Holy Spirit on Pentecost and the future anticipation of Jesus' second coming. By recalling these events, the church is making present anew the redemptive work of Christ, inspiring the faithful with the riches of the Lord's graceful presence.

The church calendar is outlined below:

Advent. Advent marks the beginning of the church year. Beginning around the end of November, it lasts about four weeks. It is a season of preparation for Christ's coming.

Christmas Season. This period begins with Christmas which celebrates the mystery of the incarnation, God-made-man. Christmas proclaims *Emmanuel!*, ''God is with us.'' This joyful season also celebrates the feast of the Holy Family, the Solemnity of Mary (January 1) and Jesus' Epiphany or manifestation to the Magi. The season ends with the feast of the Lord's baptism.

Ordinary Time 1. Between the Christmas season and Lent, the church does not celebrate any particular aspect of the Christian mystery. Rather the church reads through one of the gospels in sequence: Matthew (Cycle A), Mark (Cycle B) and Luke (Cycle C). (John's gospel is read during the Lenten and Easter season and for some of the Ordinary Time in Cycle B since Mark's gospel is short.) The good news proclaimed over a three-year cycle gives the Sunday Mass-goer good exposure to the New Testament and much material for meditation.

Lenten Season. The word *Lent* comes from an Anglo-Saxon word for "spring." Beginning on Ash Wednesday, it is a season of penance in preparation for the solemn and joyful feast of Easter. Lent lasts six Sundays and 40 weekdays, concluding on Holy Thursday with the celebration of the Lord's Last Supper.

Historically Lent was the proximate period of preparation for catechumens ready to be baptized. The *Rite of Christian Initiation for Adults* recaptures this historical thrust by preparing the elect for initiation. During Lent all baptized Christians are called on to contemplate and renew through penance and prayer their own baptismal commitment. This commitment implies walking the way of the cross to the glory of the Lord's resurrection.

Easter. Easter is at the very heart of the liturgical year and of Christian faith. It celebrates our redemption in Christ and his promise of everlasting life. The seasonal celebration consists of a Triduum (three days) from Thursday evening to Sunday night: Holy Thursday, Good Friday and Holy Saturday. Easter is celebrated on the first Sunday after the first full moon of the spring equinox and is thus a moveable feast. This dating is tied in with the traditional date given for Jesus' crucifixion on the 14th day of Nisan (the date of the Passover in the year A.D. 30 on the Jewish lunar calendar).

Easter Season. This season of joy spans 50 days from Easter to Pentecost Sunday. Readings focus on the themes of death to sin, resurrection, and living a life of grace. The example of the early Christians in Acts is often given as a model of Christians alive in the Lord. The last 10 days of the Easter Season celebrate the promise and gift of the Holy Spirit. Ascension Thursday occurs 40 days after Easter; Pentecost, 50 days after Easter. Pentecost Sunday celebrates the descent of the Holy Spirit, the event in salvation history that inaugurated the Christian church.

Ordinary Time 2. Ordinary Time resumes after the Easter season and proceeds to Advent and a new church year. Trinity Sunday is celebrated one week after Pentecost, and the feast of Corpus Christi one week later. The following Sundays in Ordinary Time look to the teaching and ministry of Jesus. Toward the end of this period the readings turn to the end of time and Christ's second coming. The feast of Christ the King is the last Sunday of the church year.

Organization in the Church

The church is organized to carry on a worldwide mission of preaching Jesus' message and serving the needs of individual people. Its structure can be viewed from the vantage point of the local, national and international levels.

Local: The Parish and the Diocese

In truth the smallest church unit is the Christian family. But the family needs support of a community to live out its Christian vocation. So most Catholics experience Christian community in the local *parish* which usually embraces all Catholics living in a given geographical area. The bishop appoints a *pastor* to serve the pastoral needs of the people and to supervise the temporal affairs of the parish plant in co-operation with God's people. The pastor, the symbol of unity in the parish, often serves with a pastoral team which coordinates the efforts of the many organizations within a parish.

In between the parish and the diocese is a *deanery* which consists of a group of parishes located in a certain geographical region. These pastors work with the bishop on a regional basis.

The *bishop* is the chief shepherd of a *diocese*, which is typically associated with a geographical area. He presides from the *cathedral*, the bishop's church. He is aided in his work by priests, and his chief consulting body is a *priests' council*. The bishops' staff works out of the *chancery* which includes organizations like Catholic Charities, the Office of Education, Liturgy Commission, Family Life Bureau and the like.

National: NCCB and USCC

The *National Conference of Catholic Bishops (NCCB)* is made up of all the bishops in the United States. This Conference meets at least once a year to discuss and set policy on issues related to the liturgy and church ministry as well as issues of social concern. In recent years the American bishops have issued important pastoral letters on peace and the economy.

The *United States Catholic Conference (USCC)* handles the public, educational and social concerns of the church. With many offices in Washington, this organization of the bishops carries on many of the administrative functions of church programs on both the national and international levels.

International: The Pope, Curia, Synods, Ecumenical Councils

The *pope* is the chief shepherd, teacher and lawmaker of Roman Catholicism. His headquarters and administrative offices are in the Vatican, an independent city within Rome's city limits.

The pope is assisted in the day-to-day operation of the church by the *curia*, the bureaucracy which runs the church. Cardinals (an honorific title given to some bishops with the right to elect the pope) and bishops head various congregations and other agencies. Some examples are the Congregations for the Clergy and Laity, the Secretariat for Christian Unity, and the Commission on Justice and Peace.

The *synod of bishops* is a representative body of bishops assembled periodically by the pope to advise him on important church concerns. It is not a legislative body.

The most important teaching body and lawmaking assembly in the church is the *ecumenical council*. There have been 21 such councils in the history of the church. An ecumenical council is made up of the pope and all the bishops of the world. Vatican II was the last ecumenical council to meet (early 1960s); it took up major issues in the area of doctrine, church life, and the church's relationship to the world.

Seven Deadly Sins

1. Pride
2. Envy
3. Anger
4. Sloth
5. Greed
6. Gluttony
7. Lust

Stations of the Cross

The stations of the cross are a type of meditative prayer based on the passion of Jesus. This devotion grew out of the custom of Holy Land pilgrims who retraced the last steps of Jesus on his way to Calvary. Most Catholic churches have the stations depicted on the side walls to help us imagine the sufferings of Jesus and focus on the meaning of the paschal mystery.

Traditionally there have been 14 stations, ending with the laying of Jesus in the sepulcher. In recent years a 15th—depicting the resurrection—is added to show the glorious conclusion to Jesus' sacrifice for us.

We pray the stations either as a group or individually by meditating on the following scenes:

1. Jesus is condemned to death
2. Jesus takes up his cross
3. Jesus falls for the first time
4. Jesus meets his mother
5. Simon of Cyrene helps Jesus carry his cross
6. Veronica wipes the face of Jesus
7. Jesus falls for the second time
8. Jesus consoles the women of Jerusalem
9. Jesus falls the third time
10. Jesus is stripped of his garments
11. Jesus is nailed to the cross
12. Jesus dies on the cross
13. Jesus is taken down from the cross
14. Jesus is laid in the tomb
15. The resurrection of the Lord

Virtues

Virtues are God-given powers which enable us to live the Christian life and to become more like God.

Theological Virtues

Faith   Personal commitment and trust in the Lord; belief in his word

Hope   Trust in God's salvation and that he will bless us with the means necessary to attain it

Charity   Self-sacrificing love of God and others; compassion

Cardinal Virtues

Prudence   Right judgment; spiritual judgment

Temperance   Moderation (especially in our appetites: food, sex, drink)

Justice   Rendering others their due (respecting others' rights and fulfilling obligations)

Fortitude   Courage (ability to overcome fear in order to work to build up God's kingdom)

The Existence of Angels and Devils

There is an interesting phenomenon today concerning the existence of angels and devils. On the one hand, some people deny the existence of any spiritual reality. They claim that belief in devils and angels is simply superstition. Even some Christians who certainly believe in God's existence question the existence of these spiritual beings; they explain scriptural references to them as examples of symbolic language. On the other hand, hardly a year goes by without filmmakers exploiting the theme of demon possession and the conflict between the spiritual forces of good and evil.

Catholics do indeed believe in the existence of angels and devils. Both scripture and tradition attest to this belief.

Angels are created, spiritual beings. Like us, they are free, knowing, loving beings created by God for union with himself. Unlike us, angels are pure spirits; they do not have bodies.

The word *angel* means "one who is sent" or "messenger." This tells us something about the angels' function in relation to us. Both the Old and New Testaments have many examples of God sending his angels.

The church has instructed Catholics to honor the angels who are our spiritual friends and guardians. The church has traditionally taught that each person has a guardian angel.

We believe that when the angels were created they were given a basic choice, similar to our choice here on earth, to accept God or reject him. Those who chose themselves over God—thereby choosing to be alienated from him in hell—are called demons or devils. God permits devils to tempt us, but he does not allow them to harm us. (The church does teach that there is such a thing as demon possession, but the church's ritual of exorcism warns against concluding too quickly that a demon possesses a person. Many examples of possessions have turned out to be the result of emotional disturbances or fraud.) By resisting the temptations of evil spirits we are given the opportunity to draw closer to God.

Appendix 2
Some Traditional Prayers

Sign of the Cross
> In the name of the Father,
> and of the Son,
> and of the Holy Spirit. Amen.

Our Father
> Our Father
> who are in heaven,
> hallowed be your name.
> Your kingdom come;
> your will be done be done on earth as it is in heaven.
> Give us this day our daily bread
> and forgive us our trespasses
> as we forgive those who trespass against us.
> And lead us not into temptation,
> but deliver us from evil.
> For the kingdom, the power and the glory are yours
> now and forever. Amen.

Glory Be
> Glory be to the Father
> and to the Son
> and to the Holy Spirit,
> as it was in the beginning
> is now, and will be forever. Amen.

Hail Mary

> Hail Mary, full of grace,
> the Lord is with you.
> Blessed are you among women
> and blessed is the fruit of your womb, Jesus.
> Holy Mary, mother of God,
> pray for us sinners now
> and at the hour of our death. Amen.

Memorare

> Remember, O most gracious Virgin Mary,
> that never was it known
> that anyone who fled to your protection,
> implored your help,
> or sought your intercession was left unaided.
> Inspired by this confidence,
> I fly unto you,
> O Virgin of virgins, my mother,
> To you I come, before you I stand,
> sinful and sorrowful.
> O Mother of the Word incarnate,
> despise not my petitions,
> but in your mercy hear and answer me. Amen.

Hail, Holy Queen

> Hail, holy Queen, mother of mercy,
> our life, our sweetness and our hope.
> To you do we cry,
> poor banished children of Eve.
> To you do we send up our sighs,
> mourning and weeping in this valley of tears.
> Turn then, O most gracious advocate,
> your eyes of mercy toward us,
> and after this exile
> show us the blessed fruit of your womb, Jesus.
> O clement, O loving, O sweet Virgin Mary.
> > Pray for us, O holy mother of God,
> > that we may be made worthy of the promises of Christ.
> > > Amen.

Morning Offering

O Jesus, through the immaculate heart of Mary, I offer you my prayers, works, joys and sufferings of this day in union with the holy sacrifice of the Mass throughout the world. I offer them for all the intentions of your sacred heart: the salvation of souls, reparation for sin, the reunion of all Christians. I offer them for the intentions of our bishops and all members of the Apostleship of Prayer and in particular for those recommended by our Holy Father this month. Amen.

Apostles' Creed

I believe in God, the Father almighty
    creator of heaven and earth.
I believe in Jesus Christ, his only Son, our Lord.
    He was conceived by the power of the Holy Spirit and
        born of the Virgin Mary.
    He suffered under Pontius Pilate, was crucified, died,
        and was buried.
    He descended to the dead.
    On the third day he rose again.
    He ascended into heaven, and is seated at the right
        hand of the Father.
    He will come again to judge the living and the dead.
I believe in the Holy Spirit,
    the holy catholic Church,
    the communion of saints,
    the forgiveness of sins,
    the resurrection of the body,
    and life everlasting. Amen.

Act of Faith

O my God, I firmly believe that you are one God in three divine Persons, Father, Son and Holy Spirit. I believe that your divine Son became man and died for our sins, and that he will come to judge the living and the dead. I believe these and all the truths which the Holy Catholic Church teaches, because you have revealed them, who can neither deceive nor be deceived. Amen.

Act of Hope

O my God, relying on your infinite goodness and promises, I hope to obtain pardon of my sins, the help of your grace, and life everlasting, through the merits of Jesus Christ, my Lord and Redeemer. Amen.

Act of Love

O my God, I love you above all things, with my whole heart and soul, because you are all good and worthy of all my love. I love my neighbor as myself for the love of you. I forgive all who have injured me, and I ask pardon of all whom I have injured. Amen.

Act of Contrition

O my God, I am sorry for my sins with all my heart. In choosing to do wrong and failing to do good, I have sinned against you whom I should love above all things. I firmly intend, with your help, to do penance, to sin no more, and to avoid whatever leads me to sin. Our Savior Jesus Christ suffered and died for us. In his name, my God, have mercy. Amen.

Angelus

The angel of the Lord declared unto Mary.
R: And she conceived by the Holy Spirit.
　Hail Mary. . .
Behold the handmaid of the Lord.
R: May it be done unto me according to your word.
　Hail Mary. . .
And the word was made flesh.
R: And dwelled among us.
　Hail Mary. . .
Pray for us, O holy mother of God.
R: That we may be made worthy of the promises of Christ.
Let us pray: We beseech you, O Lord, to pour out your grace into our hearts. By the message of an angel we have learned of the incarnation of Christ, your Son; lead us, by his passion and cross, to the glory of the resurrection. Through the same Christ our Lord. Amen.

Grace at Meals

Before Meals

Bless us, O Lord,
and these your gifts,
which we are about to receive from your bounty,
through Christ our Lord. Amen.

After Meals

We give you thanks, almighty God,
for these and all the gifts
which we have received
from your goodness
through Christ our Lord. Amen.

Prayer to Our Guardian Angel

Angel of God, my guardian dear, to whom God's love entrusts
me here, ever this day (night) be at my side, to light and guard, to
rule and guide. Amen.

Prayer for the Faithful Departed

Eternal rest grant unto them, O Lord.
R: And let perpetual light shine upon them.
May their souls and the souls of all the faithful departed, through
the mercy of God, rest in peace.
R: Amen.

The Jesus Prayer

Lord Jesus Christ, Son of God, have mercy on me, a sinner.

The Divine Praises

(These praises are traditionally recited after the benediction of the
Blessed Sacrament.)

Blessed be God.
Blessed be his holy name.
Blessed be Jesus Christ, true God and true man.
Blessed be the name of Jesus.
Blessed be his most sacred heart.
Blessed be his most precious blood.
Blessed be Jesus in the most holy sacrament of the altar.
Blessed be the Holy Spirit, the paraclete.
Blessed be the great mother of God, Mary most holy.
Blessed be her holy and immaculate conception.
Blessed be her glorious assumption.
Blessed be the name of Mary, virgin and mother.
Blessed be St. Joseph, her most chaste spouse.
Blessed be God in his angels and in his saints.

Prayer for Peace (attributed to St. Francis of Assisi)

Lord, make me an instrument of your peace.

Where there is hatred, let me sow love;
where there is injury, pardon;
where there is doubt, faith;
where there is despair, hope;
where there is darkness, light;
where there is sadness, joy.
O Divine Master, grant that I may not seek so much
to be consoled as to console;
to be understood, as to understand,
to be loved, as to love.
For it is in giving that we receive,
it is in pardoning that we are pardoned,
and it is in dying that we are born to eternal life.

Appendix 3
Selective Glossary of Terms

Abortion—The expulsion of a nonviable fetus from the mother's womb through medical or surgical procedures. Abortion is condemned by the Catholic church as an unjustified attack on innocent human life.

Adultery—Sexual relations between a married person and another who is not one's marriage partner. Adultery is a serious breakdown in the covenant love between a husband and wife whose marriage commitment is supposed to be a sign of Christ's faithful love for his church.

Annulment—An official church declaration that what appeared to be a Christian marriage never existed in the first place.

Asceticism—The religious practice of works of self-discipline like fasting, prayer and almsgiving which are motivated by the love of Jesus Christ and contribute to growth in holiness.

Assumption—The official church dogma that the body of the Blessed Mother was taken directly to heaven when her life on earth ended.

Baptism of Desire—The process by which some good, loving individuals who were never afforded the gift of faith gain salvation because of the way they lived their lives.

Beatific Vision—Seeing God "face to face" in heaven; the final union with God in eternity.

Bible—The inspired word of God; the written record of revelation.

Canon (of the Bible)—The official list of the inspired books of the Bible. Catholics list 46 Old Testament books and 27 New Testament books in the canon.

Canon Law—The code of church laws which governs the life of the Catholic community.

Canon of the Mass—The Eucharistic Prayer which includes the words of consecration. It is the central prayer of the Liturgy of the Eucharist. There are several canons available for use in today's eucharistic rite.

Canonization—The process whereby the church officially declares that a person who has been martyred for Jesus Christ and / or has heroically practiced Christian virtue is in heaven and is worthy of veneration and imitation by Christians.

Catechesis—The process of religious instruction and formation in the major elements of the Christian faith.

Catechumen—A person who is studying the main elements of the Christian faith in preparation for the sacraments of initiation.

Catholic—A Greek word which means "universal." The term *Catholic church* refers to the Christian community which is open to all people everywhere and in all ages and which preaches the fullness of God's revelation in Jesus Christ.

Charism—A gift of the Holy Spirit which enables the recipient to do good works in the building up of Christ's body. Examples include wisdom, prophecy, zeal in witnessing to Christ, discernment of spirits and exemplary loving service of others.

Charity—Love of God above all things and love of neighbor as oneself; the greatest of the three theological virtues.

Christ—Greek translation of the Hebrew word *messiah*; a significant title of Jesus meaning "the anointed one."

Church—For Christians, the community of God's people who profess faith in the risen Lord Jesus and live lives of loving service under the guidance of the Holy Spirit.

Collegiality—The bishops in union with the pope as their head sharing teaching and pastoral authority over the worldwide church.

Common Good—Those spiritual, material and social conditions needed for a person to achieve full human dignity.

Communion of Saints—The entire community of Christians—those on earth, in purgatory and in heaven.

Conscience—The practical judgment which helps a person decide the goodness or sinfulness of an action or attitude.

Covenant—The open-ended contract of love God made with the Israelites and with all people everywhere in the person of Jesus Christ.

Dogma—A church doctrine (teaching) issued with the highest authority and solemnity; a core teaching of the church.

Ecumenical Council—A worldwide, official assembly of the bishops under the direction of the pope. There have been 21 ecumenical councils, the last being the Second Vatican Council (1962-1965).

Ecumenism—The movement which seeks Christian unity and eventually the unity of all peoples throughout the world.

Encyclical—A papal letter written on some important issue and circulated throughout the worldwide church. Encyclicals are often addressed not only to Catholics but also to all Christians and people of good will throughout the world.

Eschatology—Teaching about the last things—death, judgment, heaven, hell, purgatory, *parousia* and the resurrection of the body.

Eucharist—From the Greek word meaning "thanksgiving." The Eucharist is one of the seven sacraments and the central act of Christian worship. It is also referred to as the Mass or the Lord's Supper. The Eucharist can also designate holy communion.

Euthanasia—Active euthanasia, also called mercy killing, is condemned by the church because direct, intentional means are used to bring about the death of a person or reasonable, ordinary means are not used to keep a person alive. Euthanasia is a violation of the fifth commandment.

Evangelist—A person who proclaims the good news of Jesus Christ. "The four evangelists" refers to the authors of the four gospels: Matthew, Mark, Luke and John.

Faith—One of the three theological virtues. Faith refers to (1) personal knowledge of God; (2) assent of the mind to truths God has revealed, made with the help of his grace and on the authority and trustworthiness of his revealing them; (3) the truths themselves (the content of faith); and (4) the lived witness of a Christian life (living faith).

Fathers of the Church—An honorary title given to outstanding early Christian theologians whose teaching has had lasting significance for the church.

Gospel—Literally, "good news." Gospel refers to (1) the good news preached by Jesus; (2) the good news of salvation won for us in the person of Jesus Christ (he is the good news proclaimed by the church); (3) the four written records of the good news—the gospels of Matthew, Mark, Luke and John.

Grace—The free gift of God's life and friendship.

Heresy—A false teaching which denies an essential (dogmatic) teaching of the church.

Hierarchy—The leadership of the Catholic church. The hierarchy is made up of the ordained ministers in the church: pope, bishops, priests and deacons. The pope is the symbol of unity in the church and the successor to St. Peter.

Hope—One of the three theological virtues. Hope enables us to firmly trust in God's salvation and that he will bless us with the necessary gifts to attain it.

Immaculate Conception—The church dogma which teaches that the Blessed Mother was free from sin from the very first moment of her human existence. This dogma is sometimes confused with the doctrine of the *virginal conception* which holds that Jesus was conceived of the Virgin Mary by the power of the Holy Spirit without the cooperation of a human father.

Immanence—A trait of God which refers to his intimate union with and total presence to his creation.

Incarnation—A key theological term for the dogma of the Son of God becoming man in Jesus Christ, born of the Virgin Mary. (The term literally means "taking on human flesh.")

Infallibility—A gift of the Holy Spirit which preserves the church from error when it teaches on matters related to divine revelation. It can be exercised by a worldwide council of bishops in union with the pope or by the pope alone when teaching on faith or morals.

Inspiration (of the Bible)—The guidance of the Holy Spirit which enabled the writers of the Bible to record what God wanted written.

Just-war Doctrine—Derived from the natural law and reflection on Christian revelation, this teaching carefully sets out the conditions necessary for participation in a war.

Kerygma—The core or essential message of the gospel. An excellent example of the kerygma is found in Acts 2:14-36.

Kingdom of God—The reign of God which was proclaimed by Jesus and inaugurated in his life, death and resurrection. It refers to the process of God's reconciling and renewing all things through his Son, to the fact of his will being done on earth as it is in heaven. The process has begun with Jesus and will be perfectly completed at the end of time.

Law—A reasonable norm of conduct given by proper authority for the common good. In the Hebrew scriptures the Law is summarized in the Ten Commandments. Jesus taught the law of love of God and neighbor.

Liturgy—The official public worship of the church. The seven sacraments, especially the Eucharist, are the primary forms of liturgical celebrations.

Magisterium—The teaching authority of the church. The Lord bestowed the right to teach in his name on the apostles and their successors, that is, the bishops and the pope as their leader.

Monotheism—Belief in and worship of one God. Judaism, Christianity and Islam are monotheistic religions.

Morality—That aspect of Christian living that seeks norms of Christian behavior based on God's revelation.

Mortal Sin—Personal sin which involves serious matter, sufficient reflection and full consent of the will. It results in total rejection of God and alienation from him.

Natural Law—God's plan written into the way he made things. Human intelligence and reflection can aid us in discovering the natural law and living a life in harmony with it.

Original Sin—The state or condition of sin into which all generations of people are born since the time of Adam's turning away from God.

Parousia—the second coming of Christ which will usher in the full establishment of God's kingdom on earth as it is in heaven.

Paschal Mystery—God's love and salvation revealed to us through the life, passion, death, resurrection and glorification of his Son Jesus Christ.

Prayer—Conversation with God. Joining one's thoughts and love to God in adoration, contrition, thanksgiving and petition.

Primacy—The pope's authority over the whole church.

Principle of Discrimination—This principle requires the combatants in a war to make a distinction between aggressors and innocent people.

Principle of Proportionality—This principle requires that the damage inflicted and costs incurred by a war (or a particular action in a war) be proportionate to the good expected.

Prophet—One who speaks for God. All Christians are called to be prophets, that is, to testify in word and action that God's kingdom is in our midst.

Real Presence—The presence of Jesus Christ in the sacrament of the Eucharist.

Revelation—God's free self-communication of himself to us through creation, historical events, prophets and most fully in his Son Jesus Christ.

Rights—Claims which individuals can make on other people and on society in order to live in dignity. For every right there is a corresponding duty.

Ritual—Traditional religious actions which celebrate the mystery of our redemption and serve to worship God.

Sacrament—A visible sign of an invisible grace. A traditional definition holds that a sacrament is an outward sign instituted by Christ to confer grace. There are seven sacraments: baptism, confirmation, Eucharist, reconciliation, anointing of the sick, marriage and holy orders.

Sacramentals—Sacred signs that resemble the sacraments and prepare a person to receive them.

Salvation—The process of healing whereby God's forgiveness, grace and loving attention are extended to us through Jesus Christ in the Holy Spirit. Salvation brings about union with God and with our fellow humans through the work of our brother and savior, Jesus Christ.

Salvation History—The story of God's saving action in human history.

Schism—A break in Christian unity which takes place when a group of Christians separates itself from the Body of Christ. This happens historically when the group breaks its union with the pope, for example, when the Eastern Orthodox Church broke with the Roman Catholic Church in 1054.

Social Justice Doctrine—That part of church teaching which deals with the obligations of individuals and groups to apply the gospel to the systems, structures and institutions of society.

Subsidiarity—The principle of Catholic social teaching which holds that a higher unit of society should not do what a lower unit can do as well (or better).

Synod—An official church assembly at one of these levels: diocesan, provincial, regional, national or international.

Tabernacle—The holy receptacle in which the Blessed Sacrament is reserved.

Tradition—Both the process of handing on the faith and that which is handed on. Tradition includes everything that helps make God's people holy and increases their faith.

Transcendence—A trait of God which refers to his total otherness, his being infinitely beyond and independent of his creation.

Transubstantiation—The official Catholic church teaching that the substance of the bread and wine is changed into the substance of the body and blood of Jesus Christ at the consecration of the Mass.

Trinity—The Christian dogma which holds that there are three persons in one God: Father, Son and Holy Spirit.

> *Immanent Trinity*—refers to the inner life of the Trinity, the relations of the three divine persons one to another.

> *Salvific Trinity*—refers to the active work of the triune God in salvation history; the Father as Creator, the Son as Redeemer, the Holy Spirit as Sanctifier.

Venial Sin—Personal sin which weakens but does not kill our relationship with God.

Yahweh—The Hebrew name for God. It means "I Am Who Am."

Index _____

(Some of these headings are also to be found in Appendix 3.)